A Casebook
of Murder

For Francis Camps

A CASEBOOK OF MURDER

Colin Wilson

COWLES BOOK COMPANY, INC.
NEW YORK

©1969 by Colin Wilson
SBN 402-12431-6
Library of Congress Catalog Card Number 75-102820
Cowles Book Company, Inc.
A Subsidiary of Cowles Communications, Inc.
Printed in the United States of America
First Edition

CONTENTS

(Cases considered at length are printed in roman)

Acknowledgements

I wish to thank August Derleth for the loan of his set of volumes on famous American murders, Brian Marriner for unearthing some valuable press cuttings, Mrs Gita Whetter for correcting the manuscript and proof, and Dr Francis Camps, Ludovic Kennedy and S Foster Damon for help on particular points. The London Library, as usual, went to a great deal of trouble to search out essential material.

The following books have provided valuable material from which I have quoted: Herbert Asbury *The Gangs of New York*, G P Putnam's Sons; Christopher Hibbert *The Roots of Evil*, Weidenfeld and Nicholson; Suzanne Lilar *Aspects of Love in Western Society*, Thames and Hudson; Sir Melville Macnaghten *Day of my Years*, Edward Arnold and Lytton Strachey *Elizabeth and Essex*, Chatto and Windus.

C W

Introduction

THE THEME OF this book is the sociology of murder – the changing patterns of murder in western society. But such considerations, while certainly fascinating, do not go to the root of my interest in murder. To put it simply, my interest in murder is philosophical rather than scientific.

Shortly after the Moors murder case (which is discussed in the last chapter), Pamela Hansford Johnson wrote a book called *On Iniquity*, in which she contradicted the current notion that there is no such thing as wickedness, only 'sickness'. I saw a number of reviews that treated this thesis with a kind of bored disgust, as if it was just another sign of the regrettable 'backward from liberalism' tendency of our period. Now I would not say that I am entirely in agreement with Miss Hansford Johnson about the need to clamp down the censorship on 'immoral' books. Whether de Sade or *My Secret Life* ever corrupted anybody is beside the point. I have no doubt they have; and it still seems to me important that they should be published and sold openly; they are not in the same category as dangerous drugs, and if a human being could write them, I see no reason why they should be denied to any human being who can read them. But the core of her argument seems to me obviously true. The interesting thing about Brady and Hindley – and there would not be books written about them if they were not interesting to a great many people – is that they were responding to certain social pressures with *freedom of choice*. Most murders are crimes of passion of one sort or another: murders within the family: a jealous husband kills his wife; an overwrought wife kills her husband or child, and so on. A large percentage of such murderers never come to trial because they

11

commit suicide. They have been faced with a crisis situation, have responded without self-control, and the result is disaster. There is a choice here, but it is merely the choice of running down a slope instead of trying to stop yourself from sliding down it. But the murder cases that make the headlines usually do so for a good reason: that the murders reveal a far more unusual kind of choice: that of the gambler, or adventurer, or leader. The murderer may be of a fairly high level of intelligence; he also feels a generalised resentment towards society. He pursues this train of thought – and emotion – logically, until it ends in murder. We may condemn the crime as ultimately stupid; but it would be blindness to apply *any* kind of blanket judgement: stupidity, wickedness, sickness, as if it was all of a piece. A classic example is Robert Irwin, an artist who murdered the mother and sister of his girlfriend in New York in 1937. Working as an errand boy at the age of fifteen, Irwin was suddenly struck one day – the word is inadequate to describe the impact – by the notion that 'before a sculptor can make a statue, he has to first make a mental statue'. He became obsessed by an idea he called 'visualising', trying to conjure up something, in his imagination, *in all its reality*. It seemed plain to him that if the imagination served the function for which it was intended, a man could close his eyes and read the complete plays of Shakespeare in imagination, or 'replay' some past experience in minute physical detail. (It will be immediately obvious that this is what Proust was aiming at in *A la Recherché du Temps Perdu*.) Irwin became so fascinated by this idea that he one day decided that castration would aid his efforts to channel all his energies. After an unsuccessful attempt to persuade a doctor to amputate his penis, he made the attempt himself, and almost bled to death. Life became increasingly frustrating; he worked at jobs he disliked, and came to feel that life is a trap. And one day, after a sudden disappointment, he committed his double murder. Neither of the women was sexually assaulted.

The psychiatrist Frederick Wertham was called for the defence, and his contention was that a man with such weird ideas was self-evidently unbalanced, and should be committed to a mental home. The plea was unsuccessful, and Irwin went to jail for life. Now for all I know, Wertham may have been right – I never met Irwin, or talked to anyone who knew him. But I have no difficulty at all in envisaging how a man might commit Irwin's crime, and still be completely sane. Irwin's idea seems to me to be a profound insight, of the kind from which all great art has sprung. Trying to summarise his view of Schopenhauer, Irwin explained to Wertham:

'. . . the life force . . . uses every living organism for its purpose of prolonging the race until we finally reach a stage of perfection in which we can rise above the material world. Every organism, upon reaching maturity, sacrifices itself to the task of reproduction. In other words, the driving force in back of our lives, which can be used for other purposes, we sacrifice to the task of reproduction. I realised that if I could once bottle that up without her [his girlfriend], I didn't need her. It's a great deal of fun to monkey around with a woman. It's a great deal of fun to have five dollars and spend it. But if by forgoing the five dollars you will later get a million dollars. . . .'

This last sentence describes the type of gambling impulse that is present in every great artist. A man without a vocation, or without the confidence to pursue it single-mindedly, takes the path of least resistance; of security and adjustment to social demands. A Shaw, a Proust, a Joyce, an Einstein, knows that he would be profoundly unhappy in any of the more or less comfortable positions society has to offer. His talent may never pay off, but he has no alternative than to take the long-shot. But this is to exaggerate; for if there were *no* alternative, the question of choice could not arise. His choice can be compared to doing a 'chicken run' in a stolen car, where the aim is to see who will stay in the car longest before it plunges over the cliff. The difference between Balzac and Dumas, between Shaw and James Barrie, is not simply a difference in literary talent; Barrie and Dumas played it safe, and jumped before the car got anywhere near the cliff.

Irwin, then, was caught in much the same dilemma as many other highly original thinkers. The crime cannot be explained in Freudian terms; a man who can attempt to cut off his penis

13

in order to free his imagination is not entirely a slave of his sexual impulse. But he was in America, the country that killed Poe and ignored Melville, not in Joyce's Dublin or Shaw's London. The pinch grew tighter, and a point came where he decided to hit back. For some reason, he ended by choosing two people of whom he had been fond. In the extremity of despair, any violent act seems to offer promise of release, a change for the better. If the act of violence had been somehow averted, his name might now be known in connection with art instead of with crime. Once Irwin had chosen to devote himself to his obsession about 'visualising', he had taken his basic risk. The home background was bad: poverty, misery; which meant that he lacked the fundamental stability that comes from natural optimism. The crime was the single mistaken act of choice in a chain that might have led to honour and success instead of a sentence of a hundred and thirty-nine years in Sing Sing.

Irwin's case is extreme, but it makes the point. 'Headline' murders may be the result of pressures that most people – fortunately – will never experience, and of choices that most people will never be called upon to make. Like the artist, this type of criminal possesses a certain independence of spirit that means that when it comes to the real issue – his deepest obsession – he doesn't bother to consult other people, but simply goes ahead. If the obsession happens to be writing *My Secret Life* or *The Naked Lunch*, it does no harm: at least, no immediate social harm. If it happens to be raping small girls, it subjects the whole social body to serious shock. In this latter case, the interesting question is: how did the obsession reach this point? And here again, we can study the interaction of obsession and choice.

In the autumn of 1965, two small girls, Margaret Reynolds and Diane Tift, disappeared in the area of Cannock Chase, near Walsall, Staffordshire. They disappeared on different dates, but in January 1966, their bodies were found together in Manstey Gulley, Cannock Chase, near the A34; both had been sexually assaulted. I was in New York when I received a press cutting about the finding of the bodies and, like

14

everyone else, I found myself wondering what sort of a man would take such risks for the satisfaction of a perverse sexual impulse. On 19th August 1967, a seven-year-old girl, Christine Darby, was playing with friends when a man stopped his car and asked the way to a nearby street; she got into the car to direct him. Her body was found three days later on Cannock Chase. In November 1968, a man attempted to persuade a ten-year-old girl to get into his car and failed; a woman who saw the attempt took his number, and shortly afterwards Raymond Leslie Morris, aged thirty-nine, was arrested and charged with the murder of Christine Darby. His wife admitted that she had supported his false alibi for the afternoon of the murder, and in his camera the police discovered an undeveloped photograph showing Morris in the act of sexually assaulting a five-year-old girl, the daughter of a neighbour. (She had thought it a game, and told no one.) Three witnesses indentified Morris as a man they had seen close to the scene of the murder of Christine Darby, and on 17th February 1969, Morris was sentenced to life imprisonment for the murder. (The earlier double murder is still unsolved.)

In the weeks since he was sentenced, English newspapers have published articles that help to answer the question of how a man develops into a child killer. Morris was good-looking, well-dressed, above average intelligence, and a photographer whose work was up to professional standards. (He assaulted the five-year-old child when photographing her for a soap advertisement.) He wrote poetry, was fond of reading aloud, and was a good mimic. His employers regarded him as reliable and intelligent, but 'cold'. He was never known to lose his temper. One of his brothers also described him as a man without emotions. But the most revealing portrait came from his first wife, Muriel, whom he married in 1951 and left eight years later. She spoke about his enormous charm and his talent as a mimic. She also described how he enjoyed acting fantasies: he was Humphrey Bogart in a trilby hat, or the Leslie Charteris' Saint (one of his favourite fictional characters), or the pianist Winifred Atwell, or the latest pop singer. After these fantasies, he would order her to remove her clothes and would make love to her. 'Often when we were together watching television, he'd suddenly say "Strip". And if I didn't obey at once, his eyes would go cold . . . and his cheeks very white . . . When I'd taken off my clothes he'd ask me to sit on his knee.' She mentions this extreme self-control several times. 'One minute I'd be laughing at his attempt to imitate a pop singer, the next I'd be in a cold sweat as he quietly commanded me to strip.' After they were separated, he ordered her to call on him twice a week for sex – otherwise he refused to support her; she describes him possessing her as she bent over the table. But she found it difficult to associate him with child murder. 'He always seemed so fond of children.' (They had two sons.) Morris's second wife, Carol, was fourteen years his junior, and never seems to have seen this sadistic aspect of his character. She apparently supported his false alibi because she thought it so completely impossible that he could be the Cannock Chase murderer, and saw no reason to cause him unnecessary trouble.

What emerges once again is a picture of a vaguely 'artistic' personality (although his poetry seems to have been as bad as that of the Great McGonagall), slightly feminine (he was engaged in building an elaborate doll's house at the time of his arrest), an 'outsider' as far as his environment went, with the charm of slightly spoiled younger sons, a fantasy life as rich as Walter Mitty's, an extremely powerful sexual impulse ('sex wasn't a thing he could take or leave; it was an overpowering maniacal urge'), and the need to assert himself by humiliating his sexual partner. His first wife was a slim, slightly-built girl – child-like is the word that comes to mind; the second, although she seems to have admired him inordinately, was built on more buxom lines and could certainly not be described as child-like. They were married for five years before his arrest. This, then, may explain why the need to play out mildly sadistic sexual fantasies developed into the urge to rape children.

But all these factors fail to explain why such a personality should develop into a child *murderer*. They do not even add up to a severely abnorma personality – most men have a touch of James Bond in their attitude towards women. (There is a great deal of it in Dostoievsky – accompanied by a morbid fascination for child-rape.) No, what is of interest here is that it is the feminine, the 'artistic', part of the personality that amplifies the mild abnormalities to criminal proportions. Because he is an imaginative misfit, with a sense of his superiority to his environment, he experiences severe psychological ups and downs. Shaw points out that all men are in a false position in society until they have realised their possibilities and imposed them on their neighbours. But the realisation of one's possibilities depends, to some extent, upon propitious circumstances, as well as upon that act of will, the gambling-on-a-long-shot, that we have already discussed in the case of Irwin. A character like Morris is fatally placed between two extremes. He is not talented or determined enough to persuade the world to take him on his own terms – although his will-drive and self-control are above the average – but he is too much of a Walter Mitty to feel comfortable in his environment. (This, be it noted, was basically the environment in which he was brought up; both wives were girls he had known since childhood; his mother lived in the next street, his mother-in-law a few streets away. . . .) Inevitably, the downs are more frequent, and of longer duration, than the ups.

And here we come to another central point. Shaw pointed out that we judge the artist by his highest moments and the criminal by his lowest. I have tried to show that the two temperaments may have much in common, so that the difference is not so much one of personality or circumstance as of *choice*. It is an inevitable part of our human lot to be subject to psychological ups and downs, and each 'down' presents a choice. We can either resist it, or encourage it by taking an attitude of defeat. It is important to recognise that this matter of choice is almost what we *mean* when we use the word 'human'. At any moment, I have a choice between immediate impulse or more distant purpose. I may be returning home from work and feeling extremely hungry; I pass a slot-machine, and am tempted to take the edge off my hunger with a bar of chocolate; but I know my wife is cooking my supper, and that I shall enjoy it more if I resist the impulse. There are no great moral issues involved here; both choices are on a purely physical level; but one involves more 'long range purpose' than the other. It may be that I feel I am overweight, and I have no intention of eating supper when I get home; in that case, the range of the purpose is even longer, and I derive a certain moral satisfaction from the thought that another week of this will reduce my weight by a few pounds. . . . The moral satisfaction comes from an increased sense of self-respect that is the result of the long-range choice, as well as from actual anticipation of achieving the purpose (losing weight).

Now if, for various reasons, my self-respect is at a low ebb – let us say I've had an exhausting day at work and a humiliating row with the foreman – I shall be more likely to give way to the immediate impulse, and buy the bar of chocolate. And if, on top of this, I know that the supper this evening will not be one that I shall enjoy, the temptation will be doubled. The immediate impulse has no rival, and even though I know that eating chocolate now will completely spoil my appetite for my un-exciting supper, I take a kind of pervere pleasure in giving way to my resentment, in making things even worse. This is the point where Irwin commits his double murder. In a character like Morris, it may not be as extreme as this. He experiences no long-range purpose to counterbalance the nagging sexual impulse; what is more, the sense of fatigue and disgust seems to increase the impulse, which is so powerful, so charged with anger, impatience, disgust, resentment, boredom, that a normal object will not suffice. The direction of the fantasy is already predetermined: the girl docilely taking off her clothes and bending over a table; now the imagination deliberately chooses a further extreme of the fantasy, the victim even more completely dominated and ravished, the conqueror even more dominant and terrifying. An act of choice has been made, and it has been made in the reverse direction from the one that creates the art-work, since it is bound to involve the reverse of the moral satisfaction that a man feels in an act of self-discipline. The essential component of the act is a self-abase-ment; and the self-abasement springs directly from the inability to 'fix' one's personality, to realise one's potentialities and impose them on the neighbours. I have elsewhere used the term 'promotion' for the feeling one experiences in moments of intensity, of rising above one's normal personality; this feeling I am now describing is a form of 'demotion', and a choice that arises from 'demotion'.

There is a further element in this choice of the criminal alternative that I have not touched on: what might be called, without exaggeration, the metaphysical problem of love. Blake said:

> *'What is it men in women do require?*
> *The lineaments of satisfied desire.'*

This implies that, in a sense, we are island universes, and our 'love' relations a matter of mutual satisfaction, like buying cabbage from the grocer. The love I feel for my children is another kind: a powerful and instinctive protectiveness. This same protectiveness may also form an important part of my feeling towards my wife; although for the most part, when men and women 'fall in love', it is a matter of the 'lineaments of satisfied desire'. And it could be argued that the protectiveness is an illusion, an instinct implanted in us for the preservation of the species, and that every parent who quarrels with a teenage son or daughter realises that it has now served its purpose, and that there was no real spiritual umbilical cord between himself and his offspring, just as a man who has been betrayed by his wife realises that their union was not the joining of two halves that belong together.

Now if, in fact, we are really island universes who are subject to *illusions* of union, of conjunction, then a person who recognises the casual and contingent character of human relations is a realist, although his neighbours might prefer to call him a cynic.

We know, as a biological fact, that animals that receive no affection in their earliest days become, in some strange way, incapable of giving or receiving it. In the *Encyclopedia of Murder*, I analysed the case of Peter Kürten, the Düsseldorf sadist, whose family was large and very poor; his father had criminal tendencies and served a period in jail for raping one of Kürten's sisters. During the period when Kürten was inflicting his one-man crime wave on Düsseldorf, killing or badly injuring men, women, children, horses, sheep – even a swan – he was also a good workman, involved in trade union activities, and an affectionate husband. His wife and his workmates found it impossible to believe that he was the multiple murderer who had terrorised Düsseldorf for two years. What they failed to understand was that Kürten *was* a good husband and a responsible trade unionist, but that he was fundamentally detached from his everyday life and background. He was genuinely quite fond of his wife; he even admitted that he liked two small girls whom he stabbed to death, and felt sorry to kill them. But in the last analysis, he felt that human beings are island universes. He responded to the children – aged five and fourteen – as a human being; the younger one even flung her arms round him and kissed him; but killing them was important if he was to have his orgasm. What did it matter if he liked them? If he walked off and left them alone, he might never see them again anyway, and he would still be unsatisfied. . . . An orgasm was real; one's feelings about people were illusory.

The disquieting thing about such a crime is that one could not give the murderer a convincing *reason* why his act should be condemned – I mean a reason he could not dismiss as social claptrap. Kürten would agree that society has a right to punish him, as a farmer has a right to shoot the fox that kills his chickens. But he would argue that it is no more morally wrong for him to murder children than for a fox to kill chickens.

Why do I raise such an issue? Does it have any relevance to the practical problem of murder? The answer is, surely, yes, as the Moors case proves. Brady argued, like de Sade, that human beings are small and rotten, and that the law against killing them is a social law, not a moral one. Once he had taken this step, he could tell himself that he was taking the same kind of risk as a poacher who gaffs a salmon in the river of a rich landowner, or as a big game hunter after a tiger.

Am I, perhaps, being too gloomy when I predict that the Moors case will not be the last one of its type? It was not the first: the Leopold and Loeb case can probably claim that dubious distinction, since the killers of Bobby Franks convinced themselves by intellectual argument – derived from Nietzsche – that murder was not morally wrong. And it might be said that this kind of killing was anticipated by Dostoievsky – in *Crime and Punishment, The Possessed* and *The Brothers Karamazov*. It has taken more than half a century for reality to catch up on art. The basic ingredient of this type of crime is a clever misfit with a deep sense of the insecurity of human relations, and a strong sexual appetite. In Dostoievsky's day Netchaevs and Raskolnikovs were rare because education was still the privilege of the few. The Leopold-Loeb murder might have been possible in 1870, since they were the children of rich parents; but even in 1924 – the year Bobby Franks was murdered – a man like Brady would not have had access to de Sade, nor perhaps even the educational qualifications to understand him. Such men as Irwin, Brady and Morris are the product of a relatively high level of civilisation – as are various other killers I have discussed in the last chapter of this book. It may be as well to recognise that they could – and almost certainly will – become an increasingly familiar pattern in criminology, and to pay some attention to the moral and psychological complexity of the phenomenon. We might also note, in passing, that it was not the pornography in de Sade that exercised the decisive influence on Brady, but the purely philosophical argument. If the solution is to make sure that de Sade's works do not fall into the hands of a Brady, then we had better also make sure that he is prevented from reading Nietzsche, Dostoievsky, Andreyev, Beckett, Céline, and half a dozen or so other writers whose metaphysic is close to de Sade's.

But in this preface I am not concerned with possible 'solutions'; I am trying only to explain what might be called my philosophical interest in murder. I see murder as a response to a certain problem of human freedom: not as a social problem, or a psychological problem, or even a moral problem (the word has too many social and religious implications that I would disown), but as an *existential* problem in the sense that the word would be used by Sartre or Heidegger. Once one has begun to think in these terms, it is easy to slip back into traditional religious concepts. (This explains the neo-religious movement of the twentieth century: Hulme, Eliot, Kafka, Greene, *et al.*) This should be avoided, if only to keep the issues clear.

In moments of crisis, man becomes aware that he possesses a far higher degree of freedom than he ever realised. In a sense, the problem of murder is implicit in Auden's lines:

> *'Life remains a blessing*
> *Although you cannot bless.'*

We are all subject to the 'great mystery of human boredom', which is the most common form of eclipse of the 'blessing'. But on the point of being shot, Graham Greene's whisky-priest suddenly realises that 'it would have been so easy to be a saint'. Raskolnikov realises that if he had to stand on a narrow ledge for ever, in eternal darkness and tempest, he would still prefer to do this rather than die at once. Even the American gangster Charley Birger remarked, as he stood on the scaffold: 'It *is* a beautiful world, isn't it?' We deny this freedom during every moment of our lives, except in these brief flashes of vision. But it is by far the most interesting possibility that human beings possess. And this recognition is the basis of my own philosophical vision, the central problem of all my work. We are like poverty-stricken Indians whose land is rich in oil; one day, someone is going to learn the technique of sinking wells. It will be the most important thing that has happened in human history.

Murder interests me because it is the most extreme form of the denial of this human potentiality. Life-devaluation has become a commonplace of our century. We talk glibly about social disintegration, about our moral bankruptcy, about the depth of our sense of defeat, and existentialist philosophers have been the chief exponents of this kind of pessimism. It may therefore sound absurd to say that every time I contemplate murder, I feel an odd spark of optimism. But it is so. We can accept boredom and philosophical pessimism as somehow inevitable, like the weather; but we cannot take this casual attitude towards murder. It arouses in us the same kind of morbid interest that the thought of fornication arouses in a puritanical old maid. If the old maid were at all analytical, she would see this morbid interest as a proof that sex cannot really be dismissed as nasty and disgusting; we do not feel morbid interest in a beggar covered with sores, or the carcass of a dead rat. Her morbid interest is an inverted form of the recognition that sex can be man's most vital insight into his secret potentialities. And if a murder case arouses this same sick curiosity, it is because we instinctively recognise it as a denial of these secret potentialities of freedom. Our interest in murder is a form of stirring in our sleep.

Let me reassure readers who find this approach baffling, or simply boring. All I have attempted in this book is a study of what might be called 'the changing fashions in murder'. I have tried to sketch an overall picture of the patterns of murder in various centuries, particularly the seventeenth, eighteenth, nineteenth and twentieth, and I have selected certain cases for more detailed exploration: Catherine Hayes, Neill Cream, H H Holmes. I had originally intended to include a study of another aspect of murder: what might be called 'murder for conviction'; the thugs of India, Hassan bin Saba and the sect of assassins, murder as a political weapon; but the book was already over-long. The material will form the basis of a second volume called *Order of Assassins*.

It will be observed that my references to certain other writers on murder – particularly Edmund Pearson, William Roughead and William Bolitho – are hardly complimentary. I dislike the 'murder for pleasure' approach. I consider this book, like the *Encyclopedia of Murder*, as a tentative contribution to a subject that does not yet exist as a definite entity, a science that has not yet taken shape. Such sciences are always coming into existence. Who could imagine that a history of mistletoe could be anything but a frivolous diversion? Yet when Sir James George Frazer pursued the subject, with endless digressions on mythology and magic, through the twelve volumes of *The Golden Bough*, it laid the cornerstone of the science of social anthropology. And what is social anthropology but the study of the relation of social custom and ritual to human freedom? I am not interested in criminology as such, but in the relation of crime to human freedom. I had also better admit that this volume will be rich in digressions. Whether this combination has produced anything more than a curious anthology of crime must be left to the judgement of the reader.

CW

One: The Beginnings

ONE MIGHT THINK that a crime as basic as murder would remain the same throughout the ages, and from country to country. This is not so. Murder is an individual kind of phenomenon, and it changes as frequently as courting customs. One of these days, a historian with a taste for the sensational will produce a social history of England entirely in terms of its murders. And such a historian would, I think, end by agreeing with me: that murder has not really come into its own until the twentieth century. Our age could be called the age of murder; that is, of murder for its own sake: for the fascination of crime. It has been a long, slow swing from the days when killing was a purely *natural* part of man's nature, when he killed an enemy as a butcher kills a pig. (I am not a vegetarian, but I can never enter a butcher's shop without imagining the horror of some far descendant of mine if he could stand there beside me: I can almost hear him say: 'My God, those people must have been far less civilised than one had assumed. It's only one step from eating one another. . . .') We must try to remember that this civilisation of ours has been an almost accidental product of human nature, and also a very recent one. In one of his most neglected books, *'42 to '44,* H G Wells remarks that it was only about ten thousand generations ago that human beings 'were brought together into a closeness of contact for which their past had not prepared them'. As men increased in numbers, they *had* to live together in fertile river valleys, for the rest of the land was too bleak or too wild to support them. The nomad herdsmen who remained 'outside' naturally became raiders and robbers. And Wells points out, 'The early civilisations were not slowly evolved and adapted

25

communities. They were essentially jostling *crowds* in which quite unprecedented reactions were possible . . . With the first cities came the first slums, and ever since then the huge majority of mankind has been living in slums.' Look at the plates in the old edition of Wells' *Outline of History* showing our early ancestors facing wild beasts – and clutching the branch of a tree or an elephant's shin bone. *This* is why you and I are living in a comfortable and complex civilisation: because our ancestors were the most efficient killers this earth has ever seen. Robert Ardrey has even gone so far as to argue that what developed man's intellect was the need to co-ordinate his brain and the bone club in his hand. Because of some physiological accident, man is the only creature on the surface of this planet to walk upright. And this has meant that he could use his hands for holding weapons. That use of an alien piece of bone – instead of fighting instinctively with teeth and claws – developed a certain detachment in man, turned him into a sleepwalker who has opened his eyes – the first great step towards his present ability for abstract thought.

To return to Wells' 'jostling crowds': these men were *not* 'social animals', no matter what Aristotle said. Perhaps a few of the tribal elders, the leaders, knew that the conglomerations of tribes were an important advance for these creatures of the wilderness. But the majority of the people who were born and grew up in the slums found themselves in a civilisation ready-made for them, and the question of choosing or rejecting it did not arise. They could either adapt themselves to it, or go and join the herdsmen and raiders in the wilderness. Or, of course, they could half-adapt themselves, become parasites, taking what they could grab, always watching for an opportunity to steal something. . . . This is *still* the way of life in the slums of many large cities, in Delhi, Hong Kong, Tangier, Rio de Janeiro. And it is not all that far behind us in the temperate latitudes of the west. Read Dickens' accounts of London in the 1840s. Or read Herbert Asbury's slightly more up-to-date account in *The Gangs of New York*:

'The cellars of the Old Brewery were divided into some twenty rooms. . . . During the period of its greatest renown, the building housed more than one thousand men, women and children, almost equally divided between Irish and Negroes. . . . In these dens were born children who lived into their teens without seeing the sun or breathing fresh air, for it was as dangerous for a resident of the Old Brewery to leave his niche as it was for an outsider to enter the building. In one basement room about fifteen feet square, not ten years before the Civil War, twenty-six people lived in the most frightful misery and squalor. Once, when a murder was committed in the chamber (a little girl was stabbed to death after she had been so foolish as to show a penny she had begged), the body lay in a corner for five days before it was finally buried in a shallow grave dug in the floor by the child's mother. . . .'

'Throughout the building the most frightful living conditions prevailed. Miscegenation was an accepted fact, incest was not uncommon, and there was much sexual promiscuity; the house swarmed with thieves, murderers, pickpockets, beggars, harlots and degenerates of every type. . . . Murders were frequent; it has been estimated that for almost fifteen years the Old Brewery averaged a murder a night, and the old Cow Bay tenements almost as many. Few of the killers were ever punished, for unless the police came in great force, they could not hope to leave the Old Brewery alive. . . .'

And *this* was one of the first consequences of early civilisation: a life that left room for the animal instincts, and nothing else. In another of his neglected later books, H G Wells rightly comments that the first crusade at the end of the eleventh century was one of the first times in history when a great mass of people were driven simply by an idea.[1] A strange prophet called Peter the Hermit appeared in Germany telling atrocity stories about when the Turks took Jerusalem. In his history of the Crusades, Stephen Runciman explains his success: 'Life for a peasant in north-western Europe was grim and insecure. Much land had gone out of cultivation during the barbarian invasions and the raids of the Norsemen. Dykes had been broken, and the sea and rivers had encroached on to the fields.

[1] *Crux Ansata, An Indictment of the Roman Catholic Church*, Penguin Books, 1943.

The lords often opposed the clearing of the forests in which they hunted for their game.' So what had they to lose? The 'people' streamed across Europe, and, as Wells explains : 'When they got among foreigners, they did not realise they were not among the infidel. Two great mobs, the advance guard of the expedition, committed such excesses in Hungary, where the language was incomprehensible to them, that they were massacred. A third host began with a great *pogrom* of the Jews in the Rhineland, and this multitude was also destroyed in Hungary. Two other swarms under Peter [the Hermit] reached Constantinople, to the astonishment and dismay of the Emperor Alexius. They looted and committed outrages, until he shipped them across the Bosphorus, to be massacred rather than defeated by the Seljuks.' And even when disciplined armies followed this mass of beggars and thieves, and captured Nicaea, the Emperor snatched it away from them before they could loot it.

The point makes itself. Masses of human beings here reveal their distinctively human quality, the ability to be driven by an idea . . . and the first thing they do is to rape and murder friendly foreigners and start a *pogrom* against the Jews. Yes, they could be said to be 'driven by an idea'; but the moment they felt themselves free of the restraints of their own home or village, they had only one desire: to possess that muscular farm girl, to eat those fat cows, to help themselves from the farmer's granaries and drink his wine. After all, *they* hadn't chosen civilisation; they woke up and found themselves in it. And the animal instincts were still strong. Man had to learn to be civilised the hard way – by massacring and being massacred. Even the peaceful ones, whose only desire was to farm their land or trade with the neighbouring towns, had to set up defensive organisations of armies and watchmen and police to protect them from fellow human beings who could not understand why they should not exercise animal strength or animal cunning to get what they wanted. Man was not trained to accept civilisation through kindness and reason, but through pain, as a wild animal is trained to obey with a red hot iron bar. And the ones who were lucky or intelligent enough to achieve some degree of comfort had to spend a great deal of their time protecting themselves against the unlucky majority.

All this means that, up to a few centuries ago, most crime was economic in origin. Consider, for example, the appalling story of Sawney Bean and his family, told by John Nicholson of Kirkcudbright in his *Tales of the Lowlands*: [1]

'Sawney Bean was born in East Lothian, about eight or nine miles eastward of the city of Edinburgh, in the reign of James I of Scotland [1394–1437 – the reader might note that in those days, even kings were short-lived, although forty-three would have been regarded as a ripe old age]. His father was a hedger and ditcher. . . .'

In his youth, Sawney Bean ran away with a woman 'as viciously inclined as himself', says Nicholson, 'and these two took up their habitation in a cave by the seaside on the shore of the county of Galloway; where they lived upward of twenty-five years without going into any city, town or village.

'In this time they had a great number of children and grandchildren, whom they brought up after their own manner, without any notions of humanity or civil society. They never kept any company, but among themselves, and they supported themselves wholly by robbing: being, moreover, so very cruel, that they never robbed anyone whom they did not murder.

'By this bloody method, and their being so retired from the world, they continued for a long time undiscovered; there being no person able to guess how the people were lost that went by the place where they lived. As soon as they had robbed any man, woman or child, they used to carry off the carcass to the den, where cutting it into quarters, they would pickle the mangled limbs, and afterwards eat it; this being their only sustenance: and notwithstanding they were at last so numerous, they commonly had superfluity of this abominable food, so that in the night time, they frequently threw legs and arms of the unhappy wretches they had murdered into the sea, at a great distance from their bloody habitation; the limbs were often cast

[1] It can also be found in the first series of Dorothy L Sayers' *Tales of Detection, Mystery and Horror*, Gollancz, 1928.

up by the tide in several parts of the country, to the astonishment and terror of all beholders. . . .'

'Persons who have gone about their lawful occasions fell so often into their hands, that it caused a general outcry in the country round about; no person knowing what was become of their friends or relations, if they were once seen by these merciless cannibals. . . .'

'Several honest travellers were taken up on suspicion and wrongfully hanged upon bare circumstances; several innocent inn-keepers were executed . . . [Although] a great many had been executed, not one of them all made any confession at the gallows. . . .'

Sawney and his family became experts in ambush; for they all knew it was vitally important there should be no one to tell the tale; therefore they never tackled more than two men on horseback, although they were known to ambush as many as six men on foot. No one suspected that their lonely cave might house the robbers, for when the tide came up, it reached two hundred yards into their cave – which went back nearly a mile. It must be remembered that Sawney's family had to live for the most part in darkness; the smoke of a fire would choke them, and would certainly give them away. Their food must have been uncooked.

They had continued like this for twenty-five years, and were estimated to have killed about a thousand people, when the inevitable finally happened; a victim got away. A man and his wife were on the same horse, returning from a fair. They were ambushed; the woman was pulled off the horse. If Nicholson's account is accurate, and not touched up for the sake of horror, they must have been hungry, for they quickly cut her throat, disembowelled her, and proceeded to feed – possibly a fresh, warm body was a luxury after cold, decaying bits of flesh. While the husband fought on, a party of sixteen people, also returning from the fair, appeared on the scene, and the robbers made off. At last, someone had glimpsed them, and could verify that they were men – for no doubt there were those who believed it was some monster – perhaps a giant octopus from the sea. The man told his story, and was taken to Glasgow to

ment Annual Report for 1966 shows around a total of 33,000 'offences' of every sort from petty larceny to murder (139 of the latter); of these, fewer than 6,000 were 'cleared' by the police. In the time of Henry VIII, every one of these 6,000 offenders would have been executed, trebling the actual rate of execution. Admittedly, the population of Cleveland is half as much again as the population of England in the reign of Henry VIII – six million compared with about four million. It still looks as if the crime rate in the sixteenth century was relatively low compared to our own. One must also take into account that with such a small population, much of it confined to country areas, there was far less of the 'alienation' that produces so much modern crime. Even today, most of the quiet country areas of England are relatively free of serious crime; in Cornwall, where I live, most people still do not bother to lock their doors or cars.

There is one case of the fifteenth century – a century after the execution of Sawney Bean – that should be mentioned because of its strangeness: the case of Marshall Gilles de Rais (or Retz). De Rais (1404–1440) was the richest nobleman in Europe, and made even richer by his marriage to a wealthy heiress at the age of sixteen. He fought beside Joan of Arc, but retired to his country estates (he had half a dozen or so) after the coronation of Charles VII. He had a bodyguard of two hundred knights and a private chapel with thirty canons. But he was also slightly 'unbalanced' – it must be difficult to maintain complete psychological balance if you are the richest man in a poverty stricken country – not to mention being a famous patriot who had actually crowned the King with his own hands. He was excitable, extravagant, capricious; H G Wells has pointed out (in '*42 to '44*) that if he had lived today he would probably have squandered his fortune at Monte Carlo or at horse racing. Instead, he went in for black magic. Since running five huge country estates diminished his fortune, he decided to try to recover it by discovering the philosopher's stone that would turn all base metals to gold. Gilles reminds us of certain of the Caesars – particularly Caligula; he seems to be another case of absolute power and wealth unbalancing an already over-excitable nature. Oddly enough, he blamed his downfall on an illustrated edition of Suetonius's *Caesars*, and on the remark that certain Caesars 'took a singular pleasure in putting children to martyrdom'. Gilles was, in any case, what we would now call a pedophile; his sexual preference was for young boys or girls; he also appears to have been a sadist, for having used the children sexually, he had their heads cut off. He was accused of killing about a hundred and forty children, although whether this was part of some black magic ceremony (black magic often involves 'blood from a virgin') was never clear. Gilles was not arrested for his crimes against children, but for beating a priest during a quarrel. It has been pointed out many times that his inquisitors stood to gain his immense fortune – for his lands would be forfeited to the Church and ducal court – and his trial was conducted with considerable irregularity; none of his retainers was called upon to give evidence. His personal retainers were tortured until they incriminated him, and then released. But even so, it seems unlikely that there was smoke without fire; it was hardly necessary to cook up such an incredible indictment to obtain his lands; the charge of abuse of clerical privilege and the practice of black magic would have been enough. (The Duke was so certain of conviction that he disposed of his share of Gilles' land fifteen days before the trial started.) Gilles was strangled on 26th October 1440.

The case is strange because it is so untypical of its period; it sounds like a throw-back to ancient Rome. Wells' theory about Gilles de Rais is as good as any. He points out that civilisation was largely 'congestion' rather than a true community; people seething and swarming together, always involved in hatreds and petty squabbles, like a large family living in a small house. Human nature being what it is, most of the improvements in civilised relations were brought about by external forces – the law, wealth, strong men learning to respect one another's rights – not by the sympathetic feelings of 'men of good will'. The strong and wealthy felt very little regard for their inferiors, and only contempt for Jews, infidels and people who got in their way. Expression of cruelty towards these inferiors was natural; cruelty was an accepted part of the social structure. But whereas the average lord of the manor contented himself by exercising his *droit de Seigneur* on the newly married wives of his farm workers, the excitable and 'artistic' Gilles had stranger tastes. This combination – of sexual perversion with psychopathic indifference to anything but his own pleasure – makes him, in fact, the opposite of a throw-back; he was a 'throw forward' to the age of Peter Kürten and the Moors murderers, and one of the most curious figures in criminal history.

People have always been fascinated by crime, but it was not until the beginning of the eighteenth century that there were actual compilations that give us an idea of the crime of the epoch. However, the Elizabethan age introduced a rather curious novelty: a type of play called 'domestic tragedy' (as distinguished from the usual 'tragedy, comedy and history' classification) which was an attempt to present a police report on the stage. Such plays as *The Witch of Edmonton, A Warning for Fair Women, Arden of Faversham* and *The Yorkshire Tragedy* give us an accurate picture of the kind of crime that made the Elizabethans shudder in horrified fascination. The Elizabethans delighted in blood; it was a naïve and innocent delight of the kind that makes ten-year-old boys read comic books of 'Frankenstein versus the Wolf Man'. At the end of *The Spanish Tragedy* or *Titus Andronicus* they loved the thought that the stage ought to be ankle deep in blood. It is a pity the cinema had to wait another three hundred years to be invented; James Bond would have been their idea of supreme artistic genius. (It is a mistake to think of the Elizabethan audiences as being sophisticated and sensitive to language; they couldn't tell the difference between a masterpiece like *The White Devil* and rubbish like *The Spanish Tragedy.*)

In the following pages I propose to consider some of the best known Elizabethan cases in detail: partly to demonstrate my thesis that an age can be understood through its typical murder cases; partly because of the interest of the cases themselves.

But first, we might raise an interesting preliminary question: why *do* certain murders come to fascinate the general public? In 1823, a cheat and a gambler named Weare made the mistake of accepting an invitation to a weekend cottage in the country; his hosts were three villains called Thurtell, Hunt and Probert. Thurtell killed Weare by cutting his throat with a penknife and then jamming his pistol against his head so violently that it went into his brain. Probert turned King's Evidence; Thurtell and Hunt were tried and Thurtell was duly hanged. A pointless, featureless murder of no interest, and yet it caused more sensation than almost any other murder of the nineteenth century. Why? It is impossible to guess. Five years later, a farmer named Corder murdered a mole-catcher's daughter who was pressing him for marriage, and buried her in a barn. *Murder in the Red Barn* subsequently became one of the most popular melodramas of the nineteenth century, and the book about the trial remained a best-seller for a hundred years, in a cheap little green edition printed in double columns. In this case, the interest is partly due to the 'supernatural' aspect of the case; the mother had recurrent dreams that her daughter was buried in the red barn in a certain corner, and they dug there....

What have two such cases in common? Only one thing: that you or I can read them with a certain horror that springs from identification with the murderer. In the ordinary adventure story we identify with the hero as he swims a crocodile-infested river or plods across the waterless desert in search of King Solomon's mines; we don't really envy him, but we enjoy putting ourselves into his shoes. And as we read of William Corder going to such desperate lengths to untangle himself from Maria Marten, we experience the same horrified fascination, glad not to be in his shoes, but willing to put ourselves into them temporarily, just to see what a bad end he comes to. And at the end, it is almost as pleasant as wakening from a nightmare and finding yourself in your own bedroom. . . . It is enjoyable putting yourself into somebody's shoes when you can take yourself out of them at a moment's notice.

This seems to be the only explanation of why certain crimes

fascinated the Elizabethans so much that dramatised versions of them played to packed houses. J A Symonds says of the *Yorkshire Tragedy*: 'Like the asp, it is short, ash-coloured, poison-fanged, blunt-headed, abrupt in movement, hissing and wriggling through the sands of human misery.' What happened was that a man called Walter Calverley, of Calverley in Yorkshire, had a fit of temporary insanity in which he killed his two young children with a knife, and also stabbed his wife; he was on his way out of the house to kill his third child – who was with a nurse – when he was caught. Nowadays he would have been committed to Broadmoor, for the thing was clearly unpremeditated. *Stow's Chronicle* (1580), which tells the story in a few lines, does not explain why Calverley committed the crime, whether he was an alcoholic or had suffered previous fits of insanity. The unknown author – some scholars attribute the play to Shakespeare – had to provide a motive, so he set out to draw the kind of moral lesson the Elizabethans loved. Calverley has got himself into trouble by gambling and loose living, mortgaged his lands, and is thinking of bigamy. His brother, a university student, has been thrown into prison since he stood guarantee for his brother's debts. The husband is portrayed as a snarling villain, growling: 'Bastards, bastards . . . begot in tricks, begot in tricks. . . .' The scene in which he kills both children, one of them while the mother is trying to protect it, would be too strong on stage for modern stomachs. His wife recovered from the attack, and the play concludes with a scene in which the husband, on his way to execution, sees her and expresses repentance. Calverley was, in fact, pressed to death: that is, stretched under a board upon which heavy weights were placed until he was crushed or suffocated; a curious and inhuman punishment.

After the *Yorkshire Tragedy*, the best known Elizabethan 'domestic tragedy' is *Arden of Faversham*, an altogether more expert piece of work. Again, it has been attributed to Shakespeare, and in this case, the attribution seems more likely. The story on which it is based was told by Holinshed, on whom Shakespeare drew heavily for material for his histories. Like the *Yorkshire Tragedy*, it is, by modern standards, a singularly straightforward murder case, with none of those interesting 'angles' that would excite a Fleet Street crime reporter. Thomas Arden was a Kentish gentleman, the Mayor of Faversham, who married Alice North, the sister of the North who translated Plutarch. Arden was more interested in money than sex, and Holinshed suggests that he married Alice for her powerful family connections rather than because he was in love with her. Probably her dowry was generous. And having secured her, he went back to his main business of accumulating money and land – he managed to defraud a man named Greene of some abbey lands by using his influence to get a Chancery grant of them. Alice now met a tailor called Thomas Morsby (or Mosbie, as it is spelt in the play) and became his mistress; Morsby was in the service of her father, Sir Edward North. Arden was perfectly happy about handing over his marital duties to Morsby. He invited Morsby to come and live in his house, and left him there to console Alice when he had to go on business trips. He certainly knew what was going on; there was an occasion when he saw Alice with her arms around Morsby's neck, and heard them referring to him as a cuckold. What pleased him less was the discovery that the couple were thinking of murdering him; however, he didn't take this too seriously, and continued to encourage Morsby to keep up the good work. Presumably this left Morsby too tired to do the murder himself; for he approached Greene – the man who has been defrauded – and Greene, in turn, hired two assassins with the beautiful names of Black Will and Shagbag. These proved to be a pair of incompetents, and Charlie Chaplin could have made a superb comedy out of their attempts to kill Arden. Even Shakespeare – or whoever dramatised the case – has a preposterously funny scene in which the two murderers wait for Arden by a market stall, and the stall-keeper swings his shutter into place and cracks the skull of Black Will.

Morsby tried various sophisticated and over-subtle methods of killing Arden – a poisoned crucifix, poisoned pictures, etc – but finally, they were forced to summon Black Will and Shagbag to the house to kill Arden as he sat at table. Morsby finished him off with a blow on the head from a flat iron, after he had been stabbed and throttled. They then dragged the body to a nearby field. It was snowing, so the footprints were obvious, and one of the accomplices forgot to throw the blood-stained knife and towel into the well. The law took violent retribution. Murder of a husband by his wife was regarded as a form of treason, and the penalty was to be burned alive. The servants who had helped in disposing of the body were also tried. Shagbag, Greene and the painter who had supplied poisons managed to escape; the last lines of the play mention that Shagbag was murdered in Southwark. The law was so anxious to make an example of everyone concerned in the murder that an innocent servant named Bradshaw was tried with the others, and sentenced to death, although the rest of the conspirators all asserted that he was not concerned. 'These condemned persons were diversely executed in sundry places,' says Holinshed; the servant Michael hung in chains at Favers-ham; a maid servant who had been an accessory was burnt alive, 'crying out on hir mistresse that had brought hir to this ende'. Mosbie and his sister were hanged at Smithfield in London; Alice Arden was burnt at Canterbury on 14th March, and Black Will was also burnt on a scaffold at 'Flishing in Zeland'. Greene – the man who had procured the murderers – returned some years later, and was promptly executed and hung in chains. Even a man named Adam Foule, who had merely acted as Alice's messenger to Mosbie, was sent to London with his legs tied under the horse's belly and imprisoned in the Marshalsea. Holinshed adds the legend that the imprint of Arden's body could be seen in the grass for many years after-wards; he also notes that Arden had stolen the field in which his corpse was found from a poor widow. The archives of Canterbury contain the entry: 'For the charges of brenning Mistress Arden and execution of George Bradshaw [the inno-cent servant], 43 shillings.'

The play itself is remarkably successful as drama; but it can hardly be called a realistic presentation of the case. Arden – who was obviously a vicious miser – is portrayed as a doting husband who loves his wife so much that he closes his eyes to her infidelities. Alice is made to repent fulsomely when she sees her husband's body; in fact, it was Alice who accused the innocent Bradshaw – hardly the act of a repentant woman.

In short, it is necessary to read between the lines to get the facts of the case. Arden married Alice for money, and then deliberately found her a lover. Alice was almost certainly a nymphomaniac. Why did she accuse Bradshaw, whom the others declared to be innocent? Was it because she had made advances to him and had been rejected? Why was Adam Foule imprisoned, although he had been only a messenger? Was it because the judges suspected that any male connected with Alice might have been her lover?

We also learn something of the Elizabethans from the fate of the maid, who had been merely an accessory after the fact. She was burned alive, while Mosbie, the instigator, was only hanged. Why such severity over the murder of a highly unpleasant miser? It is surely a reasonable inference that it was the sexual aspect of the case that aroused this universal morbid interest. The Elizabethan public was very like the public of today, except that it was far less sophisticated, since there were no sensational newspapers to spread the details of every divorce case. There is an immense reservoir of sexual frustration under the surface of working class life, and this case offered it an outlet. Alice Arden was one of these upper class women who spend their days in the arms of lovers; probably every woman in the case was somebody or other's mistress. . . . They all deserved burning. So when the story was made into a play, Arden had to be whitewashed – otherwise the sexual motive was made less important, and nobody wanted that. . . .

Those who followed the Max Garvie murder case in England in 1968 will note that human nature has changed very little in four hundred years. Garvie, a wealthy farmer, was murdered by his wife, Sheila (33), and her lover, Brian Tevendale (22); like Arden, he had connived at the affair. There was also some titillating evidence about wife swopping and nude parties, and the sensational Press gave the story the fullest treatment for week after week – the story of Garvie's wife's lover, the story of Garvie's mistress, the story of Garvie's mistress's husband, the story of Garvie's mistress's brother's mistress. . . . There is only one major difference between the England of 1968 and the England of 1568. If anyone turns the Garvie case into a play or a novel, everybody in it will be represented as sex-mad; there will be no innocent parties and no final repentance. Whether this is an advance on Elizabethan morality is difficult to say; but there can be no doubt that the punishments meted out in the Garvie case represent a moral advance on the part of society.

The pamphlet called *A Brief Discourse of the late Murther of Master George Sanders* was published in 1573, and an anonymous author used it as the basis of another popular play, *A Warning for Fair Women*. The case again concerns the murder of a husband by a wife and her lover; but it has one touch that, if true, gives it a certain psychological interest. A young Irish captain named Browne was introduced to Sanders, who was a merchant of Shooters Hill, London, and to his wife Anne. Browne conceived a violent passion for Anne; but she was a virtuous girl, and it was not returned. Browne therefore approached a friend of hers, a certain Widow Drury, whose side-line was fortune-telling, and persuaded her to help. The widow seized an opportunity to read Anne Sanders' hand, and told her with amazement that it indicated that she would soon become a widow, and marry a handsome man who would become wealthy and powerful. The widow claimed to be able to read what the man would look like – and, of course, her description bore a remarkable resemblance to Browne. Mrs Sanders was told that the stars would bring about her marriage to Browne in due course, and all she had to do in the meantime was treat him with common courtesy. This was enough. Obviously, if a woman is convinced that a certain man is destined to be her future husband, common courtesy will soon give way to warmer feelings.

Probably Browne meant only to seduce her; the chronicle suggests he was a roué. But having persuaded her to allow him into her bed, he made up his mind he was in love with her. They decided to kill Sanders, and Browne and a manservant fell on him in a wood near Shooters Hill and killed him; they also

43

attacked his servant, John Beane, and left him for dead. But Beane was alive; he crawled away, badly injured, and identified the murderer. He later gave evidence at the trial. Browne, his mistress, and the accomplice, were all hanged. Browne showed himself to have more spirit than Morsby; he denied her complicity to the end, and she might well have escaped the penalty if she had not suddenly decided to confess in prison. Widow Drury was also hanged.

One more case that became the subject of a drama deserves mention here: the case of the wife murderer Francis Thorney, executed in 1621. The drama is *The Witch of Edmonton* by Ford, Rowley and Dekker, and the murder scenes are almost certainly by Ford. Frank Thorney was a rather weak young man who seduced a fellow-servant, Winnifrede – who had already been seduced by their master, a certain Sir Arthur Clarington. The latter was pleased about the match and helped them with money. Thorney's father, described as 'a poor gentleman', had other plans for his son; he wanted to marry him to a pretty farmer's daughter named Susan, who was perfectly willing. Thorney was weak enough to allow himself to be swept into a bigamous marriage with the latter, although he was in love with Winnifrede. Both women were so gentle and sweet that he began to experience agonies of guilt. One day, he set out on a journey with Winnifrede, who was disguised as a page, and the innocent and infatuated Susan insisted on accompanying him part of the way, until his overburdened emotions found relief in stabbing her. He then tied himself to a tree, and made several cuts on his body to support his story of being attacked by two former suitors of Susan's. Everything went well until Susan's sister discovered the bloodstained knife in his pocket – upon which Thorney confessed.

This theme is united to the story of a 'witch', Mother Sawyer, who was burned at the same time Thorney was executed. The authors did this by suggesting that Mother Sawyer had bewitched Thorney into murdering his wife – for which there is no evidence whatever. But it might be mentioned that the authors showed a rare insight into the psychology of witchcraft, in showing Mother Sawyer as an ugly poverty-stricken old woman who is generally regarded as a witch because her ugliness excited so much repulsion; the harmless old creature is finally driven to seeking a compact with the devil out of sheer desperation at the injustice. This is the kind of insight that we tend to flatter ourselves is uniquely 'modern'.

I cannot resist a few words on the most fascinating of unsolved Elizabethan murder cases: the murder of Christopher Marlowe. It is true that, from the point of view of literary history, it was neither unsolved nor a murder. But there are too many unanswered questions about Marlowe's death to allow us to accept the story told to the Queen's Coroner. This story was as follows. On Wednesday, 30th May 1593, the twenty-nine-year-old poet and dramatist – one of Shakespeare's most powerful rivals – was supping in a room of Eleanor Bull's tavern in Deptford, which is now a London suburb. There were three others present: Ingram Frizer, a servant of Sir Thomas Walsingham, Nicholas Skeres, his friend, a definitely crooked character, and Robert Poley, a spy. They had spent the day together, and drunk a great deal. At about nine in the evening, there was a scuffle, and the hostess was informed that she had a corpse on her premises. Marlowe had been stabbed above the right eye. The story the other three told is that Marlowe had been lying on the bed, and had suddenly seized Frizer's dagger and attacked him with it, giving him a couple of cuts on the head. Frizer wrested the dagger from him and killed him in self-defence. It was said that the scuffle was due to a dispute over the bill; but for some odd reason neither Poley nor Skeres was involved in this dispute, although they were also presumably paying their share. All that is certain is that Marlowe was killed with one clean stab above the eye, and that all three men who were present had the same story to tell.

The first questions we are tempted to ask concern the nature of the struggle and the wounds. Marlowe was lying on the bed; Ingram was a few feet away, between Poley and Skeres, so that he could not escape when Marlowe grabbed his dagger and attacked him. It seems odd that Marlowe should have failed to kill Frizer if he stood behind him with a dagger. One blow driven downwards through the top of the skull would have done it. But would a man attacking another man from behind stab him in such a way as to inflict two cuts (each two inches long) on his scalp? Surely he would go for his back, or the back of his neck? And supposing that Ingram then wrestled with Marlowe and got the dagger, while Skeres and Poley looked on without attempting to interfere; would he be likely to stab him above the eye? Two men wrestling for a dagger are more likely to inflict body wounds on one another. Whereas a deep wound above the eye might be consistent with a man being attacked suddenly as he lay on his back on a bed, with his eyes closed.

The wound was described as being two inches wide and one inch deep, and Dr S A Tannenbaum in his book *The Assassination of Christopher Marlowe* reaches the conclusion that such a wound would almost certainly not kill instantaneously; the victim might linger for hours, or even days.

Dr Tannenbaum believes that Marlowe's death was premeditated assassination, and he may well be right. The three men in the room with him were all unsavoury characters. Frizer was a confidence trickster; Skeres was a robber and cutpurse; Poley was a spy, and had served prison sentences for various minor crimes. Frizer was in the employ of Sir Thomas Walsingham, and Skeres and Poley had both been associated with Walsingham in uncovering the Babington Catholic conspiracy against the Queen.

But Walsingham was an old friend and patron of Marlowe's, and all the evidence indicates that he and Marlowe were lovers. The knowledge that Marlowe was homosexual raises another interesting possibility – that he was murdered in the course of making amorous advances to Frizer. But this would not explain why Frizer was taken back into the employ of Walsingham after killing Walsingham's lover. Perhaps Walsingham and Marlowe had quarrelled? This seems the only theory that is consistent with the facts (which were unearthed as recently as 1925, when the coroner's report was found in the public archives). Or perhaps, as Francis Meres wrote five years after the murder, Marlowe was killed by 'a rival of his in his own lewd love' – ie, perhaps Frizer had replaced Marlowe as Walsingham's favourite pathic. It is even possible, as some later writers suggested, that Meres meant the quarrel was over a woman.

Two weeks before Marlowe's death, constables searched the room of his friend Thomas Kyd, author of the sensational and sanguinary *Spanish Tragedy*, and found certain theological arguments denying the divinity of Jesus. Kyd protested that these papers were not his, but Marlowe's. Atheism was a very serious matter in those days; Marlowe's schoolfriend Francis Kett was burned for it at Norwich in 1589. (Kyd's betrayal of Marlowe did him no good; after a period in Bridewell prison, he died in the following year, aged thirty-six. He had been 'put to the torture' in prison.) Marlowe was arrested at Sir Thomas Walsingham's and appeared before the Privy Council on 20th May; he was released on bail – perhaps through the offices of powerful friends. But he was in trouble; friends or no friends, he would probably end in Bridewell or the Tower – like his friend and fellow rationalist, Sir Walter Raleigh. Did Walsingham feel that Marlowe would seriously compromise him at court, and that it was time the connection between them was severed, before Marlowe dragged him down with him?

Perhaps the most interesting – and unprovable – theory about Marlowe is the one put forward by Calvin Hoffmann in *The Murder of the Man Who Was Shakespeare*. He believes – very reasonably – that Walsingham was determined to save his friend, and contrived a fake murder to get him out of England. He argues convincingly that the jury who acquitted Frizer was 'rigged', and that the body they saw was not that of Marlowe but of some other man who had been killed earlier. This supposition is supported by Dr Tannenbaum's argument that Marlowe would not have died instantaneously of the inch-deep wound over his eye.

The remainder of Dr Hoffmann's theory is even more startling. He believes that Marlowe went to the Continent, under Walsingham's protection, and continued to write. What happened to his later plays? They were published under the

47

name of Shakespeare. It is interesting that Shakespeare's first publication, *Venus and Adonis,* appeared in the September after Marlowe's death. And no Shakepearean scholar has ever tried to deny that *Henry VI, Richard III* and *Titus Andronicus* are so like Marlowe that it is generally supposed that Marlowe had a hand in the writing of them (the assumption being that they were written before May 1593, of course). Seven years after Marlowe's death the publisher Thomas Thorpe 'brought to light' a translation of the first book of Lucan by Marlowe; Thorpe later published Shakespeare's sonnets, dedicated to 'Mr W H'. (Hoffmann speculates that this was Walsing-Ham – Elizabethan names were often hyphenated like this.)

Dr Hoffmann has only one really weighty argument on his side. He speaks of Dr Thomas Corwin Meadenhall, who believed that every writer's work has certain stylistic characteristics that are as ineradicable as a thumb print. Chief among these 'constants' is the number of times he employs words of a certain number of letters. Meadenhall set out to count the number of letters in every word in several works by various writers, and apparently proved his theory. The writer's vocabulary is his thumb print, and each writer's print was absolutely consistent throughout his work. No two authors were alike.

According to Dr Hoffmann, a wealthy Baconian – an advocate of the theory that the plays of Shakespeare were written by Bacon – asked Dr Meadenhall to compare Bacon's 'thumb print' with Shakespeare's. Shakespeare's average word was four letters long – ie if one took a sentence of Shakespeare, counted the letters in it, and then divided by the number of words in the sentence, the result would be four. The words Shakespeare used with most frequency were also four letters long – words like 'each', 'plot', 'been', etc. Bacon tended to use much longer words, and his letter average was also well above four.

Meadenhall tested various other writers besides Bacon and Shakespeare. One was Marlowe. And Marlowe's thumb print was identical with Shakespeare's.

I accept that Dr Hoffmann is writing in good faith. But if he is correct, then he has proved his case, and no further argument is needed. His book should have been devoted to Meadenhall, and to demonstrations that no two 'thumb prints' *are* alike; and finally, that Marlowe's and Shakespeare's are. In these days of electronic computers, it should be possible to prove this beyond all possible doubt. If Dr Hoffmann can prove his thesis, he has accomplished the most remarkable piece of literary detective work in European history.

It might be mentioned in passing that Clemence Dane's play *Will Shakespeare,* written in 1921, four years before the Inquest Report turned up, argues that Marlowe was murdered by Shakespeare in a quarrel over a girl.

For readers who are unfamiliar with the various theories about the authorship of Shakespeare's plays, it might be worthwhile to point out that the basic problem is this: that there is no evidence whatever connecting an actor called William Shakespeare of Stratford with the plays published under his name. Shakespeare was not known in Stratford as a writer but as a businessman. The bust of Shakespeare that was put up in the Stratford church about 1630 does not show him holding a pen, but with both hands resting on a sack, a symbol of trade. There exist no manuscripts of Shakespeare, although there are of plenty of other Elizabethans. He left no manuscripts in his will, or copies of his plays, which seems odd – surely he had enough pride to keep copies of his various works in his house? His father was illiterate; so were his children; the few signatures of Shakespeare that exist support the notion that he was little better. Whether Shakespeare was Marlowe or Bacon or anybody else – that is to say, whether the actor was bribed to allow the use of his name on the title page of somebody else's work – is a matter that may never be proved; but let us acknowledge at least that it is very strange that there exists no evidence whatever to link the actor-businessman of Stratford with the playwright.

And incidentally, if Hoffmann's theory is correct, Shakespeare may well have been a murderer; *somebody* killed the man whose body was passed off as Marlowe's.

If this cross-section of Elizabethan murder is representative –

49

and there is every reason to believe it is – then the Elizabethans belonged to the age of innocence. Murder was generally committed for such straightforward motives as money or passion. No one thought of dismembering bodies or burning them in furnaces. And the attitude of the Elizabethans towards murder was also very simple. It must be borne in mind that England was still united in matters of religion, and that religion was still the supremely important subject, the cause of all the major disputes and national crises. Even a century and a half later, in the time of Dr Johnson, this was still so. That was an age when volumes of sermons became best-sellers, and Johnson could discourse with Boswell about the relative merits of the sermons of a dozen different divines. We can look back upon such an age with a certain nostalgia – but then, we are not required to live in it. Religion was absolute, in a way that it has ceased to be in Britain – except, perhaps, in some remote community in the far reaches of Scotland or Wales. Everybody went to church every Sunday, and listened to sermons on the seven deadly sins. What horrified and fascinated them about murder was not primarily that Thomas Morsby killed his mistress's husband with a flat iron, but that he had committed a mortal sin for which he would fry in hell. It was his *wickedness* – that is, his defiance of the standards they were told about every Sunday of their lives – that shocked them. If Frank Thorney killed his bigamously married wife, it must have been the Devil – operating through Mother Sawyer – who was responsible. The forces of evil were very real to them; not one of them doubted that the Devil really existed, and that he probably had horns on his head and a long tail. The gibes for which Marlowe was arrested were not directed against God or the Devil – he no doubt believed in them like everybody else – but against Adam, Jesus, Moses, and so on. ('He affirmeth that Moses was but a Jugler and that one Harriot, being Sir Walter Raleigh's man, can do more than he.')

But for all this religious streak that made the Elizabethans so interested in murder and violence, it was still an age of cruelty. Lytton Strachey describes the death of the Queen's physician, Dr Lopez, a Portuguese Jew, accused of plotting

50

with Spain against the Queen and the Portuguese Pretender, together with two others, Ferreira and Tinoco (the latter had been lured to England by a safe-conduct, which carefully forgot to mention whether he would be allowed out again):

'A vast crowd was assembled to enjoy the spectacle. The Doctor, standing on the scaffold, attempted in vain to make a dying speech: the mob was too angry and too delighted to be quiet. . . . He was strung up and – such was the routine of the law – cut down while life was still in him. Then the rest of the time-honoured punishment – castration, disembowelling and quartering – was carried out. Ferreira was the next to suffer. After that, it was the turn of Tinoco. He had seen what was to be his fate, twice repeated, and from close enough. His ears were filled with the shrieks and moans of his companions, and his eyes with every detail of the contortions and the blood. And so his adventures had ended thus at last. And yet, they had not quite ended; for Tinoco, cut down too soon, recovered his feet after the hanging. He was lusty and desperate, and he fell upon his executioner. The crowd, wild with excitement, and cheering on the plucky foreigner, broke through the guards, and made a ring to watch the fight. But, before long, the instincts of law and order reasserted themselves. Two stalwart fellows, seeing that the executioner was giving ground, rushed forward to his rescue. Tinoco was felled by a blow on the head; he was held down firmly on the scaffold, and, like the others, castrated, disembowelled and quartered.'[1]

It was later discovered that Dr Lopez was innocent.

The Queen herself was almost certainly accessory to a murder. Her lover, Sir Robert Dudley, had married a girl named Amy Robsart eight years before the Queen's accession to the throne, and the Queen was interested in making Dudley Prince Consort. In September 1560, the Queen told a foreign envoy that Lady Dudley was dying, when there was certainly nothing wrong with her. Four days later, Amy Robsart was found at the bottom of a great staircase in her Oxfordshire house; her skull was fractured. She was twenty-eight years old, her husband a year older. Elizabeth seems to have changed

[1] *Elizabeth and Essex,* Chap VI.

51

her mind about marrying her lover, or perhaps political necessity made it impossible. There seems to be little ground for
doubt that Dudley (later the Earl of Leicester) – whom the
Spanish envoy had described as 'heartless, spiritless, treacher-
ous and violent' – had his wife killed, and that the Queen knew
about it in advance. Perhaps she disliked the violence of the
method; the Simancas archives indicate that there was a plot
to poison Amy Robsart – no doubt this was what the Queen
had in mind when she said that Lady Dudley was dying.

So how can we begin to understand this strange Elizabethan
age, in which the chief objection to murder was that it was a
mortal sin, and yet in which the Queen could be privy to a
murder? Obviously, it differed from ours in respects that are
so fundamental that the Elizabethans are as alien to us as a
tribe of aborigines. They were driven by their passions to an
extent that is incomprehensible in our self-divided age, and
passion was the stuff of their literature; they could understand
Macbeth and *Othello* in a way that is impossible to a modern
scholar, no matter how closely he studies the period. When we
read Hoffmann's theory of Marlowe's escape, our main
thought is for the innocent man who was murdered to provide
the coroner with a body; the Elizabethans would have thought
this irrelevant. If Marlowe really escaped, he probably never
lost a single night's sleep over the murdered man. Neither
would the Elizabethans have agreed with the modern notion
that genius and crime are inconsistent.[1] As recently as 1926,
it was discovered that Sir Thomas Malory, author of *Le
Morte D'Arthur* (which Caxton printed in 1485) was a rapist
and an outlaw, who led a band of robbers that sacked monas-
teries and stole herds of cattle; he wrote *Le Morte D'Arthur*
in jail. (The indictment against him mentions that on 23rd May
1450, Malory 'broke into the house of Hugh Smyth and
feloniously raped Joan, the wife of the said Hugh', and on 6th
August of the same year, he broke into Hugh Smyth's house
and 'feloniously raped Joan' again as well as stealing forty

---

[1] As far as I know, this was first advanced by Pushkin in his play *Mozart
and Salieri* (1828), which is based on the rumour that Mozart was poisoned
by his rival Salieri; Rimsky Korsakov turned it into an opera.

pounds' worth of Smyth's property; it would be interesting to know whether raping Joan Smyth became a habit, and if so, whether she finally got to like it.)

One of the greatest musicians of the Elizabethan period, Carlo Gesualdo, Prince of Venosa, discovered his wife in bed with her lover, the Duke of Andria, and killed her himself, while his retainers killed the Duke. (Anatole France, who based his account[1] on earlier records, does not spare the barbarous details of Gesualdo hacking at his wife's naked body with his sword even after her death.) Gesualdo then hastened off to one of his castles and murdered his second child, in case the Duke of Andria was the father. His strange, neurotic madrigals, with their modern-sounding harmonies, were regarded as evidence of his insanity for centuries after his death; but in recent years it has been recognised that they are as important as Monteverdi's.

Records of crime between the Elizabethan age and the age of Dr Johnson are scanty; only some of the most famous have survived in historical records. The most notable murder during the reign of Elizabeth's successor James I was that of Sir Thomas Overbury by James's favourite, Robert Carr, Duke of Somerset.

Carr was a tall, blond young lout, completely illiterate. When he was eleven years old and a page boy, he met Thomas Overbury, a brilliant young homosexual. Carr came heavily under the influence of Overbury, and was presumably seduced by him. Five years later, Carr broke his leg at a tournament when the King was present. James was also a homosexual – a strange, feeble man, given to bursting into tears; he slobbered as he talked and his legs were so weak that he often leaned on the shoulders of the people he was talking to. James was soon infatuated with the tall, blond illiterate, and even took his advice on dissolving Parliament.

Overbury now became Carr's secretary – a reversal of posi-

---

[1] Anatole France: 'History of Dona Maria D'Avalos and Don Fabricio, Duke of Andria' in *The Well of St Claire*. See also Aldous Huxley's essay on Gesualdo in *Adonis and the Alphabet*.

tions that he did not particularly relish; however, it was a gain in power. And Overbury was interested in power. This was about the only thing he had in common with Carr; otherwise they were opposites: Carr, tall, pink-cheeked, open faced and not particularly bright; Overbury, swarthy, brilliant (his *Characters* is a classic of English literature), brooding, inclined to resentment.

Carr soon fell in love with a teenage beauty, Frances Howard, who was already married to the Earl of Essex. The marriage had not been consummated – Essex was abroad – and it never was. Frances Howard returned the feeling, and she and Carr became lovers. Overbury – now Sir Thomas – wrote Carr's love letters for him. But he never liked the girl. She had the face of a juvenile delinquent and the temperament of a younger Lady Macbeth. When he realised that Carr was serious about her and intended marrying her – if she could get a divorce – he began to resent her very openly. This was his mistake. The Countess of Essex was a very strong character, and basically as neurotic and unbalanced as Overbury. When her husband returned from abroad she refused to grant him marital rights, even though they slept naked in the same bed. She approached a certain Mrs Turner, a 'witch' who had concocted love potions to ensnare Carr, and obtained more powders to kill her husband. (Mrs Turner also wove spells aiming to make the Earl of Essex impotent.) Although these failed to work, Essex finally agreed to a divorce. Carr – now the Duke of Somerset – was displeased when Overbury told him he would be a fool to marry Frances Howard; the lady herself was furious. She tried to bribe a knight to murder Overbury, but he declined. So she persuaded Carr to plot against her enemy. Carr went to the King and suggested that Overbury should be made ambassador to France or Russia, and the King agreed. Carr then went to Overbury, and advised him to refuse. Overbury allowed himself to be persuaded. The King was infuriated by the refusal, and ordered Overbury to be committed to the Tower – which was what Carr and his mistress had counted on. Overbury was now at their mercy. Mother Turner was again called upon for poison; Overbury's keeper Weston was in charge of administering it. Sir Gervase Elwes, a friend of Frances Howard, was made Governor of the Tower; at first, he was ignorant of the poisoning; but when he learnt about it, he kept quiet. Overbury died on 15th September 1613, and no one was curious.

Frances Howard obtained her divorce and married Carr, who remained in royal favour. But without Overbury, Carr's stupidity became steadily more obvious. He began to cause scenes with the King – failing to recognise that what James needed most was someone on whom he could lavish affection. James found a new favourite, a Cambridge student called Villiers. And then, two years after Overbury's death, Carr's edifice collapsed. The chemist's assistant who had prepared the poisons died, and confessed before he died. The King was told, and he asked Sir Edward Coke to investigate. As a result of that investigation, Mrs Turner, Sir Gervase Elwes, Weston (the jailer) and Dr Franklin (supplier of the poison) were all sentenced, and hanged at Tyburn. Carr and his wife were tried in Westminster Hall – since they were of the peerage. Carr tried hard to put pressure on the King – apparently he threatened to blurt out details of their relationship in court, and two men stood behind him with a cloak, ready to put it over his head if he made any such attempt. But the King assured him he would not be executed. Although they were both sentenced to death, husband and wife were only confined in the Tower. By now, they hated one another, and never spoke. Both probably blamed the other for the murder. They were there for six years, then allowed to retire quietly to their country home, where Lady Somerset died of a cancer of the womb at the age of thirty-nine.

The new favourite, George Villiers, was the victim of another famous murder. He became the Duke of Buckingham under James and was made Lord High Admiral of the Navy. He made love to the Queen of France at one point, and as a consequence, appears in Dumas' *Three Musketeers* and various other novels. But after James's death, he became involved in the quarrels between the new King – Charles I – and his parliament. Charles dissolved two parliaments which wanted to impeach Buckingham. But on 23rd August 1628, a soldier called John Felton, who thought he had various causes for complaint against the Duke, waited outside the door of the room in which Buckingham was breakfasting, and stabbed him in the heart as he came out. Felton – a Puritan fanatic – hoped for immunity, since parliament had declared Buckingham a public enemy; but he reckoned without the King. Felton was hanged at Tyburn. Buckingham's rival, Robert Carr, outlived him by seventeen years. After Buckingham's death, Charles I's career began the slow downward curve that ended under the axe of Richard Brandon in 1649.

No account of murder in the seventeenth century would be complete without at least a mention of the unsolved murder of Sir Edmund Berry Godfrey, the effect of which was to cause a persecution of Catholics as brutal as any under Henry VIII. Godfrey was a man of good reputation, and had displayed a rare public spirit in his efforts of help to sufferers in the Great Plague of 1665.

Three weeks before his murder, Godfrey, who was a magistrate, had been approached by Titus Oates – a kind of seventeenth-century Senator Joe McCarthy, who talked about Catholic plots. The Gunpowder Plot of 1605 had not been forgotten, and a great many people thought a new one all too likely. On the afternoon of 12th October 1678, Godfrey left his house at Charing Cross to make a call near St Clement Danes, and did not return home. Five days later, his corpse was found in a ditch at Primrose Hill, a few miles to the north. His sword was driven into his body, so that suicide was a possibility. But, in the climate of opinion created by Titus Oates (who alleged a Popish Plot by Don John of Austria and Père la Chaise to murder Charles II and establish Catholicism in England), everyone was certain he was murdered by Catholics. Charles was tolerant towards Catholics (in fact, he *was* a Catholic, secretly), and the Queen's residence, Somerset House in the Strand, was a hive of them. Godfrey had passed Somerset House after dark on the day of his disappearance, so an investigation was conducted there. Soon a man named Praunce 'confessed' – under torture, it was later claimed. He declared that a group of conspirators knew that Godfrey intended to spend the night at the house near St Clement Danes – perhaps a brothel. He left at seven in the morning, and as he was passing Somerset House was lured into the courtyard with some story of a fight between two of the Queen's servants. There he was strangled, and his neck broken. Praunce alleged that the body was moved from room to room in Somerset House for several days, then taken to Primrose Hill and stabbed with the sword.

Three men – Green, Berry and Hill – were arrested; three more (two of whom were priests) escaped. These three were placed on trial before Lord Chief Justice Scroggs, whose reputation is as vile as that of his associate Jeffreys. Praunce gave evidence against them. They had no chance of escape; the whole country was up in arms about the Popish Plot. Titus Oates appeared against them. (He was a turncoat Catholic who had been expelled from the Jesuits for misconduct.) As far as justice goes, this must rank as one of the worst trials in English history – although, of course, that does not prove the conspirators were innocent. Green, Berry and Hill were executed for Godfrey's murder; but it is generally acknowledged that the murder remains unsolved. Why should Catholics have murdered Godfrey – who was merely the magistrate who took Oates' deposition? They must have had the sense to know it would lead to a persecution. On the other hand, Titus Oates and some of the Protestants behind him had an excellent motive for the murder. Part of Godfrey's job as a magistrate was to investigate their allegations; Godfrey may well have recognised from an early stage that the Popish Plot was basically nonsense.

It is satisfying to record that Titus Oates, like Senator McCarthy, eventually overdid it. His revelations led to massive reprisals against Catholics; five Catholic peers were sent to the Tower, and two thousand Catholics thrown into prison. All Catholics were ordered to leave London, and a bill was passed excluding them from Parliament. Another imaginative villain named Bedloe tried to top the revelations of Titus Oates, and Oates invented more freely than ever – plots for the landing of Catholic armies and the massacre of all Protestants. Finally, he charged the Queen with knowledge of a plot to murder Charles II. The King gave his brother James – later James II – permission to do something about it, and Oates was tried for perjury and libel, and sentenced to life imprisonment, with periodic whippings at a cart-tail.

The murder of Godfrey was one of those minor events that changed the course of English history. Without it, the Popish Plot furore would have died down much sooner, or perhaps never have started, and the violent measures against Catholics – including large-scale judicial murder – would never have been taken. The clashes between the Catholic James II and his parliament would have been avoided, and the revolution that brought William of Orange to the English throne would not have taken place. The full consequences of that will become clear in the next chapter.

Two: The Age of Gin

ELIZABETHAN ENGLAND DRANK beer, wine, sherry (Falstaff's 'sack'), mead and cider; they drank a lot because the water was not fit to drink unboiled. But although Thomas Dekker wrote in 1632 of a street that was almost a continuous ale-house (or tavern, as they were starting to be called), it is doubtful whether these beverages were responsible for much of the crime rate in the first half of the seventeenth century. To begin with, James I took measures to raise the price of wine from the fourpence a quart it had cost under Elizabeth, and the ordinary labourer could now afford to drink only beer; and even that had increased in price.

Somewhere around 1650 or 1660, a Dutch professor of chemistry called Sylvius discovered that a powerful spirit could be made by distilling the fermentation of juniper berries; this drink was called 'geneva' (the French for juniper). It became popular in Holland, and when William of Orange became King in 1689, geneva began to flow into England in large quantities, and the name was shortened to 'gin'. Gin was cheap and easy to make. The English quickly realised that an even cheaper and stronger spirit could be distilled from low-grade corn; and an Act of Parliament in 1690 allowed anyone to brew and sell spirits without a licence, with the consequence that every town in England was suddenly full of gin shops, many of which carried the famous advertisement: 'Drunk for a penny, dead drunk for twopence, clean straw provided.' Beer, wine and sherry had been too expensive for most labourers, but gin was within the reach of anybody who could earn or beg a penny. Inevitably, the crime rate rose; people in the slums had a great deal they wanted to forget, and twopence assured forgetfulness for at least twelve hours. In 1734, a dipsomaniac named Judith Dufour was executed for the murder of her baby; she had collected it from a workhouse – where it had been newly clothed – and strangled it, throwing the body into a ditch. the clothes sold for 1s 4d, which she spent on gin. On 6th July 1750, one Elizabeth Banks was hanged at Tyburn for 'stripping a child' – no doubt with the same motive. Eight million gallons of gin a year were consumed in England at this time, the consumption in London alone being fourteen gallons per head.

Within ten years of the accession of William and Mary, the crime rate had risen so alarmingly, and crimes of violence 'carried to a degree of outrageous passion' were becoming so common, that a new law of exceptional savagery was placed on the Statute books: the 1699 Act that made any theft of goods valued at more than 5s a capital crime. Any kind of shoplifting was a crime; and since the majority of these offenders were women and children, the execution of women and children became a commonplace. As the number of gin shops increased – at one point, one house in every six sold gin – so did the neglect and ill-treatment of children, and John Fielding – a Justice of the Peace and half-brother of Henry – spoke of children of twelve 'half eaten up with the foul distemper' of the pox. Children were trained to pick pockets, and many of them were hanged for as little as the theft of a handkerchief. The authorities were becoming desperate at this 'crime wave' (which would last more than a century), and they reacted in the manner with which we are becoming familiar: by trying to stamp out crime with cruelty.

No doubt the Elizabethan mob was as unfeeling as the mob of the eighteenth century. But the gin made it all the more obvious. Christopher Hibbert says of the period:

'Pity was still a strange and valuable emotion. Unwanted babies were left out in the streets to die or were thrown into dung heaps or open drains; the torture of animals was a popular sport. Cat-dropping, bear-baiting and bull-baiting were as universally enjoyed as throwing at cocks. . . .

'The Mohocks, a society whose members were dedicated to

the ambition of "doing all possible hurt to their fellow creatures", were mostly gentlemen. They employed their ample
leisure in forcing prostitutes and old women to stand on their
heads in tar barrels so that they could prick their legs with
their swords; or in making them jump up and down to avoid
the swinging blades; in disfiguring their victims by boring out
their eyes or flattening their noses; in waylaying servants and,
as in the case of Lady Winchilsea's maid, beating them and
slashing their faces. To work themselves up to the necessary
pitch of enthusiasm for their ferocious games, they first drank
so much that they were "quite beyond the possibility of attend-
ing to any notions of reason or humanity". Some of the
Mohocks also seem to have been members of the Bold Bucks
who, apparently, had formally to deny the existence of God and
eat every Sunday a dish known as Holy Ghost Pie. The
ravages of the Bold Bucks were more specifically sexual than
those of the Mohocks and consequently, as it was practically
impossible to obtain a conviction for rape and as the age of
consent was twelve, they were more openly conducted."[1]

The age had its ideal chronicler in William Hogarth, born in
1697, for he delighted in the portrayal of the sordid and
horrible. Anyone who wants to understand the spirit of the first
half of the eighteenth century should study Plate 7 of his
'Industry and Idleness' series, showing the idle apprentice in
bed with a prostitute. The walls are bare bricks with a few
decaying fragments of plaster; some of the floor is missing; the
'bed' is simply a sloping plank; there seems to be no window;
the room is as cold and dark as a prison cell. The prostitute is
an ugly, snub-nosed girl with small firm breasts – she is probably sixteen or seventeen. To stare at such a picture for five
minutes is to gain all kinds of insights that the literature of the
period cannot convey, because we read it with our own age in
mind.

One can begin to understand, for example, why the highway-
men of the period became popular heroes; they were hitting
back at the system. Modern writers on Dick Turpin take care
to point out that he was a brutal scoundrel, whose chief dis-

[1] *The Roots of Evil,* pp 44–6.

tinction was the manner of his death: he bought new clothes to die in, and hired five poor men to walk behind the cart as mourners; he also gave hatbands and gloves to others who would attend his execution, to give it a fashionable touch; he joked with the crowd on his way to the scaffold, chatted amiably with the executioner for half an hour, then threw himself off the ladder. He died with style; it was a gesture of defiance at the forces of money and rank that kept the poor in their places, as if to say: 'You hold all the cards, but we have more spirit than you.' It is true that Turpin's career was not marked by any spectacular bravery, or even elegance. When forced to become an outlaw for stealing his neighbours' cattle, he led a gang that simply burst into isolated houses and carried off all the money. If necessary, they tortured the inhabitants, and an occasional servant girl was raped. On the run again, Turpin met a highwayman named King, and they became partners. Turpin committed his only murder during this partnership – he shot a man who tried to arrest him. Later still, he shot and killed King, but this seems to have been an accident; he intended to shoot the man who was trying to arrest King. Turpin was now not badly off, and he moved to Lincolnshire and set up as a gentleman under the name of John Palmer; but horse-stealing got him into trouble, and he moved to Weston in Yorkshire. Here he often joined the local gentry in hunting and shooting. One day, he shot a cock, and when his companion remonstrated, threatened to shoot him too. This led to his arrest, and since he did not have the money to put up surety for good behaviour, he was committed to prison. He remained there for some time, under suspicion of horse-stealing. A letter written to his brother finally led to the discovery of his identity; the schoolmaster who had taught him to write recognised the handwriting on the envelope, and informed on him. John Palmer the suspected horse-thief was discovered to be Dick Turpin, England's Public Enemy Number One. He was executed on 7th April 1739.

It is true that there is nothing in this record that would distinguish a modern criminal; but for the poor of his time – that is, for ninety-five per cent of Englishmen – he was a man who had done what they all dreamed of doing: taking what society would not give him.

Dick Turpin never became the subject of one of Hogarth's engravings – perhaps because his trial and execution took place at York; but he engraved the portrait of an equally celebrated criminal, Sarah Malcolm, accused of a treble murder committed in the course of robbery. She was a middle-class girl whose father wasted the family's goods, so that she was eventually obliged to become a laundress. She decided to rob one of her customers, an old lady of eighty called Duncomb. When friends of Mrs Duncomb came to tea on the afternoon of Sunday, 4th February 1733, they found that Mrs Duncomb and a female servant named Harrison had been strangled, while a servant girl of seventeen was in bed with her throat cut. As Mrs Duncomb's char, Sarah Malcolm came under suspicion, and money was found in her room, as well as a silver tankard stained with blood. She claimed that the actual murderers were two brothers called Alexander and a woman named Tracy. When the brothers heard of the charge, they presented themselves to the magistrate, and declared they were innocent. No doubt they were, for they were not tried with Sarah Malcolm, and this was in a period when the law preferred to hang a dozen innocent people rather than let one guilty one escape. After her execution, her corpse was dissected, and the skeleton presented to the Botanic Gardens at Cambridge, 'where', said a writer at the end of the century, 'it remains to this day'. Hogarth was so interested in the attractive murderess – who was only twenty-two when she was executed – that he made two portraits of her.

The custom of handing over criminals for dissection to a barber-surgeon became law in 1752. For some odd reason, this seemed to worry criminals more than the thought of being hanged. It was one of many measures the government considered to try to reduce crime – upon the false hypothesis that a sufficiently cruel punishment would act as a deterrent. Another suggestion was to torture criminals before hanging them – breaking them on the wheel or burning them with hot irons – but this was rejected; there would be too many criminals to do this efficiently. But there were other ideas that seemed more practicable. For example, to leave bodies rotting on the gibbet until they became skeletons; to hang them 'in irons' – that is, in a kind of iron cage, that would prevent the corpse from disintegrating too quickly (someone suggested that it would be a good idea to hang living malefactors in irons, and allow them to starve to death; this idea was rejected because the cries might upset people); there was even a custom of dumping the body on the doorstep of the person he had wronged, to demonstrate that the law had carried out the sentence. If one had travelled around England after 1752, one would have found many good views spoilt by the gibbet with its corpse in irons; hilltops that could be seen from afar were selected as suitable spots, to deter the maximum number of criminals. Hanging in irons went out of fashion mainly because it was too expensive; as the suit might cost seventy-five pounds, and the gibbet had to be coated with lead to prevent relatives of the dead man from burning it down.

The most famous of English gallows was the one at Tyburn; it was a few yards to the west of Marble Arch, on the banks of a stream – the Tyburn – that flowed from Hampstead down to the Thames (it now runs underground for most of its length). In the time of Henry VIII, the gallows were simply a cross-beam supported on two trees; Queen Elizabeth had it changed to a triangle of beams supported on three uprights; as many as ten offenders at a time could be hanged on each beam, and the sight of thirty bodies swaying in the wind must have been an impressive sight. The phrase 'gala day' is derived from 'gallows day', gala being the Anglo-Saxon for a gallows; the hanging of notorious criminals was often the occasion for a public holiday, with a great deal of drunken merrymaking. England adopted hanging mainly because beheading large numbers of criminals was impracticable; before the time of Alfred the Great (about AD 850) criminals were often boiled alive; women were drowned in a special pit. This was given up because it was too much trouble, and an attempt to introduce the guillotine in Halifax in the first half of the seventeenth century never caught on in the rest of the country.

Beheading continued to be a fate reserved for those convicted of high treason. The most famous of English hangmen, Jack Ketch, who operated under Charles II, was a bungler as a headsman. When he executed Lord William Russell in 1683 for his part in the Rye House plot to kidnap the King, he took several strokes to do it, and the crowd became angry. Before the Duke of Monmouth was executed after his unsuccessful rebellion, he handed Ketch six guineas, and told him there would be another purse-full if he made a clean job of it. Then he felt the axe and commented: 'I fear it is not sharp enough.' Perhaps his coolness unnerved Ketch, who botched the job completely; after an unsuccessful blow that only partly severed the neck, he dropped the axe and shouted, 'I cannot do it.' Stern persuasions were brought to bear, but he was now so weak with nervousness that the head was still unsevered after four more blows, and he had to finish it with a knife. The crowd was so angry that he had to be taken away under escort.

He was hardly more efficient as a hangman, but fortunately, this hardly mattered, for his clients strangled to death if he left them long enough and pulled on their legs. (This is the origin of the phrase 'to pull someone's leg', according to J D Potter's history of hanging, *The Fatal Gallows Tree*.) It was not until the latter part of the nineteenth century, when William Marwood became public hangman, that prisoners were given a drop long enough to dislocate the neck and bring instantaneous death.

When Hogarth produced his etching of the idle apprentice being hanged at Tyburn, the public executioner was Jack Hooper, the 'Laughing Hangman', a good-natured soul of phenomenal ugliness, who did his best to make the last hours of his clients pleasant with jests and stories. Since prisoners of means usually rewarded the hangman, he probably found it a lucrative occupation. It is recorded that one of the few occasions when Laughing Jack's high spirits failed him was when he had to execute a particularly barbarous sentence on the forger Japhet Crook, alias Sir Peter Stranger, who had swindled a man out of two hundred acres of land. The sentence was to stand in the pillory, have his ears cut off, his nostrils slit open and seared with a red-hot iron, and to be imprisoned for life. The pillory could be the worst part of such an ordeal, for if the prisoner was unpopular, the crowd would pelt him with bottles and stones, often killing him. Crook survived this part of his ordeal – the crowd liked him – but neither he nor the executioner enjoyed the next part. Hooper sliced off his ears from behind with a sharp knife, and held each one up for the crowd to see, then slit his nostrils open with scissors. When he applied the red-hot iron to his nose, Crook leapt out of his chair, and the hangman decided to leave that part of the sentence uncompleted. Later in the day, Crook was well enough to drink himself insensible in a nearby tavern – no doubt on gin – after which he was taken off to jail.

The Hogarth etching conveys a clear notion of the scene at a hanging – the sellers of apples and muffins, the mothers holding babies, the 'last confessions' of the prisoner being sold to the crowd, and the prisoner himself, seated in an open cart, of the type used during the French Revolution – with lattice-work sides – reading his Bible, leaning against his own coffin, and wearing his shroud. In the background are the grassy hills of Maida Vale, all open country.

Hogarth's two pictures, 'Beer Street' and 'Gin Lane', leave no room for doubt that he attributed the rising crime rate to gin. In 'Beer Street', jolly-looking men and women drink cheerfully outside a tavern, a copy of the King's speech on a table indicates that they have been engaged in a serious discussion of politics, and an artist – ragged but cheerful – paints the inn sign. The only sign of poverty is the dilapidation of the pawnbroker's shop; a post-boy hands him a half pint through a hole in the door. 'Gin Lane' is one of Hogarth's exercises in the gruesome. A drunken mother is allowing her baby to fall out of her arms into the area below; a madman has impaled another baby on a spit; a woman is being lifted into her coffin, and a hanged man is visible in a garret. The only prosperous person is the pawnbroker, with whom a carpenter is depositing his tools to buy gin. An interesting touch here is the 'gin palace', which seems to be an open barn, full of barrels of gin, in front of which a mother is pouring gin down her baby's throat.

If a modern artist had engraved these pictures – or the even more horrifying 'Four Stages of Cruelty' – he would be accused of sadism; but in the age of Hogarth, stomachs were strong, and less violent protests would have made no impression at all. This was an age when people were used to violence. In 1731, an informer named John Waller was placed in the pillory at Seven Dials for some minor offence. He was the target for stones, bottles and cabbage stalks. Then, an hour later, a man dragged him down – he was standing upright, with his head and his hands held in the pillory – and tore off his clothes, after which the mob trampled him to death. A procuress named Mother Needham escaped alive, but died of her injuries two days later.

It was 'Laughing Jack' Hooper who hanged Sarah Malcolm, and who was saddened by it because he thought her probably innocent – that the actual killings had been done by males. (Hogarth said that her face 'showed that she was capable of any wickedness'.) But it was not the hangman's job to be sensitive about his task. Hooper's successor, John Thrift, was so timid and good natured that he suffered agonies in the execution of his task. He was visibly close to vomiting when he had to hang, then decapitate and disembowel nine of the Jacobite rebels in 1746. Later the same year, he almost came to grief over the beheading of two more of the rebels, Lord Kilmarnock and Lord Balmerino. Thrift fainted on the scaffold and had to be revived with wine, then when Lord Kilmarnock arrived, he fell on his knees and burst into tears; Kilmarnock had to comfort him and pat him on the shoulder. But he did a better job of the beheading than Jack Ketch had with the Duke of Monmouth, severing the neck with one clean blow. Lord Balmerino was less fortunate; by now, Thrift's tears blinded him, and he only lacerated the neck with the first blow; it took two more to finish the job. The tender-hearted Thrift was one of those hangmen who was also a murderer; when being booed and stoned by a crowd, he drew his sword and ran one of them through; sentenced to death, he was reprieved, and restored to his post of hangman. But his years of hanging and whipping had been too much for his sensibilities; he was subject to fits of delusion in which past victims came and made faces at him, and he died soon after his reprieve.

Another of Hogarth's contemporaries, John Price, has the dubious distinction of being the only hangman who was hanged and gibbeted. One night when drunk, he tried to rape an old apple seller, who resisted; Price beat her to death, knocking out one of her eyes and breaking her arm. He was hanged in 1718. Price's type was far more usual among hangmen than Thrift's. This is hardly surprising, since the job involved tasks that must have been a sadist's delight. A receipted bill by Thomas Turlis, the hangman who succeeded Thrift, mentions 'For whipping of Elizabeth Fletcher, five shillings, For whipping of Sarah Johnson, five shillings, For whipping of Anne Eaton, five shillings, For whipping of Jane Hodgson, five shillings', while for whipping Mary Dolley from Cavendish Square to Duke Street (tied to a cart-tail) he received ten shillings. His successor, Edward Dennis, had the disagreeable task of hanging a pretty young girl named Mary Jones, who had stolen four pieces of muslin. Her husband had been kidnapped by a press-gang, and she stole the muslin to feed her two babies, one of whom was at her breast as she was driven to Tyburn. But she has her place in history for a more interesting reason. In 1776, Sir William Meredith told her story in the House of Commons during a debate, and moved some of his audience to tears. It was a sign that the era of brutality and callousness was coming to an end, and that a new age of reform was beginning. The 'age of gin' lasted approximately one century.

But the age of crime is also the age in which we have the first adequate records of crime. In 1735, when Dick Turpin was still engaged in his gleeful depredations, a bookseller called John Osborn, of the Golden Ball in Paternoster Row, thought that it might be a profitable idea to gather together some of the lives and exploits of remarkable criminals from the pamphlets that were hawked at Tyburn, and he issued three volumes of *Lives of the Most Remarkable Criminals* in that year. Forty years later, in 1774, a gentleman named George Theodore Wilkinson brought the records up to date in the famous *Newgate Calendar.*

The high moral tone of both these works makes them tiresome to read. Their authors were recording the lives of criminals in order to make money, and they felt they had to disguise this by making their accounts sound like sermons. 'There cannot, perhaps, be a greater misfortune to a man than his having a woman ill-principled about him, whether as a wife or otherwise,' says Osborn severely, in writing of a highwayman named Picken. One is struck by the commonplace nature of most of the crimes, the lack of the kind of features that would have interested Sherlock Holmes. The first case in the volume is typical. Jane Griffin, a forty-year-old housewife with a hot temper, lost the cellar key, and went to the maid's room to upbraid her. She and the maid had already had several disagreements, and the maid returned the bad language with interest. Jane Griffin was holding a kitchen knife with which she had been cutting a chicken for the children's supper, and she suddenly saw red and stabbed at the maid. Unfortunately, it was a good blow that went straight to the heart. Today, Jane Griffin would get two years for manslaughter, and possibly psychiatric treatment; in 1720, she was hanged.

Osborn's book contains a lengthy account of the eighteenth-century equivalent of the Arden of Faversham case. Catherine Hayes was born Catherine Hall, in Birmingham, the daughter of poor parents. In 1705, when she was fifteen, she was noticed by some army officers, who persuaded her to return to their quarters; there she became their collective mistress for a while, until they moved on. She then found a job as a servant with a Warwickshire farmer named Hayes. The son of the house, a carpenter, fell in love with her; one morning, they went secretly into Worcester, and were married. John Hayes was then twenty-one. After six years in the country, his young bride began to dream of London, and persuaded her husband to move there. She was so excitable and quarrelsome that her in-laws raised no objection. In London, John Hayes became a successful coal merchant, pawnbroker and moneylender. His success in this latter occupation lends colour to his wife's assertion that he was unbearably mean. At all events, Hayes was successful in business, and in a little over ten years, made enough money to sell his shop in the Tyburn Road and take lodgings nearby. His relations with his wife had deteriorated badly. This may have been due to his meanness and her desire for luxury, or there may have been deeper causes. She later told one of her accomplices in the murder that Hayes had murdered two of his children in the country – presumably when they were new-born. If Hayes was pathologically mean, there might just possibly be some truth in this story.

Early in 1725, a young man named Thomas Billings, a tailor, came to their house, and Catherine Hayes declared him to be an old friend, or relative. He stayed with them, and when Hayes went to the country on business, Billings took his place in Catherine's bed. The two lovers made the most of their free-dom, throwing parties and spending a great deal of the money that Hayes had taken so long to accumulate. When Hayes returned, he was furious, and gave his wife a beating. But for some reason, he did not turn Billings out of the house.

Another friend from Warwickshire now arrived, a Thomas Wood. It was to him that she told the story of her husband killing her two children, and she mentioned that Hayes had also killed a man. Wood also became her lover, and her promise that her husband's estate – some fifteen hundred pounds, a fortune for those days – would be put at his disposal when she became a widow finally made him agree to help her kill her husband.

On 1st March 1725, Wood came back from a visit to the country, and found Billings, Catherine and John Hayes in the midst of a drinking session. Wood, who was young and boast-ful, declared that he had just drunk a guinea's worth of wine and was still sober, and Billings challenged Hayes to drink the same amount – six bottles. If Hayes could do it without getting drunk, Billings would buy the wine; if not, Hayes should pay for it. Hayes accepted the offer; perhaps the prospect of six bottles of free wine was too much for his miserly soul. Billings, Wood and Catherine Hayes set off for a tavern in New Bond Street, and on the way, she pointed out that this would be a good opportunity to kill her husband.

In the Brawn's Head the three of them drank a pint of 'best mountain wine', and asked for six pints to be sent up to their lodgings. Catherine Hayes paid 10s 6d for it – perhaps its quality was only half as good as the stuff Wood claimed he had been drinking.

Hayes downed the six pints of wine without much trouble, while the other three drank beer; his wife quietly sent out for another pint which Hayes, now too fuddled to count the bottles, also drank. He then fell down on the floor, woke up after a few minutes, and staggered off to bed in the next room. The bed was probably the kind that Hogarth portrayed, with its lower end actually on the floor. Hayes fell asleep on his face. Billings came in with a coal hatchet, and hit him on the back of the head with it. The blow fractured his skull, and Hayes began to kick his feet in agony, making such a noise that the woman in the room overhead came down to investigate. By this time, Wood had seized the hatchet and given Hayes two more blows, which completed the work of killing him. When Mrs Springate complained that the thudding noise had awakened them, Catherine Hayes explained that her husband had some noisy guests, but that they were about to leave. It must have been a tense moment, and both Wood and Billings were badly unnerved.

The next problem was what to do with the body. They had to get it down two flights of stairs to the street. Then suppose they bumped into a member of the watch? As soon as Hayes was recognised, they were done for. But Catherine Hayes refused to be panicked. She pointed out that if they cut off her husband's head, and disposed of that first, the body would not be identifiable, even if they had to flee from the watch and leave it in the street.

The two men were already nauseated. The bed was drenched with blood; blood had even shot up to the ceiling with the hatchet blows. Catherine Hayes suggested that they decapitate her husband with his neck over a bucket to catch the blood. The two men must have been wishing that this business had never started; but there was obviously no way out except to dispose of the body. So they placed the body on the bed so the head hung over. Catherine Hayes held the bucket underneath the neck, Billings twisted his fingers in the blood-soaked hair, and Woods sawed away at the neck with a carving knife – hatchet blows would have brought Mrs Springate down again. When the head was off, they dropped it in the pail, and left the headless body to bleed into it.

Catherine Hayes recognised that there was still danger. If the head was identified, it would be traced back to her. She proposed boiling it in a pot until the flesh came away – a revolting but sensible idea – but the others were too nervous. They became even more nervous when Mrs Springate shouted down irritably to know what was going on. Here Catherine Hayes showed a presence of mind that entitles her to be ranked with Alice Arden and Lady Macbeth; she called back that her husband had been suddenly called away on a journey, and was getting ready to go. Now the two Thomases could hardly wait to get out of the house. They poured the blood from the bucket down the sink, then had to tiptoe up and down the stairs half a dozen times to get water from the well to wash it down. When that was done, the men crept downstairs, one of them holding the bucket under his coat, while Catherine Hayes walked down behind them, talking in her normal voice, saying goodbye to her husband, in case any of the neighbours was listening. According to the sharp-eared Mrs Springate, she put up an excellent and convincing performance. Then the two men made off as fast as they could, and Catherine Hayes hurried upstairs to clean up the blood before it clotted. It was a long task, because the unpolished floorboards had soaked up the blood like a sponge; even when she had washed it and scraped it with a knife, the marks were still visible.

Meanwhile, Billings and Wood hastened towards the river – a long walk, from the present day Oxford Street down to Whitehall. It was nearly midnight. People of that time tended to go to bed early, and the watch were likely to challenge people who were out after midnight. Billings must have looked as if he was pregnant, with the pail under his greatcoat. They reached Whitehall, but the dock gates had already been closed. The tide was out, and the foreshore of the river was mostly mud;

wading across that would attract attention. They walked on along the river, past Westminster, to the Horseferry wharf – at the end of the present Horseferry Road, under Lambeth Bridge. They went to the end of the dock, and threw the head over. Instead of a splash, there was a thud as it landed on mud. But they were too frightened to worry. They threw the bucket after it, and hurried away. The nightwatchman on the wharf heard the thud, and a man on board a boat saw them throw the bucket; but it was a dark night, and no one was very curious. Billings and Wood hastened back home, now feeling slightly better. They found Catherine Hayes still scraping at the floorboards, trying not to make too much noise. The headless body still lay across the bed. The two men made up a makeshift bed in the other room, and tried to sleep. Catherine Hayes sat by them, brooding. She must have been wishing that they had disfigured the face with a knife to prevent recognition. But with luck, the head was already on its way out to sea. . . . She was still sitting there when the two men woke up at dawn.

And also at dawn, the nightwatchman, a Mr Robinson, walked to the edge of the dock to stretch his legs, and saw the bucket and the head lying in the mud. A small crowd soon gathered, and the lighterman from the boat mentioned seeing a man throwing the bucket into the river.

Back in the lodgings, the murderers were discussing what to do with the body. The first and most obvious thing was to conceal it in case someone came into the room. Mrs Hayes went out and got a large box; but it was not big enough. They cut off the arms, and the legs at the knees; but the body was still too long. They hacked off the thighs, and finally managed to pack most of the pieces into the box, leaving some of the smaller items in an old blanket. That evening, at nine o'clock, Wood and Billings crept downstairs with the trunk in a blanket. It was early and there were too many people about; but they were not going to risk being stopped by the watch. This time they went north – fortunately there was not far to go before they were in the fields of Marylebone. They tossed the trunk into a pond that Wood had located during the day, then went back and collected the rest of the body. It was Mrs Springate who let them in at midnight; fortunately, she had no reason to be suspicious, even though her husband had found clots of blood in the drain that morning. Blood was common enough.

The next day, Wood made off to the country to soothe his shattered nerves. Billings resumed his place in his mistress's bed.

The parish officers of Westminster had not been idle. They ordered the blood and dirt to be washed from the head and – a macabre touch – the hair to be combed. Then the head was set on a stake at St Margaret's churchyard in Westminster. It drew a fascinated crowd, but no one recognised it. But the next day, a young apprentice named Bennett saw it, and flew to tell Catherine Hayes that he thought it looked like her husband. She told him angrily that he could get himself into serious trouble if he spread such reports – her husband was alive and well. Bennett apologised and promised to say nothing about it. And a Mr Patrick also thought he recognised the head, and went along to a pub called the Dog and Dial in Monmouth Street – at which Hayes and his wife used to drink – to mention his suspicion. Billings happened to be working there at the time, and someone replied that the head couldn't belong to John Hayes, because Billings was his lodger, and he would know if anything had happened to Hayes. Billings immediately confirmed this, saying that he had left Hayes in bed that morning.

Mrs Hayes must have been feeling nervous; but she recognised that flight would be a mistake. When a neighbour asked after her husband, she said he was out taking a walk; the visitor mentioned the head in the churchyard, and Mrs Hayes expressed horror at the wickedness of the age. 'Why, they even say they've found bits of a woman's body in a pond at Marylebone,' she declared, and the neighbour said she hadn't heard about that.

Wood came back to town on the fifth – two days after he had fled. Catherine Hayes gave him some of her husband's clothes, and five shillings. She told him that the head had been found, but that no one had yet identified it.

The head was beginning to stink; worse still, the features

74

were already beginning to turn black. The parish officers had it placed in a large jar full of spirit – perhaps gin – and continued to exhibit it to anyone who was interested. For a short period it looked as if the mystery was solved when a woman said she thought it was her husband; but after a long look at it, she said she couldn't swear to it.

Catherine Hayes remained remarkably cool. Less than a week after the murder, she left her lodgings and moved to another in the neighbourhood, taking Billings, Wood, and Mrs Springate. No doubt she was afraid that the latter might gossip; she even paid a quarter's rent for the lady. She then proceeded to collect as many of her husband's debts as possible, even threatening to sue her husband's brother-in-law for money he owed. She wrote various letters in her husband's name to other debtors.

Inevitably, Hayes' friends began to wonder what had become of him. A man called Ashby called on her to enquire. She then told him, in strict confidence, that her husband had killed a man in a quarrel, and had fled to Portugal. Mr Ashby asked if the head found in the river belonged to the murdered man, but Mrs Hayes said no, they had buried the body entire.

All this was bound to arouse suspicion. Ashby communicated with the neighbour who had already enquired; they talked with another neighbour. And finally, a Justice of the Peace was informed. They hurried to Catherine Hayes' lodgings and knocked on the door. She was in bed with Billings; she dressed and went to the door. Billings was sitting on the edge of the bed without shoes or stockings when the officers came in. When asked if he had been sleeping with her, she said no, he was mending his stockings. The Justice remarked that he must have been doing it in the dark, since there was no candle or fire.

Wood was not present, but they arrested Catherine Hayes, Billings and Mrs Springate, and took them off to different prisons, to prevent them concocting a story. Catherine Hayes continued to assert her innocence, and asked if she might see the head from the churchyard. The Justice agreed, and they took her to the barber-surgeon – a Mr Westbrook – who was

75

keeping the head. Here, Catherine Hayes called upon all her histrionic powers, and shouted: 'Oh, it is my dear husband's head!' and proceeded to kiss the jar. Mr Westbrook came in and said he would take the head out of the jar – it was generally believed in those days that murderers would reveal their guilt if forced to touch the corpse. But Catherine Hayes was equal to anything; she seized the head and kissed it, then asked if she could have a lock of its hair. Her performance must have been a little too dramatic; the barber-surgeon replied sardonically that she had already had too much of his blood; at which Catherine Hayes fainted, or pretended to. She had already run through the emotional spectrum; it was the only thing left for her to do.

While all this was taking place, someone saw the blanket floating in the Marylebone pond, and pulled it out. The rest of the body was soon recovered. But Catherine Hayes and Thomas Billings continued to assert their total innocence.

Wood was the weak link in the chain. On the following Sunday, he came back to London from Harrow, and went along to Catherine Hayes' old lodgings. They told him she had moved to a house nearby, and someone offered to show him. His informant took him to the wrong place – to the house of Mr Longmore, one of the neighbours who had caused the arrest. There the terrified Wood was dragged off his horse, and taken to the Justice who had been questioning the others. At first, Wood declared himself innocent; but in Newgate, his nerve broke, and he made a full confession. He explained that Mrs Hayes had told him that her husband was an atheist and free-thinker, and that 'it would be no more sin to kill him than to kill a dog'. When the other two were told of the confession, they decided that there was no further point in keeping silent – especially as it might lead to torture – and also confessed. Mrs Springate was released.

It was after this that Catherine Hayes suddenly realised that the charge against her was not of murder, but petty treason – the killing of her lord and master; and that the penalty for this was to be burned alive. But she still hoped that her crime might be regarded simply as murder, since she had not struck any of the blows that killed her husband. At her trial, with the fear of a painful death hanging over her, she denied that she had any hand in the actual killing of her husband, and said that she had kept silent only because she was afraid that Wood and Billings would kill her too. When it was clear that all three would be sentenced to death, Wood and Billings begged that they might not be hanged in chains, and she again repeated her plea to be hanged rather than burned. But the judge sentenced her to be burned, and she screamed all the way back to Newgate.

She revealed a better side to her nature before her execution; she sent messages to her two ex-lovers, regretting that she had involved them in all this. When she saw Billings in chapel, she sat holding his hand and leaned her head on his shoulder. She was obviously in love with Billings.

A few days before her execution, she somehow managed to get a bottle of acid into her cell. Unfortunately, a fellow prisoner saw it and tasted it. A little spilt on a handkerchief burnt it. So the prisoner smashed the bottle on the floor.

Wood caught a fever in prison, and died before he could be executed. He is the only person in the case who seems to deserve much sympathy. His age is not recorded, but it seems fairly certain that he was still in his teens. He seems to have been a good-natured, easygoing young man who was too easily influenced.

Billings was also young. Osborn records that when he first came to stay at the Hayes' lodgings, there was a rumour that he was Catherine Hayes' son by a previous 'connection'. He was executed before Catherine Hayes, and when the executioner – Richard Arnet, Laughing Jack's predecessor – came to fetch her, she asked him if he had killed her 'dear child' yet.

Her last moments give the case a final touch of horror. It was customary to strangle a woman condemned for petty treason before burning her. Arnet lit the brushwood around her, then started to pull the strangling rope from behind; but the fire reached his hands too quickly, and he had to let go. The spectators watched her trying to push the burning faggots away

77

while she screamed. More faggots were thrown on, to try to put her out of her misery soon, 'but', says Wilkinson, 'she survived amidst the flames for a considerable time, and her body was not perfectly reduced to ashes in less than three hours'.

I have discussed this case at length, not merely because its details are dramatic in themselves, but because it illustrates what it was about murder that so interested the people of the eighteenth century. If the author of *Arden of Faversham* had been alive, he could have made a classic play of the Hayes murder. Osborn tells it with as much detail as Holinshed relates the Arden murder – no doubt because he was in London at the time, and probably went to view the head. But the kind of thing that would interest a modern reporter struck him as irrelevant. Why did Catherine Hayes want to murder her husband? She mentioned in her confession that John Hayes had been a bad husband to her, and kept her half starved; this seems consistent with his meanness. Did she find in Billings an important emotional experience after years of living with a husband who thought of little besides money?

Again, why did Hayes allow Billings to remain in the house after he had beaten his wife for throwing parties while he was away? He must have had some suspicion. He was forty-one years old – and at that time, this was the beginning of old age. Had he gone past the point of feeling sexual jealousy? There may be another reason why he wanted Billings to remain. In those days, most farmers kept their money in an old sock, or hidden somewhere in the house – as Dick Turpin discovered. Hayes was a farmer's son; he was also a moneylender; therefore it is almost certain that he kept his money – fifteen hundred pounds of it – on the premises. (It could not have been in a bank, or there would be records of Catherine's attempts to get it after his death, as well as of her collecting his debts.) They lived in two rooms, in a house in which some of the tenants were poor – Mrs Springate was a quarter of a year behind with her rent. One of them must have stayed at home all the time in case of thieves. And since John Hayes must have been out on business, his wife was confined to the premises. A lodger who could

78

be trusted was a valuable addition to the household, even if he did assume some of the husband's rights.

How did Billings feel about Wood? We may assume that Wood became her lover, for two reasons: that he was otherwise unlikely to join in the murder plot, and because Osborn speaks of her 'taking every opportunity to caress him'. She even slept with the two of them on the night after the disposal of the body. Although frightened, he continued to return from Harrow to see her, when he would have been more sensible to stay away for six months. The emotional complications of this triangle – a healthy, sex-starved woman of thirty-four, and two virile teenagers – are enough to excite the interest of any dramatist. Billings was the one who stuck by her after the murder, which may explain why she transferred her affections completely to him before the end.

A final touch of mystery to the whole story: what about Mary Springate? On the night of the murder, she complained that they had wakened her husband. What became of the husband when Mrs Springate moved out with Catherine Hayes? Why was it *Mrs* Springate who complained about the noise, rather than her husband? Could he, perhaps, have been a market porter who had to rise very early? But if so, why were they a quarter of a year behind with the rent? No, it seems more probable that he had been ill for some time. Perhaps he died in the week after the murder. And Mrs Hayes took care to become more closely acquainted with the neighbour who had opened the door to Wood and Billings after the disposal of the body. Of course, it is just as likely that the husband was simply lazy, and that he left his wife sometime during the week after the murder. John Osborn was not interested in such commonplace details, and so we shall never know.

Catherine Hayes was by no means the only woman who was burnt for the murder of her husband in the eighteenth century; there was Ann Williams, burnt in 1753 for poisoning her husband with arsenic (the dying man gave her away); Amy Hutchinson, who also used arsenic – she married her husband to spite a former lover, but decided she preferred the lover

79

after all; she was strangled before being burnt in 1750; Ann Beddingfield, a farmer's wife who persuaded her lover to strangle her husband; unfortunately, the lover decided to do it on the spur of the moment one night, without telling his mistress, who was alarmed by the noise and woke up a servant girl; although the coroner failed to notice that the farmer had been strangled, the servant girl gave it away – waiting until she had received her quarter's wages. Ann Beddingfield was burnt in 1763, and her lover hanged at the same time. The last woman to be burnt alive in England was Phoebe Harris, who was executed for husband murder in 1788 – which was, after all, the time of Blake, Wordsworth and Goethe.

The main impression one receives from the *Newgate Calendar* – apart from the savagery of the sentences – is of the savagery of so many of the crimes. The Brownrigg family – mother, father and son – were sadists who enjoyed beating their female apprentices – girls from the workhouse or Foundling Hospital who were taken on as servants in exchange for their keep. The girls were frequently stripped and hung from a hook in the ceiling while they were whipped. Brownrigg – a plumber – was supposed to supply clothes, but he bought them only one lot of clothes each, of poor quality; if they tore these, Mrs Brownrigg was likely to force them to strip and to do their work naked for several days. One of the girls who wet her bed was made to sleep in an icy coal-cellar on straw, without blankets. Even after one of these apprentices escaped and was examined by parish officials – who saw that she was a mass of cuts and bruises – nothing was done about it, except to threaten Mrs Brownrigg. Even so, Mrs Brownrigg had no difficulty in replacing the runaway with another apprentice. This was a girl called Mary Clifford, who was eventually flogged so mercilessly that the wounds – never allowed to heal – began to gangrene. The next-door neighbours, hearing groans and cries issuing from the Brownriggs' house every other day, managed to peep in through the attic skylight, and saw a girl so badly beaten that she could not reply to them. The parish officers were called again; Brownrigg tried to brazen it out, but they searched his house and found one of the girls, Mary Mitchell. When a doctor attempted to remove her leather bodice, it stuck to the open sores. The officers returned, by which time Brownrigg had called a lawyer to threaten them with serious legal action if they didn't leave his premises. They used their legal authority, and Brownrigg was finally forced to produce the other girl, Mary Clifford, who had been ordered to hide in a sideboard cupboard. She died shortly after being taken to a hospital. The Brownriggs fled but were arrested. At the trial, Mrs Brownrigg was found guilty of murder – for she was officially the employer of the girls. The father and son received six months each. When Mrs Brownrigg was taken to Tyburn in September 1767, the mob howled and threw things. The records do not mention what became of the father and son, but the *Newgate Calendar* account leaves no room for doubt that they were equally responsible – possibly more so.

Less than a year later, another couple – a mother and daughter – were hanged for the same crime, and this case has some more interesting features. Sarah Metyard was a milliner, who had several girls from the parish as her apprentices, and she treated these as badly as the Brownriggs treated their girls. After an attempt to run away, one of the girls was starved for three days and kept tied in a position that would not allow her to sit down or stand up. At the end of this time, she died, and the mother and her teenage daughter – also called Sarah – moved the body up to the attic, and told the other apprentices that she had had a fit, and was recovering. Then they announced that the girl had run away. The girl's sister doubted this story, and mentioned her doubts to a lodger in the house; Mrs Metyard killed her too, and put the body in the attic with her sister's. After two months, the stench was so great that the old woman cut up the bodies, and dumped them in a sewer. The coroner who was shown the pieces of the bodies observed the state of decay, and declared that they were corpses stolen from a churchyard and dissected by a surgeon.

Two years later, a man named Rooker came to lodge with the Metyards, and was shocked by the old woman's cruelty. By this time, mother and daughter were constantly quarrelling; so when Rooker offered the daughter a place in his house, she

81

accepted eagerly. She soon became his mistress, and they moved out to Ealing. The old lady was wildly resentful, and spent a great deal of time making disturbances. One day, after a quarrel in which hints of the murders were dropped, Rooker asked his mistress what she meant. Sarah confessed to the murders, and Rooker thought he now had the ideal way of getting rid of the mother – he assumed that the daughter would not be indicted, since she was under age at the time, and had acted on her mother's orders. He was mistaken; mother and daughter both died at Tyburn.

A great number of murders in the eighteenth century were committed by smugglers, or in the course of smuggling. The case known as the 'trial of the smugglers' will serve as a typical – and particularly violent – example. Seven smugglers were tried in 1749 for the murder of a customs man named Galley and a shoemaker named Chater, when the latter was on his way to give evidence against the smugglers. The names of the smugglers were Benjamin Tapner, John Cobby, John Hammond, William Jackson, William Carter, and a father and son named Mills. The customs officer and his witness were on their way from Southampton to Stanstead, in Sussex, where Chater would be examined by a Justice of the Peace.

Smuggling in those days was not merely a family affair; it might involve the whole village or district, and to do anything about it was as difficult as breaking up the Mafia in Sicily. So when the pair stopped briefly at an inn at Rowlands Castle, in Hampshire, they had walked into the lion's den. The widow who kept the inn confided to a customer that she was afraid the two men 'were come to hurt the smugglers'. A gang of smugglers soon gathered, and one of them asked Chater what had happened to a man called Diamond. Chater replied truthfully that Diamond was under arrest and that he was being taken to give evidence against him, although he didn't want to. At this, one of the smugglers, Jackson, knocked him down with a blow in the mouth. The two men must have realised the extent of their mistake and asked for their horses. The smugglers apologised for Jackson and asked them to stay and drink.

They saw they had no alternative, and stayed. The smugglers got them drunk, and took the letter to the Justice of the Peace. Its contents enraged them so much that they immediately proposed to hang the two men – egged on by two of their wives, who said, 'Hang the dogs; they are here to hang you.'

Now the episodes of incredible cruelty began. Galley and Chater were asleep; Jackson jumped on the bed with a pair of spurs, and slashed their foreheads with them to wake them. The men were then both whipped. After this, they were both tied on horses, and whipped along the road by the whole gang. When they fell off, and hung upside down under the horse's belly – their ankles being tied – they were quickly pulled upright and whipped again. One of the smugglers seized Galley's testicles and squeezed them until he fainted; Galley was then whipped to death.

Chater must have been wishing that they would kill him too; but first they wanted to find out what happened to Diamond; so Chater was chained up in a coal house with a man to watch him. The smugglers then buried the customs man, and went on a drinking spree for three days – the beverages being gin and rum. At intervals, the guard was changed, and several smugglers visited Chater to beat him. Then they decided that he had to be killed, and someone suggested putting a loaded gun to his head, and attach a long string to the trigger, which would be pulled by all of them at once – there were now fourteen – so that no one of them could be blamed.

Finally, the smugglers went to kill Chater. One of them slashed him across the eyes with a heavy knife, blinding him and cutting through the bridge of his nose. Then Chater was whipped again. After this, they took him to a well near a wood. There a rope was tied around his neck, and the other end was tied to some railings; he was then pushed into the well. Unfortunately, the rope was too short, and he was still alive after a quarter of an hour – the weight of his body being supported by the side of the well. Eventually, they tossed him in, head-first. When he still continued to groan after half an hour, they threw in stones until he stopped.

All this cruelty had not sickened them; they stopped to drink on the way home, and boasted about the murders openly. When officials started searching for the two missing men, it was not too difficult to find someone to drop a hint about the murderers. Seven of the fourteen were arrested; the trial was short, and six of them were executed the next day. The exception was Jackson, the ringleader, who died in prison the evening before his execution was due. No doubt the story of the spurs had got about, and the police had taken the opportunity to get some of their own back.

There is a curious postscript to this story that again illustrates the barbarity of which country people were capable. Another son of the elder Mills was a member of a gang who, only a few weeks later, whipped and kicked to death another man who was suspected of stealing two of the smugglers' bags of tea. They dumped the body in a pond, and Mills moved to Beckenham in Kent, where he became a highway robber. Another smuggler gave him away, and he was executed six months after his father and brother. Mills seems to have been the only one of the gang who was hanged for the murder. The leader, a man named Curtis, told the man they were whipping that 'he would whip him till he died, for he had whipped many a rogue and washed his hands in the blood'. Clearly, this kind of cruelty was not uncommon among smugglers.

Gin can hardly be blamed for the barbarity of the eighteenth century, for tales of equal barbarity can be told of earlier centuries. But it certainly played its part in releasing those impulses that civilsation aims to control. Reading the *Newgate Calendar*, it is impossible not to note that a large proportion of the crimes are due simply to loss of temper – like Jane Griffin's stabbing of the servant girl. In fact, apart from murders committed in the course of robbery, the most familiar type of murder was the 'crime of passion' – in the most straightforward sense. The last nobleman to be publicly executed in England was Lord Ferrars, who flew into a fury with his bailiff and shot him. Ferrars was undoubtedly mentally unbalanced; but the sentence was carried out nevertheless. The hangman was the famous Thomas Turlis. The old triangular gallows erected in the time of Queen Elizabeth had been removed in 1759, and a new one had to be built for Ferrars in the following year. (A movable gallows was used for ordinary miscreants, but a Lord obviously deserved something better.) A picture of the execution, made at the time, shows the prisoner faced by a huge grandstand, of the kind now used in football grounds, and a huge and impressive gallows nearly the size of Marble Arch. The gallows is surrounded by mounted soldiers. This impressive occasion was marred by a sordid squabble; as Turlis was reaching out his hand to take the five guineas his lordship was offering, one of his assistants leapt forward and snatched it. The dignified Turlis, who had just begged his lordship's forgiveness, turned round in a rage and unleashed a string of violent oaths. The execution was delayed until the money was restored.

The case of Captain John Porteous illustrates that the mob was still capable of taking justice into its own hands. Porteous was a tailor who married an ex-mistress of the Provost of Edinburgh, and often received favours from his wife's ex-lover, one of which was a post as captain of a band of men employed to keep the peace. Porteous was a brutal man, disliked by everybody. One day, when he was presiding over the execution of a smuggler, the crowd started to throw stones, one of which hit Porteous on the nose. He immediately fired his pistol at the nearest man, killing him, and ordered his men to fire on the mob. The soldiers fired over the heads of the crowd, but some of the shots hit people watching from windows, while Porteous continued to fire his own pistol. Nine people were killed, and many more injured. For the sake of appearances – and to avoid riots – Porteous was tried and sentenced to death, but the execution was delayed until the King could return from Hanover to review the case. The mob recognised the aim of these delaying tactics, and stormed the jail. Porteous was dragged along to the grass-market – where the previous outrage had taken place – and hanged from a pole outside a shop. This was in 1736.

Before we cease to speak of Tyburn, it might be mentioned that

85

there were a number of cases in which hanged people were revived. The most famous was of a sixteen-year-old youth, William Duell, who in 1740 raped and murdered a girl in a barn. After he had been cut down and taken to the surgeons' hall for dissection, he began to move. The surgeon bled him, and half an hour later, Duell sat up. Since the sentence of hanging had been carried out, he could not be hanged again; instead, he was transported for life.

Ann Greene was a servant girl who was found guilty of killing her newly born baby. Her friends hung on her legs to try to put her out of her misery more quickly – one can only presume the rope was badly tied – and when she was cut down, and still twitched, one of them jumped on her stomach, and a soldier hit her on the head with his musket. In the surgeons' hall, a rattling was heard in her throat and she was put into a warm bed; the next day, she was almost fully recovered. She died in 1659, nine years after her hanging, during which time she had married and had three children.

In 1728, a girl named Margaret Dickson established the basis of a lifelong reputation by hanging for an hour, and then being taken away in her coffin. Knocking noises were heard from inside the coffin – at which everyone fled. But someone had the courage to return and take her out; she not only recovered, but had to marry her husband a second time, since she was legally dead, and her marriage therefore dissolved. Her murder of her baby had also been the result of the kidnapping of her husband by a press-gang. Under the name of Half Hanged Meg, she was still a notable public figure in Edinburgh twenty-five years later.

'Half Hanged Smith' was a housebreaker who was hanged at Tyburn. After five minutes, some merrymakers in the crowd began to shout 'A reprieve', as if a man had arrived waving a document. The executioner cut him down, and he revived at a nearby house. Later, he described his sensations: 'I felt a very great pain caused by the weight of my body, and my spirits felt in a strange commotion violently pressing upwards. They forced their way into my head, and then I saw a great blaze of glaring light which seemed to go out of my eyes with a flash.

After that I lost all sense of pain until I was cut down, when I experienced an intolerable pricking or shooting' – the latter obviously the 'pins and needles' that comes when blood returns to a part of the body from which it has been cut off. This was in 1705.

Towards the last part of the century, there was a gradual change in public opinion towards violence. Tyburn gallows was removed because it hindered traffic, but also because these spectacles were beginning to offend people. This should not be taken to mean the ordinary people, who seemed to feel no sympathy for the criminal, and enjoyed the hangings in the way that schoolboys enjoy seeing other schoolboys being caned. The crowds who threw things at Elizabeth Brownrigg in 1767 were not horrified by her cruelty; it was simply a demonstration by the underdog against the 'middle classes' who could beat and starve them.

No, the change in sensibility was taking place in the educated classes, and it was the result of increased national prosperity and the gradual relaxation of religious bigotry. The *Newgate Calendar* contains an interesting example of this change of sensibility in the chapter on Thomas Colley, hanged in 1751 for drowning a woman believed to be a witch. Colley was the ringleader of a mob who seized an old couple called Osborne from the workhouse – they were believed to be a witch and a wizard. Both were stripped, and ducked in a pond; Colley kept pushing them under with a long stick. The woman died with her mouth and nose choked with mud. Wilkinson's account declares indignantly: 'It is astonishing to believe that any persons could be so stupid as to believe in the ridiculous doctrine of witchcraft,' and goes on to offer several pages of cases from the past of witches being forced to confess by torture. One realises, with mild amazement, that Wilkinson felt he was living in a rational and enlightened age, and that all this barbarity was behind him.

In fact, it would be more than fifty more years before there was an attempt to introduce even such simple reforms as preventing children from working down mines or being forced to climb chimneys as sweeps, to preventing landowners from setting mantraps and spring guns, and passing safety regulations to prevent ships from being grossly overloaded. But at least the age of Dr Johnson – who supported public hanging because he thought it deterred criminals – was giving way to the age of William Blake and Wordsworth. Blake's early poems, full of pity for children forced to sweep chimneys and girls forced into prostitution, date from the same time as the *Newgate Calendar*.

The man who was chiefly responsible for a new attitude towards crime in London was the novelist Henry Fielding, who became a magistrate in 1748, after he had failed to make a living as a playwright. Before Fielding, the law attempted to repress crime by the savagery of the sentences and by gibbets and dissection. Fielding was the first to make a simple and obvious suggestion : why not try to prevent crime in advance by having an efficient police force? This struck the government as a wildly illogical proposal; after all, each parish employed its constables and watchmen. Fielding's predecessor at Bow Street had been Sir Thomas de Veil, a good magistrate by all ordinary standards, although he boasted of making a thousand pounds a year by 'trading justice'; he was also a satyr who shamelessly used his office to procure himself 'a great variety of young ladies'. Fielding's kind of honesty and dedication was regarded as slightly insane, and after six years of struggling against the government, he died. But he had created the core of a small army of efficient policemen in Bow Street. His blind half-brother John carried on his work, and the Bow Street Runners became famous for their efficiency. In 1785, the new Prime Minister, Mr Pitt, introduced a police bill that represented the final triumph of Henry Fielding's proposals. By the year 1800, there were nine 'police offices' in London, and the century-long crime wave was at last over.

Three: Cannibals and Rapists

FROM THE CRIMINAL point of view, I find the nineteenth century far more interesting than the eighteenth. Why? Because murders that spring out of poverty and misery do not really involve much human choice – much good or evil. Bernard Shaw asked the explorer Stanley – the man who found Livingstone – what proportion of his men could lead the expedition if necessary. Stanley replied promptly: 'Five per cent.' Shaw asked if this was an exact or an approximate figure. 'Exact,' said Stanley.

Modern biology has made the same discovery, although at the time I am writing, it is not widely known. In *all* animal groups, including human, there are five per cent who possess enterprise, leader-qualities. The other ninety-five per cent are more or less passive. But, of course, there are wide extremes in the range of the dominant five per cent, from sadistic wife-beaters to Beethovens, from champion boxers to great mathematicians. In an experiment performed with rats, John Calhoun (at the Bethesda Institute of Mental Health in Maryland) showed that when rats are overcrowded, the dominant five per cent become criminals. This is obviously also true for human beings. Place them in squalor and misery, and the dominant five per cent will tend to become a criminal five per cent. The more intelligent ones will use their intelligence to escape the squalor, recognising that to become a criminal is, in a way, to surrender to the squalor as much as becoming a drunk or a drug-addict. But these will only be a tiny minority.

The criminality of about five per cent of slum dwellers is scientifically predictable, and therefore of no particular interest to a writer like myself who is more interested in questions of human freedom. Crime becomes psychologically interesting only when people are sufficiently well-off to satisfy their basic needs for food, drink, sex, security. With a few interesting exceptions, all the 'great' murder cases of the nineteenth century – Lizzie Borden, Charles Bravo, Dr Pritchard, Professor Webster – concerned the socially comfortable classes. Not the extremely rich or the aristocracy; they were seldom involved in murders, except occasionally as victims; but the middle classes. And in well over fifty per cent of these cases, the means used was poison.

In an introduction to the Folio Society edition of selections from the *New Newgate Calendar* (1960), Lord Birkett remarked that the trials of the nineteenth century do not differ very greatly from those of the eighteenth. This may be true as far as the trials are concerned; but anyone who has the original two-volume edition of Camden Pelham's *New Newgate Calendar* (1886) will immediately note a difference in the crimes themselves. Pelham's Volume One is largely a rehash of the original *Newgate Calendar* (in many cases using the original text of Wilkinson). Volume Two deals with the nineteenth century, and we are immediately in a different world. In fact, the opening case might have taken place in New York almost a century later. Three Irishmen, named Quinn, Riorton and Conolly, were standing in Cheapside and hoping for employment when a man named Barry approached them, and offered them a job on condition they took an oath of secrecy. They took the oath – and, being Irish Catholics, were convinced that their souls would be damned if they broke it. Barry then took them to a room where there was brass and various tools for shaping it into counterfeit shillings. Before they had been at work long, the Bow Street Runners came and arrested them. They were tried and condemned; but luckily, a priest told them that they need not be bound by an oath that was unlawful, and they then told the true story. Their accusers and the police officers were now arrested, and it suddenly became clear that a number of police had been supplementing their incomes for a long time by 'framing' out-of-work labourers. The three false witnesses were sentenced to transportation. Three police

90

officers were tried soon afterwards for conspiring to persuade five youths – one of them only thirteen – to commit a burglary; their aim was to arrest them and claim the reward for the conviction of housebreakers.

The Irishmen who avoided the gallows excited general sympathy, and a Lord Mayor's fund opened for them raised enough money to enable them to buy a farm in Ireland.

Even this more-or-less happy ending to the story distinguishes it from cases of the eighteenth century; fifty years earlier, the Irishmen would have been hanged, and then, possibly, the false witnesses might have been hanged, too.

The habit of transporting prisoners to Australia or America aroused a great deal of indignation among respectable colonists in those countries; Benjamin Franklin asked how the English would feel if America transported her rattlesnakes to England. In both countries, the crime rate was enormous; there were more highway robberies in New South Wales every year than there were robberies of all kinds in England. Conditions were appalling; the first colony, at Port Jackson, was founded among fever swamps, and half the prisoners had died on the long journey out. Discipline was ferocious, and the work was long and hard, so that men escaped into the bush as often as possible and became outlaws – bushrangers. Several of these were simply homicidal maniacs; Major Arthur Griffiths mentions one called 'Jeffries the Monster' who had been hangman in Edinburgh before his transportation, and who became the official flogger in the penal colony. His murders were apparently prompted simply by the pleasure of killing, for he later admitted that in a large number of them, he had not stolen anything (probably because the wretches he killed had nothing to steal). Like many of the bushrangers, he became a cannibal at one point. The crime that finally roused the community was the kidnapping of a mother and baby – presumably with the motive of sexual assault. He killed the baby with a blow on the head. Even convicts were allowed to help in hunting him down; he was eventually captured and executed.[1]

Cannibalism was not unfamiliar. A convict named Alexander

[1] *Mysteries of the Police and Crime* (1899), Vol 1.

Pierce escaped in a stolen boat from one of the island prisons, together with five other men. Hiding out in the hills, they began to starve, and one of them remarked that he could eat a man. The idea took root, and that night one of the men was killed; his heart was fried and eaten. A few days later, two more were killed, and their liver and hearts eaten. When one of the remaining three collapsed with exhaustion, he was killed with a blow from a hatchet, and partly eaten. The man who did the killing strapped the hatchet to his body in case Pierce attacked him with it in the night; Pierce decided to anticipate attack, and killed his companion, carrying off an arm and a thigh. Recaptured, he escaped again a year later with a man named Cox; Cox's dismembered body was found a few days later. When Pierce was captured, the meat and fish he had taken when he escaped were still intact; he admitted to preferring the taste of human flesh.

These early bushrangers were noted for their incredible barbarity. A man named Dignum who flourished in the area of Port Phillip in 1837 decided to murder his eight companions when food ran short. One of them, a young man named Cornerford, woke up as he was about to start, and had to be taken into his confidence. The two of them killed the other seven – by shooting them, and then became companions in a number of robberies in the area of Adelaide. Neither trusted the other, and when Dignum tried to shoot Cornerford in the back one day, the latter rode into Melbourne and gave him away. Cornerford managed to escape before their trial, and made such a nuisance of himself that he was quickly hanged when they captured him. Dignum escaped with life imprisonment on Norfolk Island, since the chief witness against him was dead.

One more story of the bushrangers before this narrative returns to England: when I was about ten years old I remember reading in *The Saturday Evening Post* of a particularly ferocious bushranger named Morgan who seems to have been a homicidal maniac – I suspect it may have been the 'Morgan' whom Major Arthur Griffiths mentions briefly. His robberies usually ended in the death of the victim. One day, he and a companion called at the home of a woman whose husband was at work, and asked for food. While she was cutting the bread, the baby started to cry in the next room, and Morgan said: 'Don't worry, I'll go and see.' A moment later, the crying stopped and the mother congratulated him on his skill with babies. When the men had left, she went into the next room, to find that the baby's throat had been cut.

The crime made the district too hot to hold the outlaws, and they had to flee. Some time later, they were rowing a stolen boat down a river when they saw a reward notice on a tree that declared there was a large sum on Morgan's head. His companion waited his opportunity, and knocked Morgan unconscious. He then severed the head, and took it into the nearest large town to claim the reward. Unfortunately, he was seized too: the woman whose baby had been killed identified him, and he was immediately executed. Major Arthur Griffiths says of Morgan: 'he was afflicted with blood madness, and pitilessly slew all his victims.' But according to Griffiths' account, Morgan was found one day riddled with bullets; so my memory may be faulty in attributing the child-murder to Morgan.

This kind of thing explains why the settlers in Australia and Virginia objected to having convicts dumped on them. When the colonial government of Tasmania was on the point of bankruptcy in 1852, it refused to take any more convicts. Queensland was asked if it had room for convicts, and countered by asking if there was not some part of Britain to which they could send Queensland's criminals. The last convict ship sailed for Western Australia in 1867. After that, England had to think of a more convenient way of dealing with criminals than sweeping them under the carpet.

This digression may have conveyed some notion of what was in store for the various criminals whom the *Newgate Calendar* mentions as having been sentenced to transportation. As the climate of public opinion caused some slight relaxation in the severity of the law, an increasing number of criminals were sentenced to transportation; in the second volume of the *New Newgate Calendar,* headings like 'executed for robbery' and 'executed for body stealing' become steadily more rare.

Another reason for the change of climate can be seen in this second volume: the increasing number of men who were convicted for provoking riots or making seditious speeches. The workers had found a voice. Men like Tom Paine, William Cobbett, John Wilkes, Henry Hunt, raised their voices against oppression. The Calthorpe Street riot of 1833 – in which a policeman was stabbed to death – began as a meeting of working men to form a union. In 1834, six men led by a labourer called James Lovelace were tried at Dorchester for attempting to start an agricultural union to raise farm wages from seven shillings to ten shillings a week. The actual charge was that they had unlawfully administered oaths to prospective members of the union. These men, who became known as the Tolpuddle Martyrs, were sentenced to transportation to Australia. What all this meant was that *some* of the 'dominant five per cent' among working men preferred protest to crime. The most sensational case of 1820 combined the two. A man named Arthur Thistlewood hatched a plot to murder the whole Cabinet while they sat at dinner at the house of Lord Harrowby in Grosvenor Square, and then to blow up the Bank of England, set fire to London, and take over the Mansion House. Thistlewood was a hater of authority; he had been imprisoned briefly after the Spa Fields riots, which he organised; he then challenged Lord Sidmouth to a duel and received another year. The thirty or so Cato Street Conspirators – as they became known – made the mistake of admitting a police informer to their ranks, and they were set upon by the police as they waited in a barn for the signal to murder the Cabinet. Most of them escaped, but a dozen of them were later arrested. One of them turned King's evidence. Thistlewood and four others were sentenced to death – the remaining six escaped execution on a technicality – and were hanged and then beheaded outside Newgate prison. When the first man was beheaded there was a gasp of horror from the crowd, but by the time the fifth head fell, the crowd was laughing.

Apart from this new element of revolutionary unrest, the reader of the *New Newgate Calendar* observes another element that was far less common in its predecessor: the increase in crimes connected with sex. There was still not a great deal of 'sex crime' in the modern sense: that is, men who could be labelled 'sexual criminals'. But sex certainly began to play an increasingly important part in the records of the nineteenth century. In Ireland, the abduction and raping of heiresses became something of a hobby. A girl of seventeen named Elizabeth Crockatt was an heiress with some two thousand six hundred pounds; there were two attempts to seize her, apparently by different men. After the first – she was kidnapped after church – her brother and uncle managed to rescue her. The second was carried out by a young man named Samuel Dick, with the help of his sister Jane, who invited Elizabeth Crockatt to stay with them. The girl agreed, and for the first day, everything seemed normal. Then, when she went outdoors in the evening, she was seized and bundled into a chaise. Jane Dick and her brother took her to another house, where she spent the day crying and refusing to eat. Finally, utterly exhausted, she agreed to sleep in the same bed with Jane. Halfway through the night, she discovered that her sleeping partner had been changed; it was now the brother, who proceeded to commit upon her offences over which Pelham decently draws a veil. The next morning, Dick rushed off to get a marriage licence; the others were now presumably confident that Miss Crockatt was anxious to become Mrs Dick, and they relaxed their vigilance – with the result that Miss Crockatt escaped, and Dick ended on the gallows.

Four years later, in 1822, a young man named Brown was so anxious to secure the hand of an heiress named Honoria Goold that he hired a gang of men to storm her house. They dragged her off, and Brown was waiting outside to sweep her on to the saddle of his horse and gallop away. When they arrived at the house of a farmer named Leahy, he proposed to her, and she refused him. Brown then locked himself in a room with her and 'in spite of her entreaties and screams, proceeded to undress her'. Pelham adds indignantly: 'The reader need not be told the rest – the purity of female innocence was grossly violated in the person of this young and lovely creature; and her destroyer arose from his bed of lust, the polluter of one whose peace of mind neither the world's sympathy nor the world's wealth could restore.' (This is typical of Pelham's style in recounting rapes.) After three weeks of refusing to marry Brown, the girl was finally set at liberty, and the abductors fled. Brown had the money to escape abroad; the others didn't; they were tried at Limerick and all sentenced to death, although four of the eight escaped on a point of law.

Now the subject of rape has arisen, we may as well pause to examine it more fully. Of the two hundred or so cases in the original *Newgate Calendar*, only four concern rape, and one of those is an assault on a youth by a homosexual. (Wilkinson is so shocked he can barely bring himself to splutter out the basic details.) Only one of these cases excited much attention: the abduction of a demure little Quakeress named Sarah Woodcock by Lord Baltimore in 1768. For three nights she wailed and protested so violently that he left her alone; on the fourth night, she undressed for bed – a four poster with curtains – then discovered Lord Baltimore waiting in it, who then 'effected his horrid purpose' twice. During the next two days she was apparently menstruating, but later in the week his lordship 'sent for her to go to bed' and she complied. And 'What passed this night is too horrible for relation'. Lord Baltimore had already sent her father a two-hundred-pound note, and now her relations managed to trace her, and got her out of Lord Baltimore's clutches with the help of a warrant from Sir John Fielding. At his trial he alleged her consent, and was acquitted. He died four years later, at the age of thirty-nine, apparently worn out by his libidinous excesses.

Fifty years later, his chances of acquittal would have been slim, lord or no lord. Juries had begun to feel more strongly about virtue in danger; the Victorian cult of the distressed damsel was established long before Queen Victoria came to the throne in 1837. In fact, a man accused of almost anything by a girl was likely to be found guilty, just to be on the safe side. In 1831, a young Irishman called Luke Dillon was sentenced to death for rape. The complainant was a Miss Frizell, who admitted that she and Dillon had met several times at parties, and that 'he professed to be her warm admirer'. She agreed to meet him one day, and they spent three hours sheltering from the rain in an empty cottage, during which time he proposed to her and she accepted. They then drove off in a carriage, and he persuaded her to stop for 'refreshment', which included fish and a glass of punch. She claimed she then lost consciousness until she woke up and found herself naked in bed. She jumped up screaming, and ran into the wall, upon which Dillon threw her on the bed and 'completed an outrage which, there was no doubt, was a repetition only of an act of violence of which he had before been guilty'. He promised to marry her again, and in the morning, she went back to the house of relations, and told them she was married. Dillon took care not to see her again, and did not answer a letter she wrote him beginning: 'My dearest Dillon' and asking him to recollect his solemn promise. When he failed to keep it, he was arrested and charged with rape.

Even this brief account of the facts makes it apparent that her story has several weak points. She had known Dillon for two years and admitted that their acquaintance 'soon ripened into an intimacy'. She agreed to marry him, and accompanied him to a private room – with a bed – for supper. She implies that Dillon gave her some powerful drug in a glass of punch; in those days, most people believed that villains could procure drugs that would render a girl immediately unconscious; but this seems unlikely. What is more probable is that she drank more whisky punch than she would admit. We can assume that Dillon then removed her clothes and raped her. But is it likely that, when she woke up screaming and tried to rush out of the room, he hurled her on the bed and raped her again? His first reaction would be to soothe her and assure her that they were already man and wife in the sight of heaven, etc. Even in a house of ill-repute (and no one suggested this one was), a screaming girl would have aroused attention. Besides, a noisy and excited girl is not likely to arouse lust, especially in a man who has already accomplished his purpose once. And even supposing that Dillon was the type of man whose desires were aroused by

97

a struggle, he would not find the task of raping a frightened virgin – or near-virgin – easy.

No, it is surely obvious that he soothed her and persuaded her to get back into bed, so that the second 'outrage' was by her consent. And since she had agreed to marry him, and eaten supper with him in a room with a bed, it is arguable that the first time was not strictly a rape either. In short, Dillon's crime was not rape; he had only done what a great many other libertines did: promised marriage and then changed his mind after receiving an advance payment of conjugal favours. This is a censurable activity, but not a crime.

Dillon's sentence was later commuted to transportation to Australia. Pelham ends his account by adding that 'the unhappy object of Dillon's machinations and brutal crime died in the month of June 1831, a victim to her own sensitive feelings. She had gone to Bangor, in Wales, in hope that a change of scene might relieve her of the melancholy which appeared to have settled upon her mind, but she died there of a broken heart.' No doubt Pelham's late Victorian readers found this perfectly understandable; the modern reader finds himself reflecting that people do not literally die of a broken heart. What did she die of? Perhaps the 'consumption' to which languishing young ladies of that day were prone? If so, she probably had it before the offence took place. But the main point is that a chronicler who can record that the girl died 'a victim to her own sensitive feelings' may be regarded as biased, and the whole account becomes suspect.

This is even clearer in the case of a publican, George Cant, who was transported for rape in 1840. The woman, Jane Bolland, went to work as a barmaid at the Windsor public house in Holborn, and claims that the landlord immediately began to make advances to her, and to ask her to leave her door open at night so he could come in. 'She told him she was not the sort of person he imagined her to be.' Later in the day, 'she became unwell', and went to bed; she could not recall who went up with her. She woke in the night to find the prisoner at her bedside, and he put one hand on her mouth; a struggle took place and she fainted. When she woke at six in the morning she found her clothes (which had not been taken off) in disorder and the bone of her stay broken. The landlord came to her door, and she called him a villain; he retaliated by calling her a drunkard. The landlord's wife also called her a drunken hussy when she accused her husband of rape. Jane Bolland left the Windsor public house, and returned to the house of her brother, with whom she usually lived. On Saturday, she was examined by a doctor, who verified that she had been raped.

The defence did not deny the rape, but declared that it had been committed by another man called Edwards, who was also living in the house. When the landlord was arrested, Edwards went voluntarily to Cant's solicitor and confessed that it was he who raped the girl, going into her room in the dark and finding her unconscious.

Edwards was cross-examined, and said that Jane Bolland had gone off to bed between nine and ten (when a public house would be very busy), apparently drunk. He had gone into her room at eleven, and had intercourse with her. She seemed quite willing. The next morning, he walked home with her to the East End, and she said that Cant had called her a drunkard and she would 'fix' him. He said she seemed quite happy.

In spite of all this, Cant was sentenced to death, although the interest aroused by the case finally led to his being transported for life.

On this evidence, there seems to be hardly any doubt that Cant was wrongly convicted. As to what really happened, there seem to be two possibilities. Jane Bolland got drunk on her first day as a barmaid. Later that evening, Edwards went to her room – which was in darkness – and had intercourse, with or without her consent. In the morning, the landlord called her a drunkard; she retaliated by accusing him to his wife, who also refused to listen. (Why? Did she know perfectly well that her husband had not left the room all night? Their bedroom was directly below the girl's.) Jane Bolland then left, swearing revenge, and accompanied by the man who had been in bed with her. It was not until the next day that she was examined by a doctor, who pronounced that she had been raped.

The second possibility is that Jane Bolland was not drunk.

Her brother declared that she had suffered from a severe attack of erysipelas in the head, and that from that time she had been insane. Erysipelas is a disease that causes severe inflammation of the skin, accompanied by fever. And so it may well be true that Jane Bolland was overcome by an attack of giddiness that made her seem drunk. It could also be that she remained passive during intercourse, giving the impression that she had no objection.

In either case, it is unlikely that Cant was the man in bed with her. If he was, he would have been unlikely to stir up her indignation by accusing her of drunkenness the next morning. Assuming, then, that Edwards was the man in her bed, how far can we accept his account? Rape was a hanging offence. If he had really committed it, he would be unlikely to have made a confession: it would merely put his neck in the noose. His action in declaring that he was the one who climbed into her bed is the action of a man with nothing on his conscience.

If Jane Bolland reached home on Friday morning and told her brother she had been raped, why did she wait until the following day to see a doctor? And what could such a medical examination – thirty-six hours after the event – demonstrate anyway? If the hymen had been recently ruptured, it would prove recent intercourse, but not rape. If she was not a virgin, it could have proved nothing at all. Doctors in those days had no method of detecting male sperm, even if any remained so long after. The only fairly certain proof of rape is the presence of bruises or scratches in the area of the genitals, but Jane Bolland admitted she was passive at the time of the assault.

Pelham's account suggests one more possibility – that Jane Bolland's whole story was a fabrication to get revenge on Cant. It is true that the defence was exceptionally generous about her: '[Mr Phillips] disclaimed all intention of impeaching the young woman's character, and was happy that he had no reason for making even an insinuation against her in regard to her conduct previous to this occasion.' That was because his line of defence was completely different, and he might only have damaged his client's chances by making the prosecution angry. (As it was, the prosecution 'rejoiced that Mr Phillips had not attempted to cast any aspersion' on Jane Bolland's character.) If the conclusive medical proof of sexual intercourse was a torn hymen, she might have acquired it after leaving the public house. (Her brother visited her at the Windsor with a man named Balfour who is not heard of again. Her lover?) She got drunk on her first day at the pub (the pot boy gave evidence that she struck him as drunk, and he must have known what a drunken woman looked like). She was thrown out, and told Edwards she intended to 'fix' Cant. That same night, she finally admitted Balfour into her bed, and in the morning, went to see a doctor with her story of rape. Cant saw that his only chance lay in bribing Edwards to claim that it was he who had intercourse with Jane Bolland, with her consent. . . . This version fits the facts. At all events, it is perfectly clear that George Cant was wrongfully convicted, as far as the evidence against him was concerned.

Compare this with a modern case cited by C R M Cuthbert,[1] Superintendent of the Metropolitan Police Lab. A married woman and her friend went to a village dance while the husband stayed at home baby-sitting. The wife flirted with a soldier, who walked home with them. At the corner of her lane, the married woman asked her friend to walk on. Ten minutes later, she came home and declared she had been raped. She was not injured in any way, but there was mud on her coat, and stains of sperm in the fork of her panties. The soldier was easily traced, and admitted frankly to having had intercourse with the woman; but he declared it was with her consent. What must have happened is fairly clear. The married woman obviously had something in mind in asking her friend to walk on. After allowing the soldier intercourse, it strikes her that her husband will be extremely suspicious and that the mud on her coat will be difficult to explain. So she invents the story of the rape. Presumably the soldier was not charged (there was clearly no evidence against him). In 1850, he would have been executed or sentenced to transportation on the word of the housewife – even though the ultra-violet and microscopic methods of detecting seminal stains had not then been invented.

[1] *Science and the Detection of Crime*, Hutchinson, 1958.

101

I have often wondered whether this cult of the distressed damsel explains one of the most baffling features of the 'crime of the century' – the Red Barn murder. When William Corder became Maria Marten's lover, she already had an illegitimate child and had lost another. Even Pelham has some difficulty making her sound innocent and virtuous: 'An unfortunate slip ruined the character of the young woman, and a second mishap with a gentleman of fortune left her a child.' She quickly became pregnant by Corder, but the baby died soon after birth. But why did he now murder her, instead of taking the obvious course of vanishing – which, in fact, he did after the murder? There was nothing to stop him from simply walking out. After the murder, he went to London, advertised for a wife (and received fifty-three replies), and married a young lady with whom he set up a school. Maria's mother's dreams of murder in the red barn led to the discovery of the body, which had been shot and stabbed. (Corder's confession denied stabbing her.)

There are two possibilities as to why Corder murdered her rather than absconding. The first is that Maria might have taken legal action – not only against William Corder, but against his brother Thomas, who was her first seducer (and the father of the child that died). In the climate of opinion in 1827, she had a strong case; the poor wronged girl, doing her best to be virtuous, but with an unfortunate predisposition to 'slips' and 'mishaps', each one of which left her pregnant.

The other possibility – a remote one – is that she was in a position to blackmail Corder about the death of her baby. Even Pelham and the anonymous author of *Murder in the Red Barn* admit that there is no reason to attribute the baby's death to anything but natural causes. Admittedly, Corder and Maria vanished for two days with the body, and Corder later told people that the baby had been buried at Sudbury, which proved to be untrue. In his confession, he says that he murdered Maria as a result of a quarrel about the place where they buried the baby. It is not clear why they didn't have it buried in the normal way, since there was no suspicion of murder.

Maria Marten played to crowded houses for another seventy-five years. And almost as famous was the victim of a similar murder. Ellen Hanley's story was novelised by Gerald Griffin as *The Collegians* (1829), dramatised by Dion Boucicault as *The Colleen Bawn* (1860), and finally turned into an opera *The Lily of Killarney* by Sir Julius Benedict (1863). She was the pretty niece of a ropemaker named Connery, who lived in Ballycahane, near Limerick.[1] The squire of Ballycahane Castle – actually a group of farm buildings – was a twenty-six-year-old ex-officer who had fought against Napoleon, and was now retired on half pay; his name was John Scanlan. Scanlan's batman in the army had been Stephen Sullivan – six years his senior – and he continued to be Scanlan's manservant in Ballycahane; the relation between the two was very close.

Everyone seems to agree that Ellie Hanley *was* an extremely pretty schoolgirl – she was only fifteen when she was murdered – although her incisor teeth were rather prominent and fang-like, making her look like one of Dracula's wives.[2] Scanlan was familiar with the brothels of Europe, and the response provoked in him by the farmer's daughter was quite impersonal; he wanted her maidenhead. Ellie was impressed by the sporting squire; but, being a Catholic, she was determined to remain virtuous. Scanlan persuaded her to elope with him, and they were married – in late June 1819 – by a defrocked priest. Almost immediately afterwards, Scanlan discovered that the marriage was legal; Ellie was his wife. He began to feel that he had paid an exceptionally high price for his maidenhead. Ellie was socially naïve and sexually inexperienced; her attitude towards her husband was one of uncritical admiration; after a few days of soft words and caresses, Scanlan began to think longingly about horses and hounds. They spent the first days of their honeymoon at Glin, on the Shannon, then moved to an island in the river. Glin is a very small and very dull village; after two weeks, Scanlan was impatient to return home. But there was a problem. When Ellie left home, she took the life-savings of her uncle – one hundred and twenty pounds in notes and twelve guineas in silver. She promptly spent a great deal

---

[1] And not in Dublin, as Pelham mistakenly asserts.
[2] Fitzgerald says they were 'double teeth', whatever that means.

of this on silk dresses. It began to dawn slowly on the sporting squire that his guardian angel had been off duty on the day he asked Ellie to marry him. He was the spoilt son of the family – his father had died when he was a child – and his impetuosity was a local legend. And now he was tied hand and foot.

Stephen Sullivan understood his employer's feelings; in fact, he shared them. He had thought it an excellent idea for the squire to add one more maidenhead to his list, and had entered into the spirit of the thing. But Ellie was very definitely not a lady, and it was easy to guess how Scanlan's mother would feel when her son introduced the future mistress of Ballycahane Castle. He was also aware that a relationship like the one between himself and Scanlan would not survive marriage. And when Scanlan's thoughts began to run on getting rid of Ellie, Sullivan was inclined to agree that it was the only solution. So one moonlit night, Scanlan suggested an excursion to an island in the river, to look at the ancient shrine of some saint. The boat was a fairly large one; Scanlan sat behind Ellie, Sullivan in front. It was agreed that when they reached mid-channel, Scanlan would give the signal, and Sullivan would seize a club and beat Ellie's brains out, while Scanlan would, if necessary, hold her arms.

This came to nothing. Scanlan gave the signal; Sullivan raised the club. Ellie thought he was joking, and laughed. Sullivan was already unnerved; he dropped the club and ignored his master's impatient signals. The excursion went off as planned, except that Ellie wondered why the two men looked so gloomy.

A few days later, Scanlan prevailed on Sullivan to try again. By this time, they had lost the large stone with a chain attached with which they had intended to sink the body; it had fallen overboard on a fishing expedition – and Scanlan bought some rope from a man in Glin. Then Ellie was persuaded to take a moonlight row with Sullivan. Scanlan provided his servant with a bottle of whisky this time, and Sullivan drank most of it rather quickly. Four miles out from land, Ellie had fallen asleep. Sullivan picked up his gun and swung it down with all his strength; but his drunkenness spoiled his aim, and he hit her arm at the shoulder, breaking it. Ellie woke up – but the next blow shattered her skull. Sullivan went on raining drunken blows on the body, until he was certain she was dead. Then he removed her clothes, with the exception of the bodice, which would take too long to unlace, tied her knees against her chin, and weighted the body with a heavy stone from the boat's ballast.

When he returned to Carrig Island – where Ellie and Scanlan had spent most of their honeymoon – the two men cleaned out the boat. Then they rowed back to Glin. Sullivan's sister Maureen was given some of Ellie's clothes and her pocket book. A friend of Ellie's called Ellen Walsh saw the men and asked after Mrs Scanlan; Scanlan told her that she had 'misbehaved', and that they had put her on board a boat bound for America.

Ellie was murdered on 14th July, less than three weeks after her marriage. The Reverend Richard Fitzgerald, who was staying with the Knight of Glin at the time of the murder (and who wrote his account of the case in 1869) states that by the time of her death, Ellie was already a living skeleton from moving from place to place with her husband and not eating enough food. This sounds like a typical Victorian attempt to throw in some extra pathos.

Scanlan and Sullivan decided to separate for the time being; there was already gossip about Ellie in Glin. And on 6th September the body of Ellie Hanley was cast up on the sand at Money Point, near Glin. The knees were still tied to the neck. One arm was missing – the one that Sullivan broke with his first blow – and one of the legs was found to be broken in several places.[1] The head was devoid of flesh, and the teeth were also missing, although the large sockets of the incisors could be identified. The stench was so appalling that they had to keep burning gunpowder to lessen it.

It took a hastily empanelled jury no time at all to decide that this was the body of Ellen Hanley, and that she had been murdered by John Scanlan and Stephen Sullivan (alias Humphreys). But the accused men were nowhere to be found. Gossip had it that Sullivan had gone to Galway and Scanlan

[1] Fitzgerald declares it was a leg, not an arm, that was missing.

to Cork, and the Knight of Glin suggested publishing a description of them in the *Hue and Cry* – the Irish 'police gazette'. Scanlan's family was horrified by the accusation, and took a great deal of trouble to stop the news from spreading. Since they were very influential in Limerick, they succeeded to a large extent. And the Limerick police decided to ask the help of the police of neighbouring County Clare for help, to overcome this problem of family influence. One day in November, Major Warburton of the Clare police was told that Scanlan had been seen at his family home in Ballycahane. He moved quickly, surrounding the house with troops. A lengthy search of the farm failed to uncover the suspect. Two dragoons glanced into an outhouse with straw inside and decided Scanlan was not there either; to make sure, one of them drove his bayonet into the straw. There was a yell, and Scanlan leapt to his feet – the dragoons were probably as startled as he was.

The great Daniel O'Connell was engaged for the defence. His account of the murder cast the blame entirely on the missing Sullivan. According to O'Connell, Sullivan realised that his master was ruined by the marriage; that his wife would never be acceptable to the social circle of Ballycahane. He offered to put Ellie on a ship bound for America. And until the discovery of the body, Scanlan went on believing that his unwanted bride was on the Atlantic. . . .

It was no good. The jury found Scanlan guilty of murder, and the judge ordered his immediate execution, afraid that his family might engineer a reprieve. On 10th March 1820, he was publicly hanged at Gallows Green, Limerick. At the last moment, public sympathy swung in his favour. As the horses pulling the carriage approached Ball Bridge over the Shannon, they stopped and refused to go forward. People murmured: 'It's the hand of God. He's innocent.' Scanlan continued to protest his innocence until he was hanged.

No one seemed to have a clue to Sullivan's whereabouts; it was generally believed that he had escaped abroad. Scanlan had rejoined the army after the murder – and then deserted a month later. But Sullivan had not been with him.

In fact, Sullivan had moved a mere thirty miles south, to

Scartaglen, and changed his name to Clifford. At about the time Scanlan was hanged, Sullivan was being married to a local heiress. But in May, his luck gave out; he was accused of passing forged money, and committed to Tralee jail. He was undoubtedly innocent of the forgery charge; but someone in the jail recognised him, and passed on the information to the Knight of Glin. On 25th July 1820, Sullivan stood trial in the same dock as Scanlan; he was found guilty, and hanged on Gallows Green on 27th July 1820. On the gallows, he made the following speech: 'I declare before Almighty God that I am guilty of the murder. But it was Mr Scanlan who put me up to it.'

For the modern reader, the case of the Colleen Bawn ('white girl') is altogether less interesting than it was to the Victorians. They saw it as a moral tale of a wicked seducer, an innocent country girl, and so on, forgetting that Ellie Hanley stole the life savings of the man who had brought her up, and then spent most of it on clothes. She may have been injured, but she was not innocent. Scanlan himself certainly provides material for moralising – spoilt, selfish and cowardly, without even the courage to commit his own murder. The most interesting person in the case is Sullivan. His attitude to Ellie was thoroughly ambivalent. His first attempt to kill her failed because she smiled at him; after this, he apparently tried to persuade Scanlan to let her return home, and even offered to take the blame for seducing her. And then, when it comes to the actual killing, he falls into a sadistic frenzy and continues beating the body long after she is dead. He then undresses her. Why? It is true that her clothes might identify her; but the clothes will have to be disposed of anyway. It sounds as if his attitude to Ellie is strangely self-divided. He has participated actively in her seduction; probably it is not the first time he has played Leporello. She is a girl of his own class. (In Ireland there were no middle classes; only the peasantry and gentlemen.) And if Scanlan had agreed to allow Sullivan to take the blame, no doubt Sullivan would have ended by marrying her; such arrangements were common in those days. (Fitzgerald is of the opinion that Scanlan's marriage to Ellie was invalid anyway.) Scanlan has her but does not want her; Sullivan wants her but cannot have her. But the act of murder itself has sexual implications, and when it comes to killing her, the frustrations and repressions explode.

And then, why should the body rise to the surface? Rope that is wholly immersed in water does not rot, and seaman's rope is tarred; it should have been as durable as a chain. If the stone had been placed inside Ellen Hanley's clothes, and the body bound with rope, it would not have risen to the surface. Perhaps Sullivan was too drunk to tie the body efficiently? Or does his attempt at disposal of the body display the same ambiguity as the murder itself? If Sullivan was killing someone he would have preferred to caress, then the act of murder had overtones of suicide.

Four: Into the Age of Violence

THE GERMANS INVENTED the useful term *lustmörd*. This does not mean – as one might suppose – lust-murder, but 'murder for pleasure', joy-murder. Unfortunately, the Germans have no corresponding term for what might be called 'business-murder', murder carried out in a purely practical spirit. For these are the two chief types of murder. I think that Oscar Wilde must probably be given the credit for founding that school of writers who are chiefly interested in 'murder-with-an-eye-to-business'. He was delighted by the remark of the forger and poisoner, Thomas Griffiths Wainewright, that he had killed his sister-in-law because he didn't like her thick ankles. His essay on Wainewright – published in *Intentions* in 1891 – is one of the first to treat murder as if it were an elaborate joke; Roughead, Pearson and William Bolitho adopted the manner. Writers of this type feel no interest in 'joy-murder' because such cases lack clear-cut motives. But it is 'joy-murder' that raises some of the profounder questions of human psychology. In the present chapter, I intend to examine some typical examples of both types.

The Germans can perhaps claim not only to have invented the word for joy-murder, but the thing itself. The earliest cases I have come across are to be found in the Journal of Master Hans Schmidt, the Nuremberg hangman in the sixteenth century. Of one murderer, Nicklaus Stüller, who was torn with red-hot tongs and broken on the wheel in 1577, he writes: 'First he shot a horse-soldier; secondly he cut open a pregnant woman alive in which was a dead child; thirdly he again cut open a pregnant woman in whom was a female child; fourthly he once more cut open a pregnant woman in whom were two male children. Görgla von Sunberg [an accomplice] said that they had committed a great sin and that he would take the infants to a priest to be baptised, but Phila [another accomplice] said he would himself be priest and baptise them, so he took them by the legs and dashed them to the ground.' Another murderer mentioned by Schmidt, Kloss Renckhart, broke into a mill and shot the miller, raped the wife and a maid, then made the wife fry eggs and eat them off the body of her husband.[1]

For some reason, German murder cases often seem to have this touch of brutality; it must be something in the German temperament. (I remember an old military man assuring me that the German temperament is naturally violent and brutal, and that all German men of genius have been Bavarians.)

Major Griffiths offers an account of a German Jack the Ripper named Andrew Bichel, who lived at Regensdorf in Bavaria. In 1808, a girl named Seidel happened to recognise a piece of dimity from which a tailor was making up a waistcoat; she thought it was the same material as a petticoat worn by her sister Catherine, who had vanished earlier the same year. On enquiry, she discovered the waistcoat was being made for a fortune-teller named Bichel. This confirmed one of her worst suspicions. Her sister had last been seen shortly before a visit to this same fortune-teller. He had told her to come in her best clothes, and to bring three changes of clothes – this being part of his method of foretelling the future. Bichel declared that the girl had eloped with a man she met at his house.

Bichel's house was searched, and a chest of women's clothes was discovered. A police dog got excited in the wood shed, and rushed to a corner where there was a heap of straw. Buried under this were the dismembered bodies of Catherine Seidel and another girl who had vanished the previous year, Barbara Reisinger. Bichel finally confessed. He had been tempted by Barbara Reisinger's clothes when she applied for a post as a servant girl. He persuaded her to have her eyes bound and her hands tied behind her, promising to show her her future in a magic mirror. He then stabbed her three times in the neck. This was all so easy – reminiscent of the method later employed by

[1] Schmidt, Hans, *A Hangman's Diary*, ed Albrecht Keller, 1928.

Christie – that he decided to do it again. But perhaps his manner made girls suspicious, or his request that they bring their wardrobe. His only other success seems to have been Catherine Seidel; at least, this was the only other murder brought home to him. Several other girls made appointments, and thought better of them. Bichel was sentenced to be broken on the wheel, but his sentence was commuted to beheading. The judge who tried him remarked that he would commit crimes that only required no courage; he might administer poison or murder a man in his sleep, but he would never commit highway robbery or burglary. All of which would seem to indicate that Bichel was an example of the 'furtive criminal'; not a man who needed to express an aggression against society, but who was attracted by the idea of secret crime. The American murderer Ed Gein – of whom I shall speak later – is a typical example. The motive of such men is always sexual (a fact that Major Griffiths did not seem to recognise). Bichel may have been a homosexual who was fascinated by women's clothes, or he may have been simply a transvestite.

Major Griffiths classifies with Bichel the crimes of the Dumollards in L'Ain (near Lyons) in the late 1850s, but here the motive was obviously peasant avarice. Madame Dumollard – the wife of a peasant – or her husband, would visit an employment agency in Lyons and ask for a servant girl. The girl would arrive at their cottage near Mollard, and never be seen again. In 1855, the body of a girl was found in a wood, with several stab wounds, and Martin Dumollard was suspected. She was a servant girl from Lyons. Several girls actually escaped from Dumollard; but for some reason, he was still not arrested. Finally, in May 1861, Dumollard accosted a girl named Marie Pichon in Lyons, and told her he was the gardener at the château at Montluel and had been sent to find a servant girl. Marie Pichon accompanied him to Montluel, but began to worry as he led her across fields. Finally, when she refused to go any farther, he tried to slip a noose over her head. She managed to escape, and found her way to a farm, where she stayed overnight. The police investigated, and eventually Marie Pichon identified Martin Dumollard as her attacker – he was a distinctive looking man with a tumour on his face and a scar on his upper lip. Clothes of several girls were found in the cottage, and Mme Dumollard led the way to a female skeleton – the girl had died of a blow on the head. Her confession – made in prison – stated that she had nothing to do with the murders; her husband would simply come and say: 'I've killed a girl in the woods of Montmain. I must go and bury her.' Some writers on the case are inclined to believe that Dumollard was a homicidal maniac and that his wife accepted his murders with peasant indifference. But it is worth noting that he tried to kill Marie Pichon by slipping a noose over her head – which would not have damaged her clothes. The corpse in the forest of Montaverne had been stabbed in the head. The other skeleton had a shattered skull. Dumollard killed in such a way as not to damage the clothes, and his wife confessed that she would wash out any bloodstains and then wear the clothes. Whether the girls were sexually attacked is not known. Dumollard's last words on the scaffold were to remind his wife that a neighbour owed him money. It is estimated that he killed ten girls, and that nine more escaped. (It was discovered that one of his victims had been alive when buried.)

There are only two English cases of the nineteenth century – if we except Jack the Ripper – that deserve classification with Bichel and Dumollard: the Ratcliffe Highway murders of 1811, and the murders of the body snatchers, Burke and Hare.

The Ratcliffe Highway[1] murders are the subject of a classic piece by de Quincey, an appendix to his essay 'On Murder Considered as one of the Fine Arts'. On Saturday 7th December 1811, a servant girl named Margaret Jewell was sent out sometime before midnight to buy oysters; she returned home to the hosier's shop in the Ratcliffe Highway (in London's East End) at 1 am to find it locked up. She thought she heard footsteps inside, but when no one answered her knock, she summoned a neighbour, who forced his way into the house, and found four corpses: Timothy Marr, his wife Cecilia, their baby, and an apprentice boy of thirteen. The violence of the murders was

[1] Now 'The Highway'.

incredible; all had their skulls smashed and their throats cut. There had been no robbery – perhaps the girl interrupted the killer. Twelve days later, a man broke into an East End public house just off the Ratcliffe Highway, the King's Arms, and killed the servant – a woman named Harrington – as she was cleaning the grate – with a blow from a crowbar, then proceeded to kill the owner – a Mr Williamson – and his wife. A twenty-six-year-old apprentice, aroused by the noise, crept downstairs and saw the murderer cutting the throats of the three victims, then searching for keys. The lodger hurried upstairs and climbed out of his bedroom window by means of knotted sheets. He quickly spread the alarm, and the murderer leapt out of the back window, ignoring a sleeping child in the same room.

A few days later, an Irish labourer named John Williams was arrested. The evidence against him was circumstantial. A mallet had been found at the scene of the Marr murders with the initials 'JP'. This was identified as belonging to a Swede named John Petersen who was at present at sea. When Petersen was ashore, he lived at the Pear Tree Inn, close to the Ratcliffe Highway, in a room where several other sailors lodged – including Williams. On the night of the second series of murders, he had returned to the room late and shouted at some German sailors to extinguish the candle. De Quincey asserts that a bloodstained knife was found in the lining of Williams' coat, but his account is perhaps not as reliable as it might be. Williams knew both Marr and the publican Williamson; in fact, he had sailed on the same ship as Marr, and been dismissed for general misbehaviour. He was also a customer at the King's Arms – and it seems fairly certain that the publican opened his door to a customer he recognised, and had gone to the cellar to get beer when his caller slammed the front door and proceeded to wield his crowbar.

Williams committed suicide before coming to trial – by hanging himself in his cell; he was buried at the crossroads with a stake through his heart.

There is one point upon which de Quincey is obviously reliable – his account of the terror that spread all over the Home Counties as a result of the murders; there was nothing like it again until Jack the Ripper. It emphasises the point that although murder was common enough, crimes of real atrocity were rare.

This is the reason that the crimes of Burke and Hare were the sensation of their day. In retrospect, they are interesting largely because of the light they throw on social conditions in a large town at about the time Maria Marten was murdered at Polstead. Both were Irishmen, in their mid-thirties at the time of the murders. Burke had been in the army as a 'substitute', then worked on the Union Canal in Scotland. He met William Hare – a tall, thin wolf of a man with a cast in one eye – in 1826, and the two men moved to a 'beggar's hotel', Log's Boarding House in Tanners Close, Edinburgh. Both had common law wives; Burke's was called Helen McDougal, a prostitute, and Hare's, Maggie Laird. When Log died, Hare took over the house. One day, a tenant called Old Donald died, owing three pounds ten shillings in rent. Hare had an idea of selling the body to the medical school – at this time, body snatchers (also known as Resurrection Men) made an excellent living. Old Donald's corpse was sold to Dr Knox, of 10 Surgeon's Square, for seven pounds ten shillings, and Old Donald's coffin filled with a sack of bark. Dr Knox asked no questions; corpses were hard to come by, and the medical students had to learn most of their anatomy from books. The medical school would pay from eight to ten pounds for a body and ask no questions.

It naturally struck Hare that there was a lucrative trade here, if one could only find corpses. The simple solution would be to make them. It was far less dangerous than digging up a newly buried body in a graveyard, for the victim could be quietly killed in the rooms of Burke or Hare, and conveyed to Dr Knox in a barrel. When a tenant called Joe the Mumper (or Miller) was ill, Burke and Hare hastened his exit with a pillow pressed over his face, and sold his body for ten pounds.

In February 1828, they decided that this was a business worth pursuing; but they almost lost their nerve over the first planned murder. A female hawker named Abigail Simpson was lured into their house and persuaded to get drunk. Burke and Hare also got drunk, and Abigail was still alive the next day.

lrunk again, and Hare suffocated her while
. Dr Knox paid ten pounds. The method
d, and the turnover was quick. An old
y Haldane; an attractive young prostitute
on – this almost became a double murder,
Brown, could hold more whisky, and left
McDougal started to quarrel; an unnamed
by Hare and his 'wife'); yet another un-
nglishman weakened with jaundice; Mary
ter (who asked after her mother, and was
Hare); an old Irish beggarwoman and her
e the boy's back over his knee after
; an old cinder woman (killed by Hare
len McDougal's from Falkirk; an idiot
d a widow woman named Docherty. It
rder – in October 1828 – that two of
ar couple named Grey – stumbled upon
plied heavily with whisky to keep them
e and Hare considered more lasting
their silence, but the couple talked to
ng could be done. Mrs Docherty had
.........y, and there were bloodstains on the bed.
Hare quickly turned King's Evidence, and so was not tried;
neither was Maggie Laird. Burke and Helen McDougal were
tried; she was acquitted for lack of evidence, but Burke was
hanged on 28th January 1829. Hare apparently gave his evidence at the trial with such gloating delight that the crowd
struggled to reach him. He vanished after the trial, and is said
to have died in London as an old beggar man, blinded by quick-
lime that had been thrown in his eyes by some workmates who
discovered his identity.

Quite clearly, the murders of Burke and Hare, like those of
John Williams, were 'economic' murders. If they were carried
out with a certain brutality, it was the brutality of 'criminal
rats', of men who had been rendered brutal by the slums and
the hardness of their lives. And if we look back over the murder
cases of the past three chapters, it will be seen that they are all,

to some extent, 'economic' murders, or 'business-murders' (Bichel being the only possible exception). Murders of unwanted mistresses, of unwanted husbands, murder in the course of robbery, very occasionally of rape – these have been the common motives. But it is during this nineteenth century that there is a slow but perceptible change in the style of murder. The industrial revolution has brought a higher degree of prosperity, and where it has not brought prosperity, it has brought a new class-consciousness, and eventually, a new self-consciousness. Most of the murders in the *Newgate Calendar* might have been committed by cunning animals; now a new note enters. It is the note of rebellion; and there are times when the rebellion becomes a psychotic explosion.

Paris during this period was as full of poverty and crime as Edinburgh. We catch glimpses of it in the memoirs of the detective Vidocq – the convict who turned police-spy and became the founder of the Sûreté – and also in the novels of Balzac, who made Vidocq the basis of his great criminal Vautrin. There were about two hundred murders a year, most of them committed in the course of theft. In France, a thief could be executed, or sent to the gallows, which was in many respects worse than the guillotine. It was common sense to murder their victim if there was any chance that he might identify them.

It was after Vidocq's retirement in 1827 that France's most notorious criminal appeared upon the scene – Pierre-François Lacenaire, the 'Manfred of the gutter', as Gautier called him, referring to Byron's rebel-hero. Lacenaire's actual crimes were unspectacular enough; in fact, he was a consistently unlucky criminal. Before his first known murder, he attempted to kill his mistress, a girl named Javotte (who was also a receiver of stolen goods), but a locket around her neck deflected the dagger, and after a quarter of an hour of wrestling, the neighbours came to investigate. Lacenaire told them it was merely a marital quarrel, and Javotte did not contradict him.

After some petty and not very remunerative thieving, Lacenaire decided that robbing bank messengers would be a good idea. In those days, the messenger would call at a house to collect money to save the depositor the trouble of going to the bank. Lacenaire requested a messenger to call at a certain address, giving a false name, and then he and an accomplice waited with knives. . . . The porter told the messenger that no one of that name lived there, and the messenger went away. Lacenaire tried again, borrowing a well-appointed flat. This time, the messenger forgot to call; Lacenaire stole the curtains and sold them.

At 271 Rue St Martin lived a homosexual begging-letter-writer named Chardon, whom Lacenaire had met in jail. He supported his bed-ridden mother, and was said to have money saved. Lacenaire and an accomplice named Avril called on him on 14th December 1834, and met him in the street. Chardon told them to go up to his room. As soon as they got into Chardon's apartment, Avril seized him by the throat and Lacenaire stabbed him in the back. Then Avril finished him off with a hatchet, while Lacenaire went into the bedroom and quickly killed the old woman with a shoemaker's awl. Their profit on this venture was about seven hundred francs. The bodies of the Chardons were not found for two days.

Two weeks later, Lacenaire decided to have another try at the bank messenger idea. Under the name of Mahossier, he hired an apartment at 66 Rue Montorgueil. Avril was temporarily in jail so this time he used an accomplice named François. They slammed the door behind the bank messenger, and Lacenaire stabbed him in the back with the shoemaker's awl as François grabbed him by the throat. However, François was over-excited and got his fingers into the man's mouth. As the man struggled, he panicked and ran away, slamming the door behind him. Lacenaire, hearing approaching footsteps, also ran away.

Vidocq's successor Allard put his best man, Chief Inspector Canler, in charge of both cases, although there was no reason to connect them. It is interesting to study the way in which the detective went about his task in those days before fingerprints or comparison microscopes. He did not use strict logic so much as a knowledge of the working of the criminal mind. Obviously,

Mahossier was not the man's name. But criminals sometimes became fond of an alias, and used it many times over. So Canler plodded from lodging house to lodging house, asking to look through the registers. It was tedious work, but after several days, he came across the name 'Mahossier' in the register of a cheap doss-house. Underneath it was the name 'Fizellier'. The lodging-house keeper couldn't remember Mahossier, but he was able to describe 'Fizellier'. His wife was able to supply the information that Mahossier had stayed there before under the name of Bâton. And Bâton sounded like the man who had stabbed the bank messenger – a distinctive man whose manner was courteous and polished, who had a high forehead and silky moustache. (Lacenaire's pictures make him look a little like Edgar Allen Poe, except for the curved, beak-like nose.) Canler seemed to recall a prisoner at the Préfecture who resembled the description of Fizellier. Canler went to the jail, engaged the man in conversation, then asked casually: 'By the way, what made you call yourself Fizellier when you stayed at Pageot's?' The man made no attempt to deny it. 'Because I don't believe in using my real name when I can avoid it.'

Next, Canler traced a homosexual thief named Bâton and placed him under arrest. But Bâton was totally unlike the descriptions of Mahossier. However, Canler again used his knowledge of criminal psychology. Why should Mahossier call himself Bâton? It might be chance. More likely, he knew Bâton. So Canler questioned people who knew Bâton, asking about his friends. And the description of a man named Gaillard sounded promising. Canler ordered Bâton's release, and talked amicably with him as they strolled towards the doors of the Préfecture. Bâton agreed that he knew a man called Gaillard, and gave a description of him: high forehead, silky moustache, a fastidious dresser....

But where was Gaillard to be found? With incredible patience, Canler went back to checking doss-house registers. Eventually, he found the signature 'Gaillard'. The keeper remembered him because he had left some papers behind – a packet of Republican songs and some poems. The stabbed bank messenger had noticed that 'Mahossier' had a copy of Rousseau's *Social Contract* sticking out of his pocket.

Avril – Lacenaire's accomplice in the Chardon murder – happened to be in jail. Now, with the usual lack of honour among thieves, he came forward and offered to help the police find 'Gaillard'. After a week of wandering around low cafés he had still not succeeded, so he was put back in jail; but he added another useful piece of information; Gaillard had a rich aunt who lived in the Rue Bar-du-Bec. The indefatigable Canler went off to see her. She admitted that she had a disreputable nephew, and said that she had had a grille installed in her door because she was afraid that he might decide to murder her one day. She added the information that his name was not Gaillard, but Lacenaire. . . .

Now, at last, the police knew the name of the man they wanted. A general alert went out. And on 2nd February the police at Beaune notified the Sûreté that they had arrested a man matching the description; he had been trying to negotiate a forged bill of exchange.

Lacenaire arrived back at the Préfecture in irons, and he greeted Canler politely. When accused of the attempted robbery of the bank messenger, he agreed; obviously, the messenger would identify him anyway. He refused to name his accomplice, but the police told him it was François – alias Fizellier. Then they told him that François had volunteered the information that Lacenaire had been the killer of Chardon. He refused to believe them. When they added that his accomplice in the Chardon killing – Avril – had tried to get him arrested, Lacenaire was thoroughly disturbed. He soon discovered that the police were not lying – that each of his accomplices had volunteered to betray him; and he decided that he would drag them down with him. He gave a full confession, implicating them both.

In prison before his execution, Lacenaire wrote the famous *Memoirs* (which Dostoievsky later published to increase the circulation of one of his magazines). He was a considerable celebrity, and many people came to see him. One man offered him an expensive coat; Lacenaire refused it on the grounds that

119

he would not have time to wear it out. The execution was carried out quietly and unannounced, on a cold and foggy morning in January 1836, just over a year after the murder of the Chardons. Lacenaire remained calm and polite and watched Avril's execution without flinching. The two men had made it up at the end. The night before the execution, Lacenaire called to his old accomplice: 'The earth will be pretty cold tomorrow.' 'Ask to be buried in a fur coat,' shouted Avril.

When Lacenaire's head was on the block, there was an accident that would have broken another man's nerve. The blade of the guillotine dropped, then stuck halfway. As it was hauled up again, Lacenaire twisted his head to look up at the triangular blade. A moment later, it fell again. Lacenaire was thirty-six years old when he died.

The *Memoirs* is an interesting book, but not because it contains any detailed descriptions of crimes. He is more concerned to explain how he became a criminal – how his parents greatly preferred his elder brother, and he reacted in the classic way by stealing, to gain attention. The story reeks of self-pity, although Lacenaire's lucid Gallic style keeps this under control. It becomes clear that Lacenaire was driven by self-pity into a suicidal state, that finally became an obsession. Rather than commit suicide, he decided to 'have the blood of society'. He experienced the same trouble as Vidocq; that once a man had served a prison sentence, he was unable to escape crime. Too many criminals knew him; he knew too many criminals. (There were reckoned to be eight thousand criminals in Paris alone.)[1] He could always reckon on being accosted by someone he had known in prison.

Before he made the mistake of trusting Avril and François, Lacenaire had always worked alone, and he prided himself on it. His *Memoirs* tell how, in Lyons, he met a man with a gold watch-chain staggering home late at night. Lacenaire throttled

[1] The population of Paris in 1836 was about 800,000, so that one person in every hundred was a criminal. Modern crime figures are not far behind this; in London in 1967 there were three crimes a year for every hundred people; in Newcastle, five to every hundred. Even assuming that each criminal may commit a dozen reported crimes a year, this is still a high figure.

him, robbed him, then threw the unconscious man into the Rhône. When the body was found, it was assumed that he had fallen in when drunk. On another occasion, Lacenaire lost heavily at the gaming tables, and followed a more fortunate player home. As he was about to stab the man in the back, a police patrol approached and he took to his heels. In his own eyes, Lacenaire was a single man against 'Society'.

Lacenaire was a highly intelligent man, driven by self-pity. His intellectual perception of the social injustice around him did not lead him to plan to overthrow the social order; it led to an ironic and embittered defeatism. He was a true romantic; looking at the world in which he found himself, he decided that his situation was tragic, and that this was inevitably so. So there was an odd fatalism about his crimes. In his own eyes, they were always justified. When an acquaintance in Italy opened one of his letters by mistake and notified the authorities, Lacenaire took him out for dinner, drove to a secluded spot, and then offered the man one of two pistols – one loaded, the other empty. When the man refused to play this odd game of Russian roulette, Lacenaire shot him through the head. But he would have been equally willing to have died himself. On another occasion, he asked the driver of a cab to deliver a letter at a house they were passing; when the man was inside, he drove away the cab and sold it. But he made no attempt to hide, and was sitting outside his usual café when the driver approached with the buyer of the cab. Lacenaire admitted his guilt with grave politeness – the cab-driver was unsure of his identity – and served thirteen months in prison for a theft that brought him only fifty francs.

The *Memoirs* make clear why he took the idea of execution so calmly. To begin with, he had convinced himself at sixteen that he would die on the guillotine, and this idea of being dedicated to the 'triangular blade' gave his life a quality of obsession. He sometimes referred to the guillotine as his 'mistress'. (He was too fastidious to gain any great pleasure from ordinary sexual activity.) If he had been a better poet, he might have written *Les Fleurs du Mal* a quarter of a century before Baudelaire. Once he had decided that he was living in a world that could never understand him, he decided that his life would be 'a prolonged suicide'. 'I belonged no longer to myself but to cold steel.' He was the true predecessor of Raskolnikov in *Crime and Punishment*.[1] He wanted to 'cancel his relations with society'.

And this is the distinctive element in so much crime of the nineteenth century. Men like Burke and Hare had not cancelled their relations with society; they were only attempting to live in it, to keep their heads above water. They had nothing against society or the human race as such. If they had accidentally stumbled on a fortune, they would have given up their trade of murder with pleasure. Dick Turpin did not want to revenge himself on society; only to live like a gentleman. As soon as a murderer begins to enjoy killing for its own sake, he has taken up a conscious attitude of alienation from society, like a disguised wolf in a flock of sheep. Even Thomas Griffiths Wainewright eventually crossed the border-line between murder-for-business and murder-for-pleasure. He started with forgery, then poisoned his grandfather for the sake of the inheritance. The motive here was to keep up his social position – he was a friend of Lamb and Hazlitt, and William Blake admired one of his paintings – and to live 'in a manner befitting an artist' – a motive with which Wilde sympathised deeply. Then he poisoned his mother-in-law – whom he was supporting – and his sister-in-law the one with the thick ankles) after insuring her life. The insurance company refused to pay up, and Wainewright vanished to Boulogne, where he dropped strychnine in the drink of the father of a girl he wanted to seduce. It is true that he had insured him for three thousand pounds, but the money would go to his next of kin, not to his poisoner. Wilde suggests that Wainewright was out for revenge on the insurance companies. It seems more likely that he had become an habitual poisoner. Wainewright was eventually tried for forgery, not murder, and sentenced to transportation.

The earliest example of 'joy-murder' I have come across is

[1] As John Philip Stead has pointed out in his introduction to the English translation of Lacenaire's *Memoirs* (1952).

the case of Gesina Gottfried, who was executed in Bremen in 1828. Details of the case are unfortunately sparse. Gesina was born in a small town in North Germany. She seems to have had the temperament of Flaubert's Emma Bovary – desire for excitement, wealth, travel. She was attractive and had several suitors. From these, she chose a businessman named Miltenberg. By the age of twenty she had two children. But her husband was a drunkard, and his business was on the verge of bankruptcy. And, like many working-class husbands of the period, he beat his wife. One day, Gesina saw her mother using a white powder to mix bait for mice and rats. She took some of it, and dropped it into a glass of her husband's beer. He was dead by the next morning. She now pursued a young friend of her husband's called Gottfried, who had displayed signs of being interested in her before Miltenberg's death. But Gottfried was shy and cautious; her patience soon wore out, and she began to slip small quantities of the white powder – arsenic – into his drink. As he became more ill, he became more reliant on her, and her chances of administering minute doses of poison increased. When her parents got wind of the intimacy with Gottfried, they opposed it. Gesina did not hesitate for a moment; she got herself invited to supper, and dropped arsenic in their beer. Then, carried away with her new-found power, she went on to poison her own two children. Gottfried – now permanently weakened – was persuaded to marry her; a day later, he was dead. His wife succeeded to his property, which had been her central motive all along.

A merchant she met at Gottfried's funeral began to court her. She didn't like him, but he had more money than her former lover. She poisoned him with the same patient deliberation that she had already shown in the case of Gottfried. When her brother turned up one day – on leave from the army and drunk – she disposed of him quickly with a glass of poisoned beer; she was not prepared to risk having him around while she poisoned her current lover. The latter was persuaded to make a will in her favour; then he died. It is not known exactly how many more she poisoned; Charles Kingston[1] mentions another

[1] In *Remarkable Rogues*, 1921.

lover, a woman to whom she owed five pounds, and an old female acquaintance who tried to borrow money. She moved from place to place during the course of these murders, and ended in Bremen, where she poisoned the wife of her employer, a master wheelwright named Rumf. The wife died shortly after giving birth to a baby, so Gesina was not suspected; it was assumed to be puerperal fever. Rumf's five children died one by one after Gesina took charge of the family. Rumf himself began to feel rather ill after Gesina's meals. One day, when she was away, he tried a meal of pork, and was delighted that it seemed to agree with him. He was so pleased with his pork that he went to look at the joint in the larder when he came home from work the next day. Gesina had sprinkled it with white powder in the meantime, and Rumf knew it had not been there that morning. So he took the leg along to the police, who quickly identified the powder as arsenic. When arrested, Gesina made no attempt to deny her guilt; on the contrary, she confessed to her various crimes with relish. Her execution followed as a matter of course.

This account of Gesina Gottfried's career sounds so fantastic that one is inclined to believe that it must be exaggerated. But a glance at Major Griffiths' chapter on female poisoners reveals that Gesina is by no means an uncommon type. Hélène Jegado, who was tried at Rennes, in Brittany, in 1851, was an habitual poisoner as some people are habitual rapists. She simply could not resist introducing poisons into food, and since she was a cook, her opportunities were unlimited. Seven people died in one house where she was a servant, including her sister. She moved on, but she was never in a house for long before somebody died. 'Wherever I go, people die,' she commented mournfully. She was a kleptomaniac, and whenever thefts were brought home to her, someone in the house died with stomach pains, or was seriously ill. When she retired to a convent for a while, the nuns began to be sick after meals. She had been poisoning for more than twenty years – and was over fifty years of age – when she poisoned a fellow-servant in the house of a M Bidard, at Rennes, and was arrested. Her past was investigated as thoroughly as her extensive travels would allow;

during the period 1833 to 1841, she was discovered to have poisoned twenty-three people, an average of three a year. Other periods were impossible to check on, but if the average was maintained, her total number of victims exceeded sixty. A Dutch nurse named van der Linden passed the hundred mark. It could be said of all these women, as it was said of another German poisoner, Anna Maria Zwanziger, that they regarded arsenic as 'their truest friend'. Griffiths quotes the jurist Feuerbach on Mrs Zwanziger as saying that 'she trembled with pleasure and gazed upon the white powder with eyes beaming with rapture'. All this makes it sound as if poisoning can become a sexual obsession with women, as more violent types of *lustmörd* can become with male sex-maniacs. There are no cases of male poisoners who became addicted to the practice for its own sake. Dr William Palmer, the Rugely poisoner who was executed at the age of thirty-two (in 1856), poisoned at least fifteen people in the course of his brief career; but in every case, there was clearly a motive. (The only exception was the death of a poor shoemaker named Abley – apparently Palmer's first murder. But in his book on Palmer,[1] Robert Graves has pointed out that Palmer was believed to be having an affair with Abley's wife. This is not improbable; next to horse-racing, the fathering of bastards was the doctor's chief delight; he was responsible for fourteen of them in the five years before his marriage.) The story of Palmer's murders is a sordid tale of a man plunging into debt, and killing to try to get out of it. The same is true of most of the other noted poisoners of the nineteenth century – which is the reason that I do not propose to devote a great deal of space to them. It might be mentioned in passing that Palmer holds the record for medical poisoners. It is true that Dr Marcel Petiot, who was executed in 1946, killed sixty-three people by poison, but he injected it with a hypodermic syringe. His victims were mostly Jews who wanted to escape from occupied France, and who believed they were being inoculated against smallpox.

It is worth studying two exceptions to the rule about the male poisoner; for the crimes of Neill Cream and George Chapman

[1] *They Hanged My Saintly Billy*, 1957.

were so motiveless that they must be classified with the poison-
ings of Gesina Gottfried and Hélène Jegado. These cases took
place towards the end of the century, when the sadistic murder
was already becoming common.

Dr Thomas Neill Cream is one of the oddest figures of the
nineteenth century, a kind of criminal Leopold Bloom; like
Joyce's hero, he was an introvert with feelings of sexual
inadequacy, given to writing strange letters to women, and
sometimes to men. He was also cross-eyed, bald-headed, and
covered with black hair like a troll. He undoubtedly suffered
from a mild but permanent form of insanity. Cream confined
his activities to Lambeth, the slum area south of the Thames,
much as the Ripper had confined himself to Whitechapel. Like
the Ripper, his victims were all prostitutes.

On the morning of 13th October 1891, a nineteen-year-old
prostitute named Ellen Donworth, who lived with her pimp at
8, Duke Street, Lambeth, received a strange letter in the post:

Miss ELLEN LINNELL [the surname of her pimp],
I wrote and warned you once before that Frederick Smith, of
W H Smith and Son, was going to poison you, and I am
writing now to say that if you take any of the medicine he gave
you, you will die. I saw Frederick Smith prepare the medicine
he gave you, and I saw him put enough strychnine in it to kill
a horse. If you take any of it, you will die.

HMB

A second letter arrived by the same post, asking her to meet
the writer at the York Hotel, and to bring the two letters with
her; presumably this was 'HMB'. The girl mentioned the
letters to an Inspector Harvey. That evening, she set out to
meet the writer, taking the letters; she mentioned to a friend
that she was going to meet a tall,[1] cross-eyed man. An hour
later, she fell writhing on to the pavement of the Waterloo
Road. She was helped home, and told her landlady that the tall,
cross-eyed man – who also had bushy whiskers and a silk hat –

[1] He was 5 ft. 9 in.

126

gave her two drinks of 'white stuff' out of a bottle. She died on her way to hospital. Analysis of the contents of her stomach revealed that she had died of strychnine poisoning.

A few days before the death of Ellen Donworth, a young prostitute named Elizabeth Masters had received a letter from a client she had met a few days before – a cross-eyed man – saying that he would call on her that afternoon. The girl and a friend waited by the window, until they saw the cross-eyed man in the street. But he was following another prostitute – a girl named Matilda Clover, who was turning round and smiling at him. The two women went out and watched Cream speak to Matilda Clover, and go into her house, where she lived with her two-year-old child. Obviously, the man liked variety. Ten days later, and only a week after the death of Ellen Donworth, Matilda Clover received a letter making an appointment, and also asking her to return the letter. It was signed 'Fred'. She met Fred that evening, and at three in the morning woke up another girl in the house with her screams. She died a few hours later, and a doctor's assistant diagnosed the cause of death as delirium tremens.

Cream was now living at 103 Lambeth Palace Road. He was so curious about the results of his pills that he asked his land-lady's daughter to go to a house in Lambeth Road and enquire whether a certain young lady who had been poisoned was dead yet! The girl refused. Cream (who was known as 'Dr Neill') told her that he knew the name of the poisoner; it was Lord Russell, who was at present involved in a matrimonial case. A few days after the murder, the Countess Russell received a letter telling her that her husband had poisoned Matilda Clover. Frederick Smith, of W H Smith and Son, also received a letter that accused him of poisoning Ellen Donworth. The writer, who signed himself H Bayne, asked that his services as 'counsellor and legal adviser' be retained, and enclosed a copy of the letter that Ellen Donworth had received on the morning of her death. 'H Bayne' said that if Smith agreed, a note should be exhibited in W H Smith's shop window in the Strand. The police advised that the note should be exhibited, but 'H Bayne' did not appear.

The Lambeth Coroner received a letter signed 'A O'Brien, detective', offering to find the murderer of Ellen Donworth for £300,000. Finally, Sir William Broadbent, a well-known doctor, received a letter signed 'M Malone' that asserted that he was the poisoner of Matilda Clover. 'The evidence is in the hands of one of our detectives, who will give the evidence either to you or to the police authorities for the sum of £2,500.' It pointed out that an accusation of this sort could ruin him for ever.

The pattern is fairly clear. Cream meets a prostitute, takes her out and buys her presents (he bought Matilda Clover some boots), then makes an appointment by letter, asking her to return the letter. He gives her medicine or capsules (he obtained empty capsules after the poisoning of Ellen Donworth, and filled them with *nux vomica*, which contains brucine and strychnine). Then he becomes immensely curious about the result of the poison, and also experiences a desire to make as much of a stir as possible. He wants to disturb people. He is obviously a man who feels totally insignificant, and who wants to prove to himself that he really does exist. Although the motive of the letters would appear to be to obtain money, he fails to show up for either of the appointments he makes.

After these murders, Cream went to Canada for a few months, having first got himself engaged to a girl named Laura Sabbatini in Berkhamsted. He returned to England on 2nd April 1892. And on 11th April two more prostitutes, Alice Marsh and Emma Shrivell, died of strychnine poisoning. And Cream, with the curious dislike of the medical profession he had already shown, told his landlady's daughter that another lodger, a Dr Harper, was the murderer of the two girls. Dr Harper himself later received a letter accusing him of the deaths of Alice Marsh, Emma Shrivell and Ellen Donworth, and demanding £1,500 to suppress the evidence. Cream also told a young photographer named Haynes that he had definite proof not only that Harper had killed the three named above, but also Matilda Clover and another prostitute named Lou Harvey. (It later transpired that Cream had spent the night with this girl, and later persuaded her to take capsules; she pretended to swallow them, but kept them in her hand. Later, she threw them away.) Cream insisted that Haynes call at the house of Matilda Clover, to verify that she had died of poison. Finally, Haynes went to Scotland Yard to lay information against Dr Harper – but without mentioning Cream's name (Cream had made him give a promise to this effect).

Cream's letter to Dr Harper – demanding £1,500 – was passed on to the police. Ellen Donworth and Matilda Clover were exhumed, and found to have died of strychnine poisoning.

Meanwhile, Cream was recognised by the young constable who had seen him leaving the house of Emma Shrivell and Alice Marsh. Constable Comley followed Cream back to his address, and thereafter kept a watch on him. Cream noticed he was being watched, and indignantly approached Scotland Yard, asking one Inspector McIntyre (who was the man Haynes had already seen about the murderous misdeeds of Dr Harper) to investigate the matter and save him from further nuisance.

Obviously, it did not take McIntyre and Constable Comley long to get together and exchange information. On 3rd June, Cream was arrested in his rooms. The result of the trial was a foregone conclusion: he himself had supplied most of the evidence. He was sentenced to death, and hanged on 15th November 1892.

Quite obviously, the verdict should have been 'guilty but insane'. It is difficult to find a single action connected with the murders that could be described as remotely normal. Cream was living in some kind of strange dream world; nothing was real. When Leopold Bloom writes letters to upper-class housewives containing lewd suggestions and the request that they should 'soil his letter unspeakably', the act may be abnormal, but its motivations are clear enough. But how can one explain what motivated Cream to have the following circular printed in Canada and shipped back to England?

'Ellen Donworth's death. To the guests of the Metropole Hotel. I hereby certify you that the person who poisoned Ellen Donworth on the 13th day of last October is today in the employ of the Metropole Hotel, and your lives are in danger as long as you remain in this hotel.

W H MURRAY'

To Laura Sabbatini he wrote shortly after his arrest:

'Was at Bow Street yesterday, and heard *such good news* that I have not been able to sleep since. A member of Parliament sent me word that he had over two hundred witnesses to clear me if I wanted them.'

Cream was obsessed by sex, in a perfectly ordinary sense. He told one prostitute that he lived only to indulge in women. In reading the account of the case, one is reminded of the anonymous author of that immense Victorian compendium of erotic experience *My Secret Life*, who apparently never had a thought that was not connected with sex. The evidence of various women makes it clear that Cream aimed to sleep with a prostitute more or less every day of his life. It is more than likely that his softening of the brain was due to syphilis. After he saw – or thought he saw – the prostitute Lou Harvey take two capsules full of strychnine, he was convinced she was dead. Some time later, he saw her in Piccadilly Circus and she spoke to him. They went into the Regent Hotel for a drink, and it was only then that she asked if he did not recognise her. He said no. She then identified herself, and Cream leapt to his feet and hurried out. Yet it was after this that he included her in the list of Dr Harper's 'victims'.

The poisoning of Ellen Donworth was not Cream's first murder. In 1878 – when Cream was twenty-eight – a chambermaid named Kate Gardener died of chloroform poisoning behind Cream's house, in circumstances that pointed to murder rather than suicide. (Cream had written a paper on chloroform during his days as a medical student.) In 1880, a girl named Julia Faulkner died in Chicago as a result of an illegal operation performed by Cream. The death may have been due to an accident of the kind that is likely to occur in the course of an abortion; but, knowing Cream's strange obsession, the abortifacient may have been strychnine. In 1881, a Miss Stack died of medicine prescribed by Cream, and he wrote a blackmailing letter to a chemist, accusing him of her death. Later in the same year, he poisoned the epileptic husband of his mistress, Julia Stott. No suspicion was directed at Cream – the death was attributed to natural causes – until he contacted the coroner and accused a chemist of poisoning Stott. Cream even insisted on an exhumation. As a result, he was tried for murder, and spent ten years in jail. (He was in jail from 1881 to 1891, which disposes of a theory that he was Jack the Ripper. Cream's last words on the gallows were, 'I am Jack the. . . .') During that time, his father died, leaving Cream $16,000. And on leaving jail, he hastened to the city that obsessed him, London.[1] And within a few days, Ellen Donworth died.

It has also been suggested that George Chapman was Jack the Ripper, and this is at least a possibility, since Chapman was actually living in Whitechapel at the time of the Ripper murders in 1888. The chief argument against it is that a man who has been killing prostitutes with a knife is not likely to change his method to poisoning with arsenic. Chapman – whose real name was Severin Klossovski, and who was born in Poland – came under suspicion in 1902 when a glass of brandy he had prepared for his sick wife was drunk by his mother and the nurse. Both became violently ill. Mrs Marsh – mother of his wife, Maud – thereupon called in a doctor, who decided that Maud was being poisoned with arsenic. Chapman – who was thirty-six at the time – finished Maud off with a large dose; but his doctor refused to sign the death certificate, and discovered arsenic in Maud Chapman's stomach. When the police reviewed Chapman's career, they became fairly certain that he had killed two earlier wives in the same way. Chapman's trouble – like Cream's – was women. But unlike Cream, Chapman married

[1] Cream was obviously fascinated by London, where he studied medicine at the age of twenty-six at St Thomas' Hospital, Lambeth; it was then that he discovered the delights of the Waterloo Road and its prostitutes. Oddly enough, his first wife – who died suddenly in 1877 – lived in a town called Waterloo, Canada. On returning to Canada with his medical degree, Cream chose to practise in a town called London, Ontario.

them. After a bigamous second marriage to a Polish lady in London, his first wife turned up, and the three of them lived together for a while. Finally, both women left him. After a trip to America, he lived with a woman named Annie Chapman – whose surname he later adopted – and then met Mary Spinks, an alcoholic, who became his first known victim. She died after living with Chapman for two years. By this time, Chapman had become a tavern keeper (with his wife's money). A year later, he married his barmaid, Bessie Taylor, and in due course, Bessie Taylor died in agony. Maud Marsh was also Chapman's barmaid before she became his wife, and died of arsenic poisoning.

Why Chapman poisoned his wives will never be known. Obviously, the motive was not sexual, as in Cream's case. What seems most likely is that Chapman was simply insane – perhaps suffering from a brain tumour, or some venereal disease that caused outbursts of violent rage. He treated his women very badly; he beat Bessie Taylor even when she was weak after a spell in hospital. (This was after he had started to poison her.) Chapman was suspected of being Jack the Ripper at the actual time of the murders; he had a barber shop in the basement of George Yard Buildings, where the Ripper's first victim died. Chief Inspector Abberline remarked in 1902, when he heard of Chapman's arrest: 'You've caught the Ripper then?' But I doubt whether he really believed it himself. By 1902, the police were fairly certain the Ripper had been dead for more than a decade.

In the seventeenth century, poison was known as 'succession powder'. The Marquise de Brinvilliers, a nymphomaniac who was beheaded in 1676, poisoned her father and her two brothers simply to gain possession of the family wealth. Two centuries later, a young barrister named Charles Bravo died of antimony poisoning at the Priory, Balham. His beautiful but alcoholic wife Florence was suspected of administering tartar emetic, but never accused, and the case has been the subject of endless discussion ever since. John Williams is of the opinion that Florence Bravo did it.[1] Yseult Bridges believes that Bravo

[1] *Suddenly at the Priory*, 1957.

himself accidentally took the poison with which he had been slowly poisoning his wife.[1] Agatha Christie has suggested that Florence Bravo's former lover, Dr Gully, did it.[2] Many writers on the case suspect Mrs Cox, Florence Bravo's companion.[3]

The point to observe here is that the case is as baffling today as it was in 1876. Murder has lost its old simplicity. It is no longer a simple question of inheritances or the removal of a husband by a lover. Motives are more complex, and in some cases unfathomable. A sociologist of the seventeenth century – if such things had existed – might have predicted that when social poverty and misery disappear, the crime of murder would disappear too. Nothing of the sort has happened. As civilisation gradually eradicates the poverty that made the crimes of Burke and Hare possible, the murder rate rises. It begins to look as if man will never outgrow the practice of murder. If he lacks a motive, he will murder without one.

The real significance of Lacenaire was that he was the first great 'loner' in the history of nineteenth-century crime. Perhaps this is why Major Griffiths applies to him the description 'one of the most cold-blooded destroyers of life the world has ever known'.

Half a century after the death of Lacenaire occurs the case that has become the symbol of the 'man on his own', the criminal loner: the unknown who killed five women in Whitechapel in 1888. The facts are too well known to require a lengthy summary. Five women died between 31st August and 8th November; all were killed by a sadistic maniac with a knife, who (except in one case, where he was interrupted) opened the bodies and took out some of the inner organs. Two unsolved murders of women earlier the same year may also have been the work of the Ripper, although in these cases the women were stabbed, not mutilated. The first victim, a prostitute named Mary Anne Nicholls, picked up her murderer sometime after 2.30 am on Friday, 31st August. In a street known as

[1] *How Charles Bravo Died*, 1956.
[2] *Sunday Times Magazine*, 20th October, 1968, *Poison at the Priory*.
[3] Elizabeth Jenkins, *Six Criminal Women*, 1949.

133

Bucks Row he clamped a hand over her mouth and drove a knife into her throat, severing the windpipe, then, when the woman lay on the ground, cut the throat with one powerful sweep. He turned his attention to her abdomen and made several slashing stabs in a normal downward direction on the right side of her stomach. (This, of course, indicates that the killer was left-handed; the throat wound, running from left to right, confirms this.) The killer was apparently not interested in her genitals. In most rape cases, the victim is left with her legs spread apart; Mary Nicholls' killer placed hers tightly together, and pulled down her skirt. He then cleaned his hands and knife on her clothes, and walked away. She was found twenty minutes or so later, at 3.45, by a carter on his way to work.

Annie Chapman was forty-seven years old – five years older than Mary Anne Nicholls – and looked sixty. She was dying of consumption and malnutrition, and the skin under her eyes was permanently blue. She was turned out of a cheap lodging house at two in the morning, when the keeper discovered she lacked the few pence necessary to pay for a bed. It is not known how long she wandered around looking for a pick-up, but probably she walked around for three hours or so before meeting Jack the Ripper. She met him in Hanbury Street, not far from the place where Mary Nicholls was murdered. They made their way down a passageway between two houses, into the backyard of No. 29 – a yard into which prostitutes often took their customers. There, against the fence, the man pressed his hand violently over her mouth, and drove the knife into her throat. It is unlikely that she struggled; she was undernourished, and weak from hours of walking the streets. It had been only a week since the man had killed Mary Nicholls, but sadistic frenzy was more powerful than ever. He was reasonably certain he would not be disturbed this time, so he took his time.

At some point, the murderer seems to have decided to remove the head completely, and proceeded to saw away at the neck; but when it was almost removed, he changed his mind, and tied a handkerchief round her neck to hold it together. The obsessive tidiness that he had manifested in the 'laying out' of Mary

134

Nicholls now appeared again; he removed two brass rings from her fingers and placed them neatly at her feet, together with a few coins. But for some reason he decided to leave this body in the normal rape position, with the knees bent and the legs wide open. And he left her dress pulled up over her breasts. Twenty minutes later, he went quietly down the passage again. While he had been killing Annie Chapman, a man had come into the yard next door to go to the lavatory, and had actually heard her say, 'No, no,' and the sound of a struggle. The neighbour was incurious, and the murderer was too obsessed by his strange need to care about interruption. He was like a male dog copulating with a bitch on heat; he had to finish before he became interested in anything else.

Certain things about the Ripper can be inferred from what has already been said. The neat laying out of Mary Nicholls' corpse, the trinkets placed round the feet of Annie Chapman, the handkerchief tied round the throat to hold the head on – all these bring to mind Neill Cream's weirdly irrational activities already discussed. This man was probably a full-blown psychotic, the kind who believes that voices speak to him from the air. Secondly, he was a sex-pervert of many years' experience. He had worked up morbid fantasies that included disembowelling women. In cases of violent sex crime, it is not uncommon for the genitals themselves to be attacked with a knife, and Paul de River (in *The Sexual Criminal*) cites a case in which the victim's intestines were torn out through her vagina. The Ripper was not interested in the genitals; his fantasies were all about cutting bellies. It was the womb itself that fascinated him. Freudians will draw a great many inferences from this – about hatred of the mother, perhaps of younger brothers and sisters stealing the parents' affection, etc. I would draw only one inference: that this destruction of the womb indicated a suicidal tendency in the Ripper; it was the place that bore him about which he felt ambivalent.

What did the Ripper wish to do with the organs he took away? In a letter written to a member of the Vigilance Committee a man who claimed to be the murderer said that he had fried and eaten half a kidney removed from a later victim, and he enclosed the other half. This letter is generally agreed to be genuine, since the half enclosed *was* a human kidney, and was 'ginny' – affected by the large quantities of gin its former owner had drunk. The victim (Catherine Eddowes) had been a heavy gin drinker. At that time, it was common for the poorer classes to buy the intestines of animals – the part normally thrown away – and to eat them fried into a crisp state.

This desire to eat the body of a victim is rare, even among sex murderers. One of the few examples I can call to mind is Albert Fish, executed in 1935 for the murder of ten-year-old Grace Budd in New York; he cooked and ate parts of the body with carrots and onions. But by this time, Fish was a pervert of long experience, who began with a taste for being spanked, and graduated to such curious activities as driving needles into his scrotum, and inserting cotton wool soaked with methylated spirit into his anus, then lighting it. He preyed on boys as well as girls, and sometimes castrated them. He was fifty-eight years old when he murdered Grace Budd, so the eating of parts of her body might be regarded as the culmination of a lifetime of sexual perversion. On the other hand, the parallel does not necessarily indicate that the Ripper was middle-aged or old. The Birmingham YWCA murderer, Patrick Byrne, who decapitated the girl he assaulted just before Christmas 1959, and cut off one of her breasts and tried to eat it with sugar, was only twenty-eight. But he later admitted that he had been fantasising for years about torturing girls, and particularly about cutting one to pieces with a circular saw. Melvin Reinhardt has pointed out, in *Sex Perversions and Sex Crimes,* that most sadistic sexual murders are preceded by years of this kind of violent fantasising.

The Ripper's next attempt at murder was a failure as far as the satisfaction of his tensions was concerned. A man driving into the back yard of a working men's club in Berners Street at about 1 am saw a woman's body lying against the wall, and rushed into the club. The Ripper was either in the yard at that moment, or had only just left it as he heard the approach of the horse and cart. The victim's name was Elizabeth Stride, a Swede who was also known as Long Liz. She was an alcoholic and a pathological liar – one of her favourite stories being of how she had been on the Thames steamer *Princess Alice* that sank with seven hundred passengers in 1878, and that her husband and two children had been drowned. She added that she had escaped by climbing the mast, and that a man above her had kicked her in the mouth and knocked out her bottom row of teeth. (Like most of the Ripper's victims, she had many teeth missing; women of her class never visited a dentist.) But she never had any children; nor was she on the *Princess Alice*. The Ripper had only just managed to sever her windpipe when the appearance of the horse and cart interrupted him.

He hastened along Commercial Road – this murder had been farther afield than the others – and in the area of Houndsditch, was in time to meet a prostitute who had only just been released from Bishopsgate police station, where she had spent a few hours for being drunk and disorderly. He had no difficulty persuading her to accompany him to Mitre Square, a small square surrounded by warehouses, only a few hundred yards away. A police constable patrolled the square every fifteen minutes, and at 1.30 he saw nothing unusual. Possibly the Ripper pressed Catherine Eddowes into a doorway in Church Passage, which connects Mitre Square with Duke Street. He then worked as quickly and silently as ever; the hand over the mouth, and the knife thrust upwards – perhaps with the thumb on the blade – into the windpipe. And now, bending over her in the corner of the square, the killer went almost insane with the delight of having another victim under his knife. At some point, he allowed himself a few delicate cuts at the face, slashing upwards across the right cheek, removing the lobe of the right ear, underlining both the eyes, and cutting through the upper lip.[1] All this took him about a quarter of an hour. He now strolled off through the passage to the north of the square, pausing to wash his hands in a sink (which was still there when I looked at the scene of the murder in 1961). The policeman discovered the

[1] Dr Francis Camps discovered sketches made by the doctor who was called to the scene of the crime; they were in the basement of the London Hospital. His article 'More About Jack the Ripper' was published in the London Hospital Journal and later in *The Criminologist*, February 1968.

body a few seconds after the Ripper left it, and sounded the alarm at 1.45 am. A watchman who had been only a few yards away, in the warehouse of Kearley and Tonge, was dispatched to find more policemen. The Ripper, strolling along Creechurch Lane and across Houndsditch, heard the police whistles, and no doubt smiled with satisfaction. He stopped in Goulston Street to wipe the blade of his knife on a piece of his victim's apron – which he had cut off – and then chalked on a wall: 'The Jewes are not the men to be blamed for nothing.' Then, chuckling to himself, he went on. The East End of London was full of Jews, and whenever there was a case of violent murder, someone was bound to bring up the 'blood accusation', the notion that part of the Jewish religious ceremonies was the ritual slaughter of Christians. He felt like stirring things up a little. Like Neill Cream.

It was a few days after this that Mr Lusk, Chairman of the Whitechapel Vigilance Committee (which aimed at patrolling the streets) received the half-kidney, with the inch of renal artery still attached, which the Ripper had removed from his last victim. The kidney was in an advanced stage of Bright's disease – a kidney disease – which seems to rule out all possibility that it was a hoax; Catherine Eddowes was suffering from Bright's disease. It was accompanied by a letter, which is reproduced on p 146. (It was an earlier letter to the Central News Agency, signed 'Jack the Ripper', that gave the killer his nickname.)

What is generally agreed to be the last of the Ripper murders took place six weeks later, on 9th November. Possibly the intensive activity of police and vigilantes made the streets too dangerous for the killer.

With his usual sense of dramatic timing – which Neill Cream would have envied – the Ripper chose the evening of the Lord Mayor's Show, which would pass through Houndsditch. Outside a narrow passageway called Miller's Court, off Dorset Street, he picked up a twenty-five-year-old Irish prostitute named Mary Jeanette Kelly; she was a stoutish, heavily-built young woman, with long black hair, a great deal better looking than any of the previous victims. But like the others, she was a heavy drinker of gin; and like them, she was a down-and-out.

She was several weeks behind with her rent, and a few hours before her death, tried to borrow half-a-crown from an equally broke acquaintance.

She took a customer back to her room about midnight, but perhaps he had no money; at all events, she was out again a couple of hours later, and spoke briefly to an ex-night watchman named Hutchinson. After she left him, he saw her picked up by a swarthy-looking man in Commercial Street. He thought the man looked too well-dressed to be hanging around the East End at such an hour, but had no suspicion that it was the Ripper. He had a gold watch chain and a heavy moustache that curled up at the ends. Hutchinson followed the couple, and saw them go into Miller's Court. Mary Kelly lived in a small room that used to be the back parlour of 10 Dorset Street. This was shortly after 2 am. Two witnesses later testified to hearing a cry of 'Murder' at sometime between 3 and 4 am. Perhaps the Ripper had intercourse with Mary Kelly, and then let her fall asleep. She was a powerful young woman, and her cries would have brought police within minutes. He killed her by clamping his right hand over her mouth, and driving his knife into the carotid artery on the right hand side of her throat – using his left hand. Blood spurted up the walls and over the killer; but he was almost certainly naked. He spent two more hours in the room. Mary Kelly was his most attractive victim so far; he could drink the cup of his strange obsession to the dregs. He could leave Mary Kelly unrecognisable as a human being.

He discovered the three-month-old foetus of a child in her womb. Was this, perhaps, an ultimate thrill? His psychosis had something to do with a horror of birth; now he had destroyed a baby as well as the mother.

He was very thorough; he even removed the nose and ears. It is not clear how the Ripper managed to see well enough to do all this. He took care not to light the candle – the muslin curtains were thin, and there were two panes missing from the window. But at some point, he lit a fire in the grate, burning all the clothes he could find, and it flared up so strongly that it melted the handle of a kettle that stood nearby.

At about six o'clock, Jack the Ripper left 13 Miller's Court.

And walked out of history. There were no more murders. It is true that parts of the body of a prostitute named Elizabeth Jackson were found in the Thames in June 1889, that a woman called Alice Mackenzie was found with her throat cut and gashes on her abdomen in July 1889, and that a woman named Frances Coles was found dying of injuries to her throat and stomach in 1891. The Ripper did not confine himself to cuts on the abdomen; his pleasure came from plunging his hands into the victim and pulling out the intestines. He probably performed most of the mutilations by the sense of touch alone. He did not bother to dispose of the bodies; he left them where they were. And he would not have left a woman dying; his hand was as skilful as a butcher's.

When I wrote my entry on Jack the Ripper in my *Encyclopedia of Murder,* I stated that the book by Donald McCormick, *The Identity of Jack the Ripper,* was the most authoritative to date. Since that time, two others have been published, Robin Odell's *Jack the Ripper in Fact and Fiction,* and Tom Cullen's *Autumn of Terror.* Dr Camps' article with the sketches of Annie Chapman, and an article on the Ripper's handwriting by C M MacLeod, have appeared in *The Criminologist,* in February and August 1968.

I do not propose to review the various theories here at length. William Stewart was of the opinion that Jack the Ripper was a sadistic midwife – his starting point was the foetus in Mary Kelly. The Member of Parliament Leonard Matters produced a completely unsubstantiated story about a mysterious Doctor Stanley, whose son died from syphilis contracted from Mary Kelly, and who spent three months of 1888 hunting down the woman responsible for his son's ruin – killing the prostitutes he questioned, to avoid warning Mary Kelly. Donald McCormick's theory is hardly more probable. He accepts the evidence of a writer called William Le Queux, who was also a pathological liar, that the 'Russian monk' Rasputin wrote a book on great Russian criminals, naming the Ripper as a homicidal doctor named Pedachenko.[1] Donald McCormick buttresses his

[1] In the appendix of my book *Rasputin and the Fall of the Romanovs* I have shown at some length that Le Queux was incapable of telling the

theory with many quotations from unpublished diaries and manuscripts of one Dr Thomas Dutton, but he offers no more evidence for the actual existence of Dr Dutton than Matters did for Dr Stanley. In fact, Dr Dutton actually existed – Tom Cullen told me he had seen his obituary notice – but until his *Chronicles of Crime* are published it will be impossible to assess the reliability of any of his facts – for example, his assertion that Annie Chapman, Martha Turner, Mary Nicholls and Mary Kelly all attended the same clinic in Walworth up to the time of their deaths, and that Pedachenko worked in Walworth at this time.

Robin Odell is of the opinion that the Ripper was a *shochet*, a ritual Jewish slaughterman. This is possible, but it strikes me as psychologically improbable – as improbable as the notion of a gynaecologist becoming a sex maniac. The essence of sadistic sex crime is the *fantasy* beforehand, and fantasy flourishes in a vacuum. The only case of a butcher committing sadistic murder that I can call to mind is of the French murderer Eusebius Pieydagnelle, on whom Zola based *La Bête Humaine* (according to Arthur Koestler, who compiled the volume called *Sexual Anomalies and Perversions* which purports to be a summary of the work of Magnus Hirschfeld). He became a butcher because he was fascinated by blood. But, significantly, Pieydagnelle did not start murdering until his family insisted he become a lawyer. It was after this that he became depressed and experienced the compulsion to kill; otherwise, the slaughter of cattle completely satisfied his sadistic compulsions. This seems to me the chief argument against Mr Odell's theory.

On the whole, I am inclined to feel that Tom Cullen has produced the likeliest theory of the Ripper's identity so far, in his book *Autumn of Terror*. In *Mysteries of the Police and Crime* (1899), Major Arthur Griffiths mentions three men whom the police strongly suspected of being the Ripper. One was an insane Polish Jew, one an insane Russian doctor (the

truth where Rasputin was concerned. Since writing the book, I have spoken at length to Rasputin's daughter Maria, who assured me that her father never wrote any such book, because he was not remotely interested in Russian criminals.

origin of 'Pedachenko') and the third – whom they suspected most strongly – 'was also a doctor', who disappeared immediately after the Mary Kelly murder. Griffiths had his information from Sir Melville Macnaghten, chief of the CID, who became a policeman six months after the Kelly murder. Macnaghten had made notes on these three men, but they had never been published. In 1959, my friend Dan Farson was asked to compère a TV documentary on the Ripper (in which I took part). He took the sensible step of approaching the Dowager Lady Aberconway, Macnaghten's daughter, and asking her if she had the notes. She had, and they named the three suspects. The mad doctor was called Michael Ostrog, an ex-convict, the Polish Jew was called Kosminski, 'a hater of women'. And the other doctor was an M J Druitt, who disappeared soon after the Mary Kelly murder, and whose body was taken out of the Thames on 2nd January. He was the chief suspect.

What Mr Cullen did, when it came to his turn to pursue the identity of the Ripper, was track down 'M J Druitt'. He did so with remarkable thoroughness – so that his book actually contains a picture of Druitt's gravestone. Druitt was born in 1857, the son of a highly respectable and conservative Dr William Druitt; his full name was Montague John Druitt. He attended public school – Winchester – won prizes, excelled at cricket, and was a formidable debater. (All of this indicates that Druitt was certainly a member of the 'dominant five per cent' – the first requirement for a Jack the Ripper.) But after Winchester, his career took a downward curve. At Oxford, he was a failure; although popular, he took only a third class degree. He became a barrister (not a doctor), but had no clients. In 1888, the last year of his life, he took a job as a teaching assistant at a private school in Blackheath, at a school Benjamin Disraeli had attended more than half a century before. By 1888, it had degenerated into a version of Dickens' Dotheboys Hall, according to Mr Cullen. In a state of depression, he threw himself into the Thames on 3rd December 1888, and was fished out on 2nd January 1889. He had written a suicide note to another master at the school, and his pockets were filled with stones; the inquest was held at Chiswick. (For some odd reason, he travelled upriver from Blackheath to Brentford to commit suicide.) His mother never recovered from the shock, and died of brain disease and 'melancholia' in 1890.

Macnaghten definitely believed Druitt to be the Ripper, but no one knows why he was so sure. Early in 1889, a Mr Albert Backert, of the Whitechapel Vigilantes, refused to disband his committee, feeling that the Ripper would strike again. He was sworn to secrecy by the police, and told that the Ripper was dead – that he was fished out of the river two months ago (this was in March). Obviously, they were referring to Druitt. And this is the point where we need some clinching piece of information. Did he confess to being the Ripper in his suicide letter? Did his family believe he was the Ripper, and tell the police so during the month they were searching for him? (If they held such a suspicion, then his disappearance would certainly be the signal for alarm; he might be anywhere in England preparing fresh slaughter.) The only trouble with this statement is that it comes from the papers of the elusive Dr Dutton; so again, we must withhold total assent until these papers are published, or at least, definitely shown to exist.

The Druitt theory fits in with certain of the known facts about the Ripper. Druitt was a gentleman, and nearly all the descriptions of the Ripper – or of the men seen with the victims before their death – involve 'toffs'. On three occasions, he is described as wearing a brown deerstalker hat – the kind Sherlock Holmes is supposed to have worn. A woman who saw a man leaving the scene of the Berners Street murder said he looked like a young gentleman. Looking through the evidence given at various inquests, one is struck by the number of times the Ripper is described as being well-dressed.

The main trouble with the Druitt theory is that we know nothing about him that suggests that he was capable of any kind of violence. There must still be alive a few schoolboys who studied under him in 1888, in these days when octogenarians are becoming increasingly common; Mr Cullen found several octogenarians to talk to him about Jack the Ripper. There is nothing in the Druitt story that is inconsistent with increasing melancholia and self-pity. He is brilliant and popular at Win-

143

chester, and still very popular at Oxford. But his personal charm fails to increase his practice, and he lacks the necessary toughness to plod on through the years of discouragement; finally, in a burst of self-pity, he writes a suicide note and kills himself. . . . There is nothing in the story as we know it that *contradicts* this picture. And so, unless someone can unearth something more definite about him, the identity of Druitt with Jack the Ripper must remain merely a possibility.

While speaking of hints and possibilities, there is another one that I might as well mention at this point. When I wrote a series on Jack the Ripper in 1960 for the London *Evening Standard*, I received two letters that made the same assertion: that Jack the Ripper died in a mental home somewhere near Ascot (or Windsor) a few years after the murders. One letter was anonymous, and had an Ascot postmark; the lady who wrote it (I forget how I knew it was a lady) told me that she could assert with authority that Jack the Ripper died in the mental home belonging to her father, between Ascot and Windsor, and confirmed – what I had suggested in my articles – that he was the son of well-to-do parents. The second letter, from an Irish gentleman, told me that the painter Walter Sickert had taken a room in Whitechapel shortly after the murders, and that his landlady was convinced that Jack the Ripper was one of her former tenants. He was a young man who had behaved very oddly, came in at all hours, and sometimes burned clothing in his grate. Then he was taken away by his father and another man – a doctor who ran a mental home near Windsor (which is close to Ascot). I noted the coincidence, and I offer it now, for what it is worth. The lady's letter specified that Jack the Ripper died in 1892.

There is also a story that the medium Robert James Lees ran the Ripper to earth – his daughter told my first wife as much in the late 1940s. (She lived in Leicester.) According to this story, Lees dreamed of one of the murders before it happened, and later recognised the murderer on a London bus. Lees followed him, according to his own story, and discovered that he was a distinguished physician – in fact, some versions of the story assert that he was one of the royal physicians. The story ends with the Ripper's arrest by the police and confinement in a mental home, and with a pension from the Privy Purse for Lees. Cullen points out that there is no record of such a pension.

But Lees was, in fact, involved with Queen Victoria – he went to the palace as early as 1868 to try to establish contact between the Queen and her deceased husband, Prince Albert. The Queen herself was extremely interested in the murders, and even made suggestions as to how the murderer should be caught. So it is probably true that Queen Victoria asked Lees if he could discover the identity of Jack the Ripper through the spirits. Whether this was because she had some suspicion that the Ripper was connected with the palace will, presumably, never be known.

One of the letters commenting on my article was from T E A Stowell, a brain surgeon (now retired), who had his own theory of the identity of Jack the Ripper – a theory he based upon certain papers belonging to Sir William Gowers, the physician, which Mr Stowell had examined after the latter's death. Since Mr Stowell told me his theory in confidence, I am not in a position to divulge it; and in any case, I think it less likely than the Druitt theory. But Mr Stowell *did* point out to me that in 1888, a great many 'gentlemen' and members of the aristocracy would be able to display the anatomical knowledge that the Ripper undoubtedly possessed, since most of them were hunters and used to dressing game, from hare to venison. It is another argument in favour of the 'toff' theory. Finally, Mr Stowell believes that his suspect, a homosexual, died in a mental home near Ascot in 1892, of general paralysis of the insane, a disease that is due to syphilis.

The Ripper left no clues: but there is one piece of evidence that is slightly less ambiguous than all the rest: the letters. The first one was posted on 28th September; that is, between the death of Mary Nicholls, and the double murder. Compared to Neill Cream's missives, it is thoroughly illiterate:

'Dear Boss,
   I keep on hearing the police have caught me, but they won't fix me just yet. I have laughed when they look so clever and

145

talk about being on the right track. The joke about Leather Apron gave me real fits. . . .'

Leather Apron was an early suspect named Pizer, who was arrested and then released. The letter rambles on in this semijocular tone, promising to 'clip the lady's ears off' next time. It is signed 'Jack the Ripper'. On the day after the double murder – a Sunday (when no newspapers came out), the man posted another letter to the Central News Agency, regretting that he had not time to get the ears. It will be remembered that the lobe of Catherine Eddowes' right ear was cut off, so it is possible that the Ripper was trying to get the ears when he was interrupted by the footsteps of the policeman. On the other hand, these early letters signed 'Jack the Ripper' may well have been hoaxes. Although no details had been published, the whole of the East End knew about the double murder within a few hours.

C M MacLeod's analysis of two of the Ripper letters strikes

me as one of the most constructive pieces of evidence that I have seen. He feels that the letter accompanying the half of a kidney is almost certainly genuine, judging by the handwriting characteristics alone. The letter reads:

Mr Lusk
    Sir
        I send you half the kidne I took from one women presarved it for you tother piece I fried and ate it was very nice I may send you the bloody knif that took it out if you only wate a whil longer
        signed   Catch me when you can Mister Lusk

Mr MacLeod draws attention to the 'knife-edged, or dagger-like strokes', evidence of aggression and nervous tension. The second letter Mr MacLeod analyses is the one beginning 'Old boss you wor rite it was the left kidny', which (unlike the one above) is signed 'Jack the Ripper'.

Mr MacLeod is of the opinion that the letters are not written by the same person. He speaks of the 'huge ornate capitals' of the first letter, and the lack of capitals in the second. The 'J' of 'Jack' is smaller than the 'K'. In the second letter, 'I' is written 'i'; in the first, 'I' is a huge flourishing capital. This seems to mark a sense of inferiority in the second writer; yet his small r's are enormous, sprawling things, and Mr MacLeod quotes a colleague as believing that this type of 'r' invariably indicates a craving for attention. He summarises:
    'If there was only one real Jack the Ripper, I should cast my vote for the writer of sample 1. He shows tremendous drive in the vicious forward thrust of his overall writing, and great cunning in his covering up of strokes; that is, the retracing of one stroke of a letter over another, rendering it illegible while appearing to clarify. . . . Whereas, although sample 1 appears

to be written better than sample 2, it is in fact extremely difficult to decipher; whereas sample 2, except for the atrocious spelling, is fairly readable.

'I would say that this writer was capable of any atrocity, and of carrying it out in an organised way. I would say he had enough brains and control to hold down some steady job which would give him a cover up for his crimes. He has imagination, as revealed in the upper-zone flourishes. Those hooks on the t-bars, among other signs, indicate tenacity to achieve a goal.

'I would have looked for this killer among men such as cab-drivers, who had a legitimate excuse to be anywhere at any time. I should have sought a hail-fellow-well-met who liked to eat and drink; who might attract women of the class he preyed on by an overwhelming animal charm. I would say he was in fact a latent homosexual (suggested by the lower zone strokes [of the y's] returning on the wrong side of the letter) and passed as a 'man's man'; the roistering blade who made himself the life and soul of the pub and sneered at women as objects to be used and discarded. . . .

'The writer of sample 2 may or may not have done any of the killings; but I would tend to think not. He certainly had the sadistic urge; but I question whether he had the drive and organisation to carry them through. I would rather believe that his extreme self-contempt coupled with his strong desire to be noticed would turn him into the sort of person who enters a police station demanding to be arrested for a crime he obviously cannot have committed. He could be the sort of toady who hangs around with the flashy type. . . .' He suggests that the writer of sample 2 could have been a pickpocket or petty thief.

Whether all Mr MacLeod's suggestions are accurate or not, he is at least examining available evidence and drawing scientific deductions based upon his long experience as a graphologist. His picture of the Ripper strikes me as in many ways more plausible than the idea of a well-dressed young barrister or doctor. There is only one aspect of the Druitt identification that gives it, as far as I am concerned, a certain plausibility: his lack of a job. A regular job provides a person with a certain stability of background, regular acquaintances and habits. It is the man who spends too much time sitting alone in his room, or wandering around without a regular home or regular sexual relief, who commits the extremely violent murder. Musil showed psychological insight when he made his sex-murderer Moosbrugger (in *The Man Without Qualities*) a wandering journeyman. Let me reinforce this point with some examples.

On 9th September 1898, two schoolgirls disappeared from the village of Lechtingen, near Osnabrück. The bodies were found later in woods near the village; the murderer had hacked them to pieces and scattered the pieces through the woods. In July 1901, on the Baltic island of Rügen, two sons of a carter vanished – aged six and eight. They were found in the same condition as the girls; their heads had been beaten in, then cut off, the arms and legs amputated, and the internal organs scattered over a large area. A travelling carpenter named Ludwig Tessnov had been seen talking to the children earlier in the afternoon, and there were blood spots on his clothes. Enquiries by the Rügen magistrate revealed that Tessnov had been the suspect in the earlier case, but had claimed that the stains on his clothes were wood-stain, and been released for lack of evidence. Luckily, by the year 1901, Paul Uhlenhuth had developed his method of testing blood stains, and Tessnov's clothes were sent to him. He was able to identify some stains as definitely human, others as being of sheep's blood. Three weeks before the murder of the two boys, seven sheep had been disembowelled and scattered over a field in Rügen. The evidence against Tessnov was overwhelming and he was executed.

Tessnov killed boys and girls – and no doubt there were others – between 1898 and 1901. The murderer Adolf Seefeld was homosexual, and killed twelve boys between 1908 and 1935. Seefeld was a travelling watchmaker. He was executed in 1936. Seefeld did not mutilate his victims.

On 28th August 1946, a young couple were petting in a car at Sandon Point, near Sydney, Australia, when a man peered through the windscreen. Cecil Kelly opened the door to ask what he wanted, and was struck on the head with a steel bar. His fiancée, an attractive model, jumped out of the car, and was also struck on the head. The man raped her, then lifted her back into the car. He kept her there for the rest of the night, and raped her five more times. Towards morning, he lifted her lover's body into the car, pushed it down towards the cliff, and then set the car on fire. He assumed the girl was dead, but she managed to roll out of the burning car.

The killer was easy to trace; some time before the murder he had called at a house and asked for water. He had then mentioned that he meant to try a nearby colliery for a job. The police found him working at the colliery – he was a thirty-nine-year-old transient named Mervyn Garvie, who lived in a wooden hut. His photograph shows a powerful man with a bull-neck and trap-like mouth, obviously a man of strong character. What happened is clear enough; he saw the couple petting; he was sex-starved, and in a state of sexual excitement that meant that he thought of nothing but rape. Basically, he was of the same type of character as Mr MacLeod's Jack the Ripper; the writer of sample 2 would have contented himself by peering in at the window and masturbating; Garvie raped the girl six times.

He was sentenced to life imprisonment, and was later killed by a fellow prisoner.

In August 1935, a boy named Danny Kerrigan was lying on the ground beside his girlfriend, Marjory Fenwick, in a lovers' lane known as Cuddies Strip, near Perth, Scotland. They sat up and the girl rearranged her clothes; then they got up to walk off. There was a shot from some bushes behind them, and shot-gun pellets whizzed through the girl's hair. They turned. There was another shot, and Danny Kerrigan was hit square in the face and chest with a charge of buckshot. A man appeared beside her as she bent over the body, and she asked him to stay with Kerrigan while she ran for help. But as she ran, the man ran beside her; at the stile, he pulled her backwards on to the ground. She pretended she had fainted; the man removed all her clothes, gagged her with her own suspender belt, and raped her. The girl managed to run away, taking her coat, and her assailant went off with her clothes. Ten days later, Marjory Fenwick identified him as John McGuigan, an Irish labourer who lived in a tent a mile away. He was known as a peeping-Tom in the area. The Scottish jury produced a curious verdict: that McGuigan was guilty of raping the girl, but not of murdering Kerrigan; he received a ten-year sentence.

In 1958, Robert J Thompson, a transient 'jack of all trades', was tried for the murder of a fifty-two-year-old woman, Mrs Harriet Ann Hicks, near Mexico City. Thompson, a Canadian, made a habit of picking up American women tourists and offering to show them archaeological remains. He then forced them – or sometimes persuaded them – to take a drink containing chloral hydrate, 'knock-out drops' – and while they were unconscious, beat them and raped them. Two of his victims – women in their fifties – died as a result of this treatment (one of them of pneumonia from a night of exposure); four more recovered to find themselves naked and badly bruised; one of them was in a motel bedroom. All were robbed. All six cases took place over three months. Thompson was also wanted in the United States for robbery and sexual assault. This case resembles the Ripper murders in that Thompson's desire was to *beat* and assault women; the fact that the woman was unconscious – he gave them enormous doses of chloral hydrate – made no difference.

I have cited this list of cases because they underline my point that this type of crime is most often committed by a 'man on his own', often a tramp. Spending night after night alone, living as an outcast from society, he reaches out to take sex as a burglar reaches out to take property. According to the inventive Le Queux, Pedachenko was accompanied on his murder sprees by a female accomplice named Winberg and another friend named Levitski. If anything in the Ripper case can be stated with certainty, it is that Jack the Ripper worked alone, and almost certainly lived alone. If he was not interned in a mental home, then he undoubtedly committed suicide. One third of all murderers commit suicide – and this is largely because such a high proportion of murders are family murders – the husband kills his wife or children in a fit of rage or obsessive anxiety, then kills himself. In cases of sex murder, there is a tendency for the murderer to grow more and more careless, and to leave clues behind, as if wanting to be caught. (The Chicago sex murderer Heirens scrawled on a wall 'For God's sake catch me before I kill more'; Byrne, the YWCA murderer, left a note saying: 'I never thought this would happen.') In 1946 there was a series of murders in Taxarcana, Texas, usually at the time of the full moon. In the first case, a man and his fiancée were knocked unconscious in a lovers' lane, and the girl was raped; a month later, in similar circumstances, a man and a girl were both shot, and the girl was mutilated with a knife as well as raped. A month later, a seventeen-year-old youth was shot, and his fifteen-year-old girlfriend was raped and tortured for four hours before she was finally shot and mutilated. A fourth murder attempt was partially unsuccessful; a farmer was shot and killed with a rifle as he read the evening paper, but his wife, although shot, managed to run to a neighbour's house. Then the murders stopped. A few days later, a man committed suicide by leaping under a train; he fitted the description of the man who raped the first woman. A car was found burning nearby, and it seems probable that this was the car used in all the assaults. Here, as can be seen, the crimes became more and more sadistic – as in the Ripper case – and then ceased.

So whether or not Montague John Druitt was actually Jack the Ripper, the police were probably correct in their assumption that he committed suicide after the Miller's Court murder.

Five: The Age of Detection

WHAT SHOULD BE quite clear by now is that up to 1800 or so, crime was purely a social problem, the outcome of poverty and man's animal nature. Throughout the Anglo-Saxon period, it was not a serious problem – no doubt because communities were smaller – and the death penalty was rare. Under King Ethelbert, in the seventh century, most crimes from fornication to murder were punished by fines. With the increase of cities, crime increased, and the punishment became more and more savage; that is to say, the authorities held the naïve idea that the answer to crime was punishment. This attitude had already begun to change by the time of Burke and Hare – otherwise, Hare would not have escaped. (The police had a watertight case against the two of them without Hare's evidence, since they had the body.) There was not a jury in England or Scotland that would not have been happy to hang Hare as well as Burke, Hunt as well as Thurtell.

I have cited the Lacenaire case to show how the new police of London and Paris began to recognise that the answer to crime was *organised* crime-fighting. And, very slowly, the methods became more sophisticated. In 1802, Thomas Wedgewood attempted to take the first photographs, utilising a discovery made in 1725, that silver salts darken when exposed to light. He succeeded in taking photographs, but as soon as they were exposed to daylight, they went dark. Nicéphore Niépce discovered that this could be prevented if the photograph was washed in nitric acid or ammonia immediately after it was taken; then the unaffected silver chloride was dissolved away, leaving only that which retained the photograph. He took his first successful picture from nature in 1826, the view out of his

153

workshop window. The view shows sunlight on both sides of the courtyard because the plate had to be left exposed all day. It was a long time before photographs could be taken quickly enough to make it worth while for criminal investigation. In the early days of 'mug shots', the criminal had to be held still by two or three brawny detectives while he was exposed to the camera for five minutes.

No doubt the preservation of the head of Catherine Hayes' husband deserves to rank as one of the first successful collaborations between the forces of science and the law. A century and a half later, photography made such gruesome experiments unnecessary. For example, on 8th November 1876, two children playing on the banks of the Seine noticed a bundle caught against some piles, and called passers-by to drag it to land. It contained the head and parts of the body of a woman. The head was photographed, and the photographs sold cheaply in the streets of Paris. One day, a man in a café recognised it as the wife of a soldier named Billoir. Billoir at first declared that his wife had left him; but a search of his room revealed bloodstains and some human hair. He now changed his story and asserted that his wife had died when he kicked her during a quarrel, and that he had decided to get rid of the body when he discovered she was dead. The doctors replied that was impossible. A corpse bleeds far less than a living body because the heart has stopped; the amount of blood proved that Mme Billoir had been stabbed to death; moreover, there was no bruise on her. Billoir was guillotined. Here is a case that parallels that of Catherine Hayes in many respects – except that it cost the police far less trouble to bring home the crime to Billoir.

The man who took the first great step in scientific crime detection was Alphonse Bertillon, who took up his duties in 1879. But before speaking of Bertillon, let us examine a classical case of the pre-scientific era – a case that sounds as if it had been invented by Georges Simenon.

On 26th January 1869, a restaurant owner in the Rue Princesse, off the Boulevard St Germain in Paris, decided to investigate his well, the water of which tasted foul. He went into his basement, and looked through a narrow window halfway down the well and a few feet above the surface of the water. There was a parcel floating in the water, and after some difficulty, the restaurateur fished it out. It contained the lower part of a leg. A young detective, Gustave Macé, was called, and he peered into the well. He saw another parcel floating below the surface. It proved to contain another leg, encased in part of a stocking. There was a laundry mark on the stocking, but this played less part in the investigation than it would in a modern case.

The legs were declared to be those of a woman, and Macé went about his task in the same painstaking way that Canler had traced Lacenaire – looking through the file of women missing during the past six months – eighty-four of them – and trying to trace them all. Weeks of work gradually eliminated them all. But Macé had discovered more clues. A human thighbone had been found in the nearby Rue Jacob. On 17th December another thigh, wrapped in an old shawl, was pulled out of the river. Two days later, a laundry proprietor had seen a man in a long coat scattering pieces of meat from a basket into the river. When questioned, the man explained that he was baiting the river for fish, because he intended to spend all the next day fishing. But after this, chunks of flesh were fished out of the river and from St Martin Canal, some of them fairly large. On 22nd December a police officer had met a man wandering up the Rue de Seine with a parcel in one hand and a hamper in the other. They questioned him – in case he was a robber – but he explained that he had just arrived by train from Mantes, and had been unable to find a cab; he pointed to railway labels on the parcel to prove his story. The police thought he looked so honest they allowed him to go. But his description sounded very like that of the enthusiastic fisherman.

Macé had another clue. One of the parcels fished out of the well was sewn up in black glazed calico, and the stitches had a professional look. Macé was beginning to get a picture of the suspect – short, plump, round-faced, with a black moustache, and a cheerful, confident manner – and almost certainly a tailor.

Meanwhile, the great Alexandre Tardieu, one of the first police pathologists – now near retirement – had examined the legs, and pronounced that they were a man's, not a woman's. All Macé's early weeks of labour had been wasted.

Why had the killer dumped the legs in a well, rather than in the Seine? Obviously, it must be someone who knew the house. Macé investigated the building that contained the restaurant. The concierge was old and inefficient; practically anybody could wander in and out. Macé got her to talk about former tenants, and asked if there had ever been a tailor in the house. No, she said, but there had been a tailoress. It sounded an unlikely lead, but the indefatigable Macé followed it up. For whom did the girl work? Various people, said the old lady. Other tailors used to pass on work to her. There was one in particular who caused her endless work; he used to spill water on the stairs. What water? asked Macé. Water from the well. . . .

So there had been a tailor who knew about the well. Macé managed to trace the seamstress, who was now a café *chanteuse*. She obviously had nothing to hide. She told Macé that the man he was asking about was Pierre Voirbo. He had once been her lover, but now he was married and living in the Rue Mazarin.

Macé asked if Voirbo had any special friends. The girl named a certain Désiré Bodasse, an old man who often drank with Voirbo. She had no idea of his address, but she knew that his aunt lived in the Rue de Nesles.

Macé traced Mme Bodasse, and she told him that her nephew lived in the Rue Dauphine. He had not been seen for a month but that was not strange. He was like that. He had been a craftsman who manufactured tapestry; now he was retired. He was pathologically mean; on one occasion, he had vanished for six weeks, and it turned out that he had been ill in hospital, masquerading under another name so the hospital authorities could not trace him to get him to pay for his treatment.

They went to look at Bodasse's apartment. The concierge said she was certain he was in – she had seen a light behind the curtains the night before – but he would not answer the door. He liked to be left undisturbed – he was an eccentric kind of recluse.

Mme Bodasse came to look at the legs in the morgue, and declared that she recognised the stockings, as well as a scar on one of the legs. It was her nephew Désiré, beyond all doubt.

The more Macé heard of Pierre Voirbo, the less Macé liked the sound of him. He was a man of dissolute habits, and he was a police spy. He pretended to be a rabid anarchist, and made speeches at Left Wing meetings, while all the time he was reporting the activities of the comrades to the secret police.

Macé decided to break into Bodasse's apartment. Everything looked in order, although there was dust on the furniture. Someone had been in recently, for an eight-day clock was still ticking. But Bodasse's strong box was empty. In the back of a watch, Macé found a piece of paper with the numbers of various securities on it. The securities were nowhere to be found.

It seemed fairly certain that Voirbo returned periodically to the flat, to give the impression that Bodasse was still alive. Macé borrowed a couple of men from the secret police to watch the flat. This was a bad move. They knew Voirbo, and when he came to the flat, they accosted him openly and asked him what was going on. Macé's quarry was alerted.

Meanwhile, Macé discovered that Voirbo had changed his lodgings since he married. The landlord of his old lodging said that he had paid his rent before he left. How? With a five-hundred-franc share of Italian stock, which the proprietor had changed for him at the corner. It was the kind of security that could be cashed by the bearer. Macé hastened to the money-changer. He had kept the counterfoil of the share, and the number was one of those in the watch.

The cleaner of Voirbo's old room also had an interesting story. Voirbo was normally the untidiest and laziest man on earth. But on the morning of 17th December she had found his room not only tidied but scrubbed; he explained he had dropped a bottle of cleaning fluid on the floor, which made such a smell that he had cleaned out the whole place.

Macé knew he had no evidence. Even the matter of the stock could be easily accounted for – Voirbo would say it was a loan, or the payment of an account. Macé decided to see Voirbo himself. He was a plump young man of thirty, but the face and eyes revealed that he was a man of some resource and character. He acknowledged frankly that he had been rather worried about Bodasse's non-appearance, although he was aware that his old friend had peculiar habits. He behaved as if he was Macé's colleague rather than a suspect – which, in a sense, was true enough. Macé had no alternative than to accept his offers of assistance, and hope that evidence would finally appear. He even attended a revolutionary meeting with Voirbo and heard the police spy make an inflammatory speech to his Republican colleagues.

Voirbo told Macé that he was fairly certain of the identity of the killer of Bodasse – it was an alcoholic butcher named Rifer. He was probably assisted by three criminal acquaintances, whom Voirbo also pointed out. Macé checked on them. Two of them had perfect alibis, in that they were in jail in the second part of December.

And Voirbo, with the calculation that was typical of him, now began encouraging Rifer to drink heavily – very heavily. There was nothing Macé could do about it. One night, Rifer had a fit of DTs, and smashed all his furniture, which he threw into the street. He was arrested – not over-gently – and taken to an asylum, where he died in the night.

The next morning, Macé arrived early at his office – and found Voirbo already there. Macé decided to arrest him. But it was so early that he was there alone, and Voirbo was a formidable man. Macé excused himself, and said he had to answer a letter immediately. Then he sat down at his desk, and while Voirbo read a newspaper, wrote careful instructions to his subordinates to surround Voirbo and arrest him. He placed the letter in the outer office, then engaged Voirbo in conversation until his men came in and made the arrest.

Voirbo was calm and sardonic; he was sure Macé had no evidence. And of course, he was right. He was thoroughly searched – and Macé realised he had made a wise decision; Voirbo had a ticket to Havre, and had intended to flee to America. The ticket was in the name of Saba; was Voirbo's choice of the name of the great assassin accidental?

Voirbo would admit nothing. Macé went to his apartment and talked to his wife – a quiet girl, who had brought a dowry of 15,000 francs (about £600 at that time). She obviously knew nothing about her husband's activities. She allowed Macé to open the box which, she said, contained her dowry (in securities) and the 10,000 francs-worth of shares he had brought to the marriage. (This was the exact value of Bodasse's securities.) The box was empty. Macé proceeded to search the house, from attic to cellar. And it was in the cellar that he found what he was looking for – Bodasse's securities, soldered into a tin box, and suspended on a string inside a cask of wine.

Macé needed only one more proof to make his case water-tight – that Voirbo had dismembered the old man in his old lodging at Rue Mazarin. A young couple had moved into the room, and Macé asked them to describe the arrangement of the furniture when they moved in. They did, and it became clear that the only place in which the old man could have been struck down on the floor was a certain spot in the centre of the room, where a table had stood. If Bodasse had been killed there, then he had probably been dismembered on the table. The floor revealed no marks of blood; but Macé observed that it sloped slightly, and that the tiles under the bed had cracks between them. He decided to stage a grand denouement scene. Voirbo was brought to the room, perfectly calm. Macé took up a jug of water, and said: 'I am assuming that Bodasse was killed where I am standing. I shall now pour water on the floor, and try to get an idea of how the blood ran.' Voirbo became notice-ably nervous. He watched the water that flowed under the bed and formed a pool. A mason was called in to take up the tiles. He did so, and the undersides were found coated with a dark brown substance that was clearly blood. Voirbo's nerve broke, and he made a confession on the spot: which is worth quoting at length:

'Tell me who you really are' [said Macé].

'My real name is not Voirbo, but for the present I shall not tell you what it is – later on we will see. I am an illegitimate child; however, I know my father, and must acknowledge that

I am not proud of him. Everybody, including my wife, believes me to be an orphan; but my parents are still in existence. I see my mother occasionally – I help her more or less, for she is poor and old in years, and, besides, the unfortunate woman worships me in spite of all my shortcomings. I likewise love her! My father is a bad man. When I was quite a child he was in the habit of beating me frequently; and as I grew up he continued to do so brutally, and occasionally in his fits of anger he would shake his clenched fist at me saying: *"You – you shall perish by my hand!"* I trust you may never know the precise meaning of those terrible words. In the main my father was right enough; I was indeed a good-for-nothing fellow. Not wishing to die by his hand, I tried to kill him; but, doubtless guessing my thoughts, he kept on his guard. I left the house, anger in my mind, hatred in my heart. Even now I still hate my father, as much as, and even more than, formerly, because of the suffering he subjected my poor mother to, and the harsh treatment he inflicted on me in my childhood. Perhaps he is the cause of my misfortunes.'

'Does he bear the same name as yourself?'

'He does not. I told you I was a *bastard* – my father never acknowledged me; his only way of testifying to his paternity was by means of blows.'

'Then tell me his name, since it is different from yours.'

'I cannot do so, for you know him. You must have had something to do with him under very painful circumstances. I will recall him to your memory, but not now.'

'What did you do when you left your parents' home?'

'I battled for life, in which everything is either chance or trickery – I did my best, and that unsuccessfully, to make up for bad luck by more or less fair means. I was an obscure personage, and I longed to shine; I was poor, and I worshipped wealth. My marriage with Mademoiselle Rémondé would have given me a modest competency, and perhaps, with such a good woman as she is, I might have taken to work again and atoned for my faults.'

'Say rather your crimes.'

'*Crimes;* you are right. Yet, I sometimes forget that I am

a criminal, and like a great many scoundrels I was anxious to settle down and become an honest man. Some manage to succeed, I am acquainted with such men – as for me, I have failed. If that selfish old man, Désiré, had lent me the ten thousand francs I begged him to advance me I would never have killed him. I had told the Rémondés that I possessed that amount – so I had to produce it; my marriage was at that price. I begged and implored Bodasse, but nothing could move him; on the contrary he laughed at me, laughed at my matrimonial projects, and at every argument I brought forward; then— well, I murdered him.'

'At your own lodging!'

'As you have proved.'

'How did you manage to entice him to your room?'

'On Monday, 14th December, after leaving the baths and dining together at the restaurant in the Rue Grégoire-de-Tours, I invited him to take a cup of tea at my place. He followed me without the least mistrust – besides, he was often in the habit of coming to my room, not, let me tell you, because he wanted to see me, but in the hope of meeting some of my work-girls. On the night in question, I told him that my betrothed was going to spend the evening there, with a relative, and, in order to make him believe all the more that I had company, I left him for a few minutes while at the restaurant, and went and lit some candles in my room. I had also thrown open the shutters so that he might see the light from the street. My determination had been taken. No sooner was he in the room, when he asked me, as he sat down by the side of the table, why I had hoaxed him, since there was nobody there? I replied that my betrothed was coming. Then, passing behind him, and without his noticing it, I seized one of the flat irons standing on my work-table – that's the one, there – and without any argument, without saying a word, I dealt him, unawares, a terrific blow on the skull. Not a sound escaped him. His head sank on to the table, his arms hung down inert. I was astonished, and satisfied with my strength and skill.

'Then, blowing out the light, I opened the window and pulled the shutters to. In silence and darkness I listened to discover if he stirred. But I heard nothing – except his blood which fell on the floor, drop by drop! This monotonous drop – drop – drop – made my flesh creep. Still I kept on listening, listening. All of a sudden I heard a deep sigh, and something like a creaking of the chair; Désiré was moving – he was not dead! Suppose he were to cry out. This thought restored all my presence of mind to me. Lighting a small lamp, I saw that the body had moved sideways; he was then still living. He was certainly no longer in a condition to make himself heard – to call for help; but his death-agony might be spun out – and I did not want to see him suffer a long while. I therefore took a razor, approached him from behind and placed my hand under the chin of my ex-friend. Yielding to my pressure, the head rose up and then fell backwards. The lamp was shining full on his blood-smeared face; his round eyes were not yet lifeless – for a moment they fastened on the blade of the razor I was holding above him, and suddenly assumed such an expression of terror, that my heart beat violently. It was necessary to put an end to it. The same as a barber does when about to shave a customer, I pressed the blade just below the Adam's apple, where the beard commences, and with a vigorous sweep I drew the blade from left to right. It entirely disappeared in the flesh – the head fell lifeless on the back of the chair. My first gash had severed the carotid artery and the larynx. A death rattle, and his last breath issued from the wound I had made. A rush of blood spurted out, and fell in part on a sugar-basin, which had been left uncovered on the table.

'I now let the body slide gently to the floor and, fearing lest I might be seen through the openings in the shutters and the muslin curtains, I fastened a thick blanket before the window, which, in my hurry to draw the shutters to, I had forgotten to close. Returning to Bodasse's body, I examined it for a moment, and saw that death had done its work! So as not to stain my clothes, I took everything off with the exception of a pair of drawers and my socks; then, taking a sponge and wash-hand basin, I commenced by wiping up the blood which had fallen in almost every direction. I threw the discoloured sugar in the stove. Then, laying the corpse on a board, I wholly undressed the upper part, cutting the clothes away with my scissors. The lower portion of the trousers, which I had separated some little distance above the knee, I threw back over the legs. They were in my way, those two legs which became the starting-point of your inquiry. I therefore detached them from the thighs, hacking them off by means of that butcher's chopper you found at my residence. But I did not chop like a butcher would when cutting up a quarter of beef – I pressed the sharp edge on the flesh, and then struck the back of the chopper with the metal bobbin you have there – it does not make the least noise.

'The legs now being off, I put them in the trunk I kept in the little closet – oh, how heavy they were! Although the man was but small in stature, and in spite of the absence of the legs, Désiré struck me as still being much too big. I commenced cutting up the body altogether – but the head, already half severed from the trunk, would not keep still. Every time the least motion was given to the bust it moved, swaying either to the right or to the left, and splashed my face with drops of blood.

'It was horrible! So I severed it completely from the body, and contemplated it for a moment as I held it in both hands – I can see it – see it still. What a terrible *tête-à-tête!* On ceasing my inspection I placed it in a pan, with the face downwards, so that I might no longer see it.

'I then cut off the arms, and completely flayed the bust. I thought that, once freed from the outer skin, the flesh, after a longer or shorter stay in the water, would be sure to be taken for the remains of some animal. And, in truth, it certainly did look like so much butcher's meat. After having opened the belly with a knife, the handle of which broke off during the operation, I removed the entrails, liver, lungs and heart to the water-closet close to the door of my room. In order to dispose of the body more easily I cut it up into small pieces, which I then packed in the same trunk as the legs. There being no door-keeper to the house I was enabled, without disturbing anyone, to get an unlimited supply of water, at the foot of the stairs, to scrub the room out with. What a quantity of blood there is in a human body! I thought I should never see the end of it. Oh! what a terrible winter's night I passed! I was red with perspiration yet I shivered with cold, my weary fingers were no longer able to handle the scissors I used for cutting.'

'What did you do with Bodasse's clothes?'

'I burnt them in the stove, with my own, as well as the chair and board which were wet with blood. During the remainder of that night, as well as the whole of Tuesday, I never stirred from my room, but on the following night I carried the pieces of flesh out of the house and scattered them everywhere. I had soon only the legs left. Fearing lest they might be recognised, I had decided to drop them down the well of the house in the Rue Princesse. Having formerly visited a girl, named Gaupe, there, I was aware of the existence of the well, and knew also the secret of gaining admission to the premises. On the night of 21st December, after having tied these two limbs in wrappers that I was in the habit of using, and having pasted railway labels on them with the intention of showing, if I were surprised, that I had just come back from a journey, I went out, towards one in the morning, bearing my funeral burden which was carefully tied up.

'By way of extra precaution, and to make anyone I might meet believe that I was a belated traveller, I threw a rug over my shoulder and carried a basket, in which I placed various articles which I had shortly before received from Langres. I was going along full of anxiety, when all of a sudden police constables Ringué and Champy barred my way at the Carrefour de Buci. Knowing the rotation of their duty and the usual rounds of the force, I was certain that, at such an hour, I ought not to meet a single policeman on my way. Therefore I stood speechless on finding myself face to face with them. Never in the whole course of my life have I experienced such fear. But recovering, fortunately, my self-possession I was able to deceive them, and continue on my road.

'The very first time I called here I recognised those two officers and, as you rightly guessed, I did my best to avoid meeting them again. This encounter in the Carrefour de Buci had perplexed me and, whilst going in the direction of the Rue Princesse, I asked myself whether it would not be better to alter my plans and to throw the remains I was carrying into the

Seine. Before entering the street, I again hesitated; but my evil genius urged me onward. I entered my former work-girl's dwelling without making the least noise; and once in the yard I was careful to see that no lights were burning in the windows. I removed the cover from the well and slipped my lugubrious bundle down it by means of a string I had rolled round it, and which gradually unwound; it disappeared in the water without the least noise. After having again made sure that nobody was watching me, I regained the street, and quietly returned to the Rue Mazarine, by way of the Carrefour de Buci, feeling sure I should not meet the same constables there. On getting back to my room, I looked in my glass and grew frightened at my own pallor. My interview with those two constables had curdled the blood in my veins. I was trembling with cold and yet in a perspiration, as at the time when I was cutting up Désiré's body. But the thought of the old man's ten thousand francs and of my betrothed gave me fresh courage. I went to bed and fell asleep as I thought of them. That, Mr Commissary, is the true account of my crime.'

'But what became of the head? You have not told me that.'

'The head is safe enough. You will probably never find it, even if I tell you what I did with it. Had I only done the same with those confounded legs, I should now be quietly seated at the fireside, with my wife.'

'Tell me, though, what did you do with the head?'

'As it was the part which could most easily be recognised, I poured lead into it by the ears and mouth. At two o'clock in the morning, I threw it into the middle of the Seine, from the top of the Pont de la Concorde. You may be quite sure that it will never rise to the surface. I melted the lead by means of that zinc worker's mould you have in your possession, and which a customer forgot at my place one day.'

'That customer was probably a criminal of some kind or other?'

'If you like.'

'An accomplice, maybe?'

'No, I alone conceived, prepared and executed the project of Bodasse's murder.'

'But was your victim's death an absolute necessity?'

'Yes, since I was in want of ten thousand francs, and Désiré happened to possess that amount.'

'You might have stolen it from him – that would have been bad enough; but after all, it would not have been a murder.'

'No matter who might have stolen his hoard, he would always have suspected me.'

'You are scarcely thirty years of age, and your life is already terribly burdened with crime.'

'True enough – but I was determined to make myself a position at all costs. To effect this, I played against society at large, a bold game, of which my head was the stake. I have made every effort to save it and in spite of all my energy the game is lost, and quite lost this time.'

Macé strongly suspected Voirbo of being involved in other murders. One of Voirbo's aliases was Saba, an agriculturalist of Aubervilliers, and he had all the necessary papers. There had been a murder at Aubervilliers, and Voirbo had the press cuttings about it. There was also a cutting about the murder of a servant girl in the Rue Placide in Aubervilliers. But before Macé could investigate these crimes, Voirbo succeeded in cutting his throat with a razor smuggled into jail in a loaf of bread. Before this, he had made a determined attempt to escape, but had been caught.

He had made only one mistake in a perfect murder – to sew the legs into the calico bags, which had given Macé his first clue. But for this, Macé would have been confronted with an insoluble crime. Voirbo would also have stood a fair chance of escape if he had continued to deny the murder after Macé's little 'demonstration' in the Rue Mazarin; for in those days, there was no conclusive test for human blood. In his room, Voirbo had another press cutting about a double murderer called Avinain,[1] a butcher, whose advice to posterity, delivered

[1] Charles Avinain had a prison record dating back to 1833, and he escaped from the criminal settlement of Cayenne in 1865. His routine of murder was curious. He would approach a farmer with hay to sell, and offer him a better price than he could get at market. The victim was lured to a

from the steps of the guillotine, was 'Never confess'. Voirbo should have remembered this.

In the 1870s, France was in ferment, and political turmoil always brings crime. If one considers the patient months that Macé spent solving the Voirbo case, and then remembers that Voirbo's murder was one of the two hundred or so in 1868, it can be seen that the old detective methods were becoming inadequate. Vidocq and Canler relied on their memory for criminal faces; in Macé's time, there were far too many faces. Even photography was inadequate; for, obviously, an archive of one hundred thousand photographs is completely useless unless they are classified in a way that will enable the police to compare the description of a criminal with photographs that might match it. And how does one go about describing someone? Just as an experiment, try describing the face of someone sitting opposite you on a bus, as if you had to describe it for the police. Unless it is a fairly distinctive face, with a broken nose or completely bald head, there is very little to say. This was the Sûreté's problem.

When the twenty-five-year-old Alphonse Bertillon became a clerk at the Sûreté in 1879, most of the old identification procedures were practically useless. Bertillon was a dreary, pedantic young man whom most people found rather repellent; but he came from a cultured and scientific family, and the chaos irritated him. He was certain there *ought* to be some simple way of arranging the hundred thousand photographs and descriptions.

Bertillon's story would be ideal for Hollywood. He compared photographs of criminals to see if there was some way of

rented shack by the river near Clichy, and killed with a hammer; he was then dismembered and thrown into the river, and the wagon and hay were sold. After two lots of remains in the river had been identified as Isidore Vincent and Désiré Daguet, a man who had escaped the murderer led the police to his shack. Avinain had arranged a trapdoor with a spring, through which he escaped, but the police caught him as he tried to emerge from a cellar. He undoubtedly killed other victims. There is a legend that the man who caught him, Chief Inspector Claude, had seen Lacenaire in a café back in 1833, and had told an associate that he sensed the man was a killer.

classifying noses and faces. Then he thought it might be a good idea to take measurements of criminals when they were arrested – height, reach, circumference of head, height sitting down, length of left hand, left foot, left leg – Bertillon chose the left-hand side because it was unlikely to be affected by work. He was subject to constipation, stomach upsets, headaches and nosebleeds; but he had a certain stubbornness that made him ignore the knowing smiles of colleagues. A doctor named Adolphe Quetelet had asserted that the chances of two people being exactly the same height are four to one. If that was so, and the same thing applied to the other statistics, then you needed only two or three measurements of each criminal to raise the odds to a hundred to one. When the prefect of police ignored Bertillon's letter about this method, Bertillon bought himself a set of filing cards, and started to work on his own, staying in the office until late at night. Macé revealed a lack of insight when he read Bertillon's report, and said it was too theoretical. The prefect, Andrieux, told Bertillon to stop making a nuisance of himself. And three years went by before Bertillon could persuade a new prefect, Jean Camecasse, to give him an interview. Camecasse was as sceptical as his predecessor, but he was impressed by the clerk's persistence. He told Bertillon that they would introduce his method experimentally for three months. This was obviously absurd; it would take more than three months to build up a file, and a method like Bertillon's depended on accumulation. But with the great Macé himself opposed to the whole idea, he knew his only chance lay in working on and praying for luck. His card index swelled at the rate of a few hundred a month. But with more than twenty thousand criminals in Paris alone, the chances of identifying one of them was low. Towards the end of the third month, Bertillon had towards two thousand cards. Theoretically, his chance of identification was one in ten – fairly high. But it must be remembered that a large number of his criminals were sent to jail, often for years, so most of his file was lying fallow, so to speak.

On 20th February 1883, luck was with him. His system led him to identify a petty criminal who had been measured three

168

months earlier. It was a very small triumph, but it was enough to make Camecasse decide to allow the experiment to continue. This was not far-sightedness. The post of prefect was a political appointment; Camecasse was hoping for fame. Unfortunately, a new prefect had been appointed by the time Bertillon became a celebrity; but history allows Camecasse the credit. As the file swelled, identification became more frequent. Before long, it averaged one a day. But what Bertillon needed was a really sensational case, something as newsworthy as Macé's pursuit of Voirbo. He had to wait until 1892 for it, but when it came, it spread his name all over the world. And the reason for the notoriety of the case was more or less accidental.

Since the early 1880s, a terrifying group of people known as the Anarchists became steadily more well known. People were not all that interested in their idealistic doctrine of the inherent goodness of human nature – which means that man does not need Authority to keep him virtuous. In 1881, Russian anarchists – they called themselves Narodniki – blew up Tsar Alexander II with a bomb; in Chicago, in May 1884, someone hurled a home-made bomb into a crowd of policemen who were about to break up a meeting of strikers, killing seven of them. Eight anarchists were condemned to death; one of them blew himself up with a bomb, and wrote in his own blood: 'Long live Anarchy!' Four of the anarchists were eventually hanged. In France, anarchists like Malatesta, Grave and Reclus spoke darkly of the 'propaganda of the deed', and the bourgeoisie shuddered. On May Day 1891, three anarchists were arrested for taking part in demonstrations at Clichy, and badly beaten-up by the police. At their trial, the prosecuting attorney Bulot demanded the death penalty for all three – although no one had been killed in the riots. The judge, Benoist, acquitted one of them and gave the other two prison sentences of three and five years. In March the following year – 1892 – a tremendous explosion shook the house in which Judge Benoist lived, destroying the stairway. Two weeks later, another explosion blew up Bulot's house in the Rue de Clichy. Luckily, no one was killed in either explosion. But the panic was tremendous. Large quantities of dynamite had been stolen from quarries at

Soiry, and the Parisians wondered where the next explosion would occur. A Left-Wing professor was arrested for the first explosion, and he agreed that he had planned it; however, a man named Ravachol had carried it out. Ravachol was known to the police – not as an anarchist, but as a burglar who was suspected of murder; he had killed an old miser and his house-keeper, two women who kept a hardware store, and an old miser who lived in a forest hut. He was also believed to have robbed the tomb of a countess to steal her jewellery. The alias of this forty-year-old criminal seemed to be Konigstein.

On the day of the Rue de Clichy dynamiting, Ravachol dined in the Restaurant Véry in the Boulevard Magenta, and tried to convert a waiter named Lhérot to anarchism. Two days later, he returned, and Lhérot noticed a scar on his thumb, which had been mentioned in descriptions of Ravachol. He notified the police, and the man was arrested.

Here was Bertillon's chance to prove his system to the world. Luckily, 'Konigstein' had been briefly under arrest at St Etienne as a suspect in the murder of the old man, and the police there had taken his measurements before he managed to escape. Bertillon himself measured Ravachol, and the measure-ments corresponded exactly. The idealistic anarchist Ravachol was the murderous criminal Konigstein, and for the time being, at least, the anarchist movement was discredited. On the even-ing before Ravachol's trial, the Restaurant Véry was blown up by a bomb, which killed the proprietor and a customer – it was obviously retaliation for the arrest of Ravachol, and an attempt to intimidate the judges. It succeeded; Ravachol was only con-demned to prison. But the judges of St Etienne were less scared of anarchist bombs; with Bertillon's proof in their hands, they were able to bring home the five murders to Ravachol, and he was executed on 10th July 1892. For the next few years Paris rocked with bombs – there was even one in the Chamber of Deputies – and President Carnot himself was assassinated. Bertillon luckily escaped the wrath of the anarchists.

But, absurdly enough, the method known as 'Bertillonage', which had revolutionised almost every police force in the world, was already out of date by this time. In India in the 1860s, a civil servant named William Herschel had observed that no two fingerprints are ever alike. He put it to use in his job of paying off pensioned Indian soldiers. These men could seldom write, and they all looked alike to English eyes. And when they realised this, the pensioners began collecting their pensions twice, or returned and collected other people's pensions. When Herschel noticed that fingerprints were always different, he made them sign for their pensions by placing the index finger on an inked pad, and pressing it gently at the side of his name on the list. The swindling ceased. Some years later, a Scot named Henry Faulds made the same discovery, and wrote a letter to *Nature*, declaring that this might be a means of identifying criminals. The year was 1880, two years before Bertillon was allowed to start making his experiments in measurement. Faulds and Herschel were later to be involved in bitter disputes about priority, but these do not concern us here.

A disciple of Darwin, Sir Francis Galton, became interested in Bertillonage because he thought it would help in the study of problems of heredity. He became friendly with Bertillon, and this interest in police work led him to write to Herschel about his methods of fingerprinting; he had read the exchange of letters between Herschel and Faulds in *Nature*. Galton settled down to the study of fingerprints, and soon decided that there were only four basic classifications; the core of his method was the triangle, or 'delta', in the centre of a fingerprint. In 1892, Galton's book *Fingerprints* came out. So in the year of his greatest triumph, Bertillon had become redundant. He refused to acknowledge it – for years he fought grimly for his system, betraying an unfortunate lack of the truly scientific spirit. But fingerprinting was bound to prevail in the end; it was so much simpler than Bertillonage.

The first murder ever to be solved by a fingerprint took place in Necochea, Argentina. A twenty-six-year-old woman named Francesca Rojas ran into the hut of a neighbour saying that her children had been murdered. The two children, aged four and six, lay dead in bed, their heads beaten in. She accused a man named Velasquez, who was in love with her. She wanted to marry another man, and she claimed that Velasquez had threatened to kill 'what she loved most'. She had returned from work to find the children dead. . . .

Velasquez was arrested and badly beaten, but he denied the murders, while agreeing to the threat. The police methods in Necochea were primitive; they tortured Velasquez for a week, without result; then the police chief tried making moaning noises outside the woman's hut, hoping to frighten her into confession by pretending to be a ghost.

A police inspector named Alvarez went out to investigate from La Plata. And he knew something about the work of a Dalmatian named Juan Vucetich, head of the Statistical Bureau of Police in Buenos Aires, who had developed his own finger-print system after reading an article by Galton. Alvarez went into the woman's hut and searched for clues. All he could find was a bloody thumb-print on a door. Alvarez sawed off the portion of the door and took it back to headquarters. Then he sent for Francesca Rojas, and made her give her thumb-print. Alvarez knew very little about classification, but it was quite obvious that the two prints were identical. When he showed the woman the two prints through a magnifying glass, she broke down and confessed – she had murdered her own two children because she wanted to marry a young lover who objected to them. This Argentine Lady Macbeth, who tried to rid herself of illegitimate children and an unwanted lover with one blow, obviously deserves to stand very high on a list of the world's worst women.

In England, Major Arthur Griffiths and Sir Melville Macnaghten were both on a panel whose task was to consider the comparative merits of fingerprinting and Bertillonage. Sir Francis Galton had still not completed his system of classification, and the British had made a typical compromise involving both systems. And then another British civil servant, Edward Richard Henry, solved the problem that was baffling Galton. Henry had some experience of Herschel's old system in India. Henry worked in Bengal, and became increasingly dissatisfied with the system of Bertillonage, even though the file cards also contained fingerprints. Bertillon's system depended upon a fanatical accuracy in taking the various measurements, and the Indian police lacked the fanaticism. Henry visited Galton's laboratory in 1899, and examined his findings. And it was Henry who finally invented the classification that Galton had been seeking for so many years. A straight line drawn across the delta would cross various ridges, which could be counted. He also distinguished five types of arches or whorls, and assigned them letters. A combination of these numbers and letters gave a formula through which a fingerprint could be quickly located from thousands of others.

Henry's methods were triumphant in India. When his book *Classification and Uses of Fingerprints* came out in England in 1900, he was appointed to sit on a committee in London to decide whether Bertillonage should be dropped altogether. It was. The British police were the first in the world to adopt the new system completely. He was also made Assistant Commissioner of the CID. His enthusiasm soon had a fingerprint department at Scotland Yard working as smoothly as it had at Calcutta. The method first proved its value on Derby Day, 1902. Criminals arrested for various offences at the Derby – picking pockets and so on – were dealt with quickly in court the next morning, and since there was no time to investigate their records, they got off with minimum penalties. Sir Melville Macnaghten decided it was time to stop this. He had the fingerprints of fifty-six men arrested on Derby Day sent to the Yard. Let him tell the rest of the story in his own words:

'The first prisoner on this occasion gave his name as Green of Gloucester, and assured the interrogating magistrate that he had never been in trouble before, and that a racecourse was, up to this time, an unknown world to him. But up jumped the Chief Inspector, in answer to a question as to whether "anything was known", and begged their worships to look at the papers and photographs, which proved the innocent to be Benjamin Brown of Birmingham, with some ten convictions to his discredit. "Bless the fingerprints," said Benjamin with an oath, "I knew they'd do me in!" ' [1]

[1] *Day of My Years*, pp 148–9.

Twenty-nine of the fifty-four were found to be old offenders, and received sentences twice as long as would otherwise have been awarded.

The first Englishman whose murderer was brought to justice by\a fingerprint was the manager of a tea plantation at Jalpai-guri, in Bengal. In August 1897, he was found dead in bed, his throat cut. All the servants had fled; so had the man's Indian mistress. In the dead man's wallet there was a calendar with a right-hand thumb-print in blood. Police enquiries revealed that, two years before, the manager had had his servant, a man named Charan, arrested for some theft, and Charan had sworn vengeance. Charan's prints were, of course, in the file, and it was found that the bloody thumb-print was his. But the court did not feel like imposing a death sentence on the evidence of a thumb-print; Charan was sentenced for the robbery, but not the murder.

The first English murder case involving fingerprints took place in Deptford in 1905. At 7.15 am, on 27th March of that year, a passing milkman saw two men emerge from a shop at 34 High Street, Deptford, and slam the door behind them. It was a paint shop, and the manager, an elderly man called Farrow, ran the shop with his wife.

At half past eight, the shop boy arrived and found the place closed up; he went to fetch the shop's owner, and they forced a kitchen window. Farrow was found dead on the ground floor, his head battered in; his wife was found dead in bed. What had happened was clear enough. The two men had broken into the shop, and Mr Farrow had heard the noise and hurried down-stairs – where he was beaten over the head with jemmies and left for dead. The men went upstairs, and killed his wife in the same way. They found the cash box under her husband's pillow and emptied it. Farrow was not dead; after the men left the shop he staggered to the door and looked outside, where he was seen by a little girl who thought nothing of a bloodstained man; then he locked the shop door, and died.

The police were on the scene by 9.30, and soon found a thumb-print inside the cash box. It was photographed and

174

enlarged. The police now checked on local criminals, and discovered that two brothers named Stratton were missing from their usual haunts. They were known as a violent and brutal pair, who had been in the hands of the police several times. They were picked up later in the week and fingerprinted. The thumb-print in the cash box was identical with that of the elder brother, Alfred. The police had no other evidence against them, since the milkman had been unable to identify them. Sergeant Collins, the fingerprint expert, would be the most important prosecution witness.

It was obviously an important case, and the future of fingerprinting might stand or fall by it – for a few years at least. Neither the judge – an elderly gentleman named Channell – nor the jury knew anything about fingerprints. The defence decided to take no chances, and called two of their own fingerprint experts. One of these was none other than Henry Faulds, the Scot who had discovered fingerprinting and declared that it should be used for police work. Through an unfortunate accident, he had never received the credit that was his due. When Sir Francis Galton had written to ask *Nature* for the addresses of the two men who had been conducting a correspondence about fingerprinting, the editor accidentally sent him only the address of Herschel. Herschel, like Galton, was a generous and disinterested sort of person, who immediately handed Galton all his results – with the consequence that Galton never had reason to consult Faulds. But Faulds, unfortunately, was an obsessive egoist who wanted credit for his discovery. (It will be remembered that Herschel actually discovered fingerprinting first, but Faulds was the first to publish the discovery.) For years, Faulds fought a violent battle to gain recognition; the British felt this was rather unsporting, and ignored him. So now Faulds decided to make himself felt by opposing the Crown case. The other 'expert' was yet another disappointed egoist, Dr Garson, who had first sneered at fingerprinting (he was a champion of Bertillonage), then decided to change horses, and invented his own system. And it was Garson's appetite for recognition that swung the case against the Strattons. Sergeant Collins gave a lecture on fingerprints and drew sketches on a blackboard. Garson and Faulds made no attempt to deny that no two fingerprints are ever alike, but they *did* assert that the print on the cash box was not identical with the print of Alfred Stratton's thumb. To the judge and jury, all fingerprints looked alike, and they were inclined to credit the assertion that the two prints were not really identical. Collins replied that the discrepancies were the kind that are bound to occur when fingerprints are taken, because lines will look thicker or thinner according to the pressure applied and the angle at which the finger is pressed on to the paper. He demonstrated this convincingly by taking fingerprints of the jury on the spot, and showing exactly the same discrepancies. But the seeds of doubt had been sown. The prosecutor now played his trump card. Garson was called back to the stand, and was asked whether it was not true that he had written a letter offering to testify for the prosecution? Yet he was now testifying for the defence. Clearly, this was a man who would change his opinions for the sake of being an important witness in an important trial. The judge remarked that he was obviously untrustworthy. And the last hope of the Stratton brothers vanished. They were found guilty, and both of them proceeded to shout abuse at the court, dissipating the impression of wronged innocence they had been aiming for. The judge sentenced them to death. England's first fingerprint murder had established that a fingerprint alone is enough to hang a man.

Sir Melville Macnaghten has a gruesome little story to tell of another fingerprint case. In 1911, a policeman in Clerkenwell noticed a finger stuck on a spike on top of a gate to a warehouse yard. A man had obviously been climbing over the gate when he had slipped and fallen backwards into the yard. A ring on his finger caught on a spike, and its top drove into the finger, so the man was left hanging, until his struggles tore the finger off his hand. The finger was taken to the Yard and identified as belonging to a thief who proved to be missing from his haunts. A few weeks later, a policeman who arrested a suspected pickpocket observed the bandage on his right hand. The man's finger proved to be missing, and the constable recalled the story of the finger from Clerkenwell. The man was accused of

176

attempted robbery, and convicted on the purely circumstantial but very damning evidence; he received a year in prison.

It was fingerprinting that revolutionised crime-fighting; but other discoveries were of equal importance. I have already mentioned the case of the sex murderer Tessnov, who was convicted when stains on his clothes were proved to be of human blood. The story of how this came about is almost as interesting as the story of fingerprints, although it will have to be dealt with more briefly. When blood is left exposed to the air, it slowly separates into two parts: a colourless liquid known as serum, and a thick, brown substance, which consists of blood cells. The serum part of the blood has amazing properties. If, for example, a human being is bitten by a snake, the serum immediately proceeds to develop the chemicals necessary to neutralise the poison; and if the dose of poison is not too great, it will be destroyed by this defence system of the body. In the 1890s, a doctor named von Behring took one of the greatest strides forward in the history of medicine when he discovered that if horses are injected with dead diphtheria germs, their serum can be injected into children suffering from diphtheria, and will destroy the germs. Snake-bite serum obviously works on the same principle.

Blood serum can be made to develop defensive properties against many other substances besides diphtheria germs and snake venom: against quite harmless substances like milk, egg-white and other kinds of blood. In these cases, the serum of the blood attacks the protein in the alien substance and causes it to turn into a harmless, insoluble substance. In 1900, Paul Uhlenhuth obtained serum from rabbits that had been injected with egg-white. If he then took a tiny drop of egg-white, and introduced it into a test tube of the clear serum, the serum immediately turned milky. So obviously, if a murder case ever hinged on whether a certain stain on a man's clothes was egg-white or sperm, it could be tested easily and quickly. For it did not seem to matter how old a stain was; the serum would react just as definitely. Moreover, serum made by injecting goat's milk would not turn cloudy if cow's milk was introduced into it;

and conversely, serum made from cow's milk would not react to goat's milk.

The next step was obvious. If serum was made by injecting rabbits with human blood, it would react by precipitating the protein of human blood, but not of animal blood. So testing a bloodstain became very simple. The bloodstain was left in salty water to dissolve the blood, then a drop of this salty water was poured into serum that reacted to human blood. If the bloodstain was animal blood, the serum remained clear; if it was human, it immediately darkened.

The case that gave wide publicity to the new method of detecting human bloodstains took place in Berlin in 1904. On 11th June of that year, a boatman on the River Spree fished a paper parcel out of the river, and found in it the headless torso of a young girl, still clad in petticoat and child's bloomers. Medical examination quickly revealed that the child had been raped. She was soon identified as nine-year-old Lucie Berlin, who lived at 130 Ackerstrasse, a gloomy lodging house for slum families. Lucie had last been seen at about 1 o'clock on 9th June, when she had asked for the key to the lavatory, which was up two flights of stairs – it was kept locked for the use of tenants only. But it seemed she had never reached the lavatory. By evening, her parents decided to notify the police. The problem was that Lucie had been repeatedly warned never to go off with strange men; child rape was fairly frequent. This made the police suspect that she had never left the house, even though neighbours spoke of seeing her walk off with a man wearing a straw hat. A prostitute who lived on the floor above Lucie's parents was among those questioned, but it was obvious that she knew nothing of the murder, for she had just returned from three days in jail for insulting a client. Her name was Johanna Liebetruth; the man in the room with her identified himself as Theodore Berger, of another address. But the police began to wonder about Berger when it was discovered that he actually lived with Johanna as her pimp. He had been avoiding marrying her for eighteen years, but now proposed to do so very shortly. Why? And on the morning the body was discovered in the river, a man fitting Berger's description was seen near the river with a rectangular parcel.

Lucie Berlin's head and arms had now been found in the river, and Berger was taken to see them. But he persisted in denying that he knew anything about her death. Johanna was questioned for hours until she finally told an interesting story. She had returned from jail on the morning of the 11th and heard about Lucie's disappearance. She noticed that a certain wicker suitcase was missing, and became convinced that Berger had slept with another woman. Berger finally admitted that he had, and that he had given her the suitcase because he had no money to pay her. This story struck Johanna as likely enough. When Berger wanted sex, 'he was like a bull'. He might well have taken a woman back to his room, driven by the need for sex, and then admitted that he had no money afterwards. Johanna was furious nevertheless – and it was at this point that Berger placated her with the promise of marriage.

When Berger was asked if he knew the suitcase, he quickly denied it. This was odd; he had been with Johanna for eighteen years; he *must* have seen it. It looked as if the suitcase was the clue that they were still seeking. If there had been blood in the apartment, it had been scrubbed away immediately after the murder.

An alert was put out for the wicker suitcase. And on 27th June, it turned up; a bargeman who never read newspapers had found it, and he knew nothing of its value until his aunt mentioned it in a conversation about the murder.

The suitcase was the evidence they needed. Johanna definitely identified it as hers. And stains inside it were proved to be of human blood. What had happened was pieced together at the trial. Lucie Berlin knew Theodore Berger well and called him 'uncle'. Berger was occasionally in the apartment of Lucie's parents, and Lucie sometimes came into Johanna's. Johanna mentioned in the course of conversation that on the day before she went into jail, Lucie had been playing with Berger's dog on the floor of the kitchen, and at one point had lain on her back with her legs up in the air. Johanna had noticed that they were very full and shapely legs for a girl of nine. Berger had no doubt

179

made the same observation. Two days later, deprived of the sex that he needed very frequently, he noticed Lucie on her way upstairs to the lavatory. There was also an old lady, who was walking downstairs, and she recollected Berger standing and staring at her until she went out of sight. Berger invited Lucie into the room; she knew him and trusted him. But when he began to caress her, she became alarmed and struggled. Berger seized her by the throat, choking off her scream, and assaulted her. Later, he carefully dismembered the body on newspapers, and wrapped up the parts, which he took down to the river in the early morning.

Berger was still protesting his innocence when he was executed.

The ability to distinguish human from animal blood was a great advance; another followed almost immediately. Not only would the serum distinguish between the blood of a man and the blood of a sheep; it would also distinguish between various types of human blood. Something of the sort had been guessed by Dr Theodor Billroth thirty years before, when he tried giving blood transfusions; 146 people out of 263 died, and Billroth reasoned that this must be because all human blood is not exactly alike. A great deal of investigation finally revealed that blood seems to have three distinct types or groups, which were labelled A, B and O, and that there is a 'typeless' group, called AB

One of the first important criminal investigations to make use of this new discovery took place in the north German industrial town of Gladbeck in 1928, and it concerned a strange sex crime. In the early hours of 23rd March, cries were heard from in front of 11 Schultenstrasse, and a few hours later a nineteen-year-old youth, Helmuth Daube, was found dying in his own blood. His throat had been cut, and for a few hours, a theory of suicide was held, until a detective pointed out that the razor or knife was missing, and that the youth's genitals had been cut off. Daube lived in the house near which he was found, and the police had little difficulty finding the youth with whom he had spent the previous evening, Karl Hussmann, a year older than Daube. Hussmann was hurried to the scene of the crime, and a police officer noticed that his shoes were soaked, as if they had been washed, and were also bloodstained. Certain of Hussmann's clothes were also found to be bloodstained. His story to account for the stains on the shoes was that he had trapped a cat that had been chasing birds, and had killed it. Later, he also insisted that he had come across a frog on his way home – after saying goodnight to Daube in front of the latter's house – and had torn it to pieces.

Research into his background revealed that he was a homosexual with strong sadistic tendencies. He had met Daube two years before. Daube was passive, feminine, rather dreamy; Hussmann was dominant and given to violence. It seems likely that he first forced his homosexual attentions on Daube on a school hiking expedition. When Daube fell in love with a girl, Hussmann was furiously jealous, but the affair broke up, and the old relation between Daube and Hussmann was resumed. But Daube wanted to break away. Schoolfriends testified to seeing Hussmann hurting Daube, once by bending back his finger to force Daube to sit on his knee. The night before the murder, a group of students had met to discuss another hiking party, and Daube had indicated that he did not mean to go. What had then happened was fairly clear. Hussmann had tried to force his will on Daube; the thought that the youth whom he regarded as his property was about to break with him excited a murderous jealousy. As Daube turned away from saying goodnight, Hussmann seized him from behind and cut his throat. He then emasculated him. The back of Daube's head had struck Hussmann's nose, causing a nosebleed, but this did not become apparent until later.

Preliminary tests revealed that the blood on the shoes and coat was human blood, not from a frog or cat. Hussmann was unconcerned; he said he had had a nosebleed, and that they could not prove otherwise. The detective in charge of the case was inclined to be overawed by Hussmann, whom he regarded as being socially superior to himself.

A week after the murder, the clothes were sent to Viktor Müller-Hesse, in charge of the Forensic Laboratory at Bonn University. Although the earlier examination had destroyed many of the bloodstains, Müller-Hesse had no difficulty in proving that the bloodstains on Hussmann's jacket were Type O – Hussman's own type – while those on the shoes were of Type A – Daube's group.

The evidence was complete; it should have hanged Hussmann. But the jury were not quite convinced by all this talk of blood groups. They ended by deciding that although they were by no means convinced of Hussmann's innocence, they were not absolutely certain of his guilt. Hussmann was acquitted. Even so, the case drew universal attention to the importance of blood groups in criminal investigation.[1]

It is true that if Hussmann and Daube had belonged to the same blood group, the case would never have reached court. It is only as recently as 1966 that two young biologists in England, Margaret Pereira and Brian Culliford, have discovered what might be termed 'the blood fingerprint' – that every individual's blood is as unique in character as their fingertips. The protein in blood has characteristics that are never the same in any two individuals. In the future, a spot of blood at the scene of a crime will be as important as a fingerprint. This work was a development of work done on blood groups by Robin Coomb of Cambridge and Barbara Dodd of London University, whose methods of finding the blood group of an old bloodstain were successful on the vest worn by King Charles I at his execution. In the future, a spot of blood the size of a pinhead will be able to prove innocence or guilt.

It is tempting to speculate how many of the great mysteries of the past might have been solved if the police had been able to use modern methods. The Ripper murders would fairly certainly remain unsolved; in the few parallel modern cases I can think of (I shall speak of them in the next chapter) the murderer has either remained uncaught, or was caught by chance. But some of the domestic mysteries – the Bravo case, for example – would almost certainly not remain mysteries; a fingerprint on a bottle would have been enough. One of the great Victorian

[1] I am indebted to Jürgen Thorwald's *Crime and Science* (1966) for providing details of the Hussmann and Lucie Berlin cases.

causes célèbres, the Pook case, would have been solved within hours if there had been tests for human blood in 1871. The victim, a servant girl named Jane Clouson, was found lying in a lovers' lane at Eltham, south London, her face and head horribly lacerated. She died shortly afterwards without speaking. The constable found a lathing hammer near the scene of the crime – a cross between a hammer and a chopper; this had made more than a dozen wounds, through one of which the girl's brain was protruding. It was discovered that she was two months pregnant. The young man who was believed to be responsible was Edmund Pook, the son of a Greenwich printer, in whose house Jane Clouson had been a servant for two years; shortly before her seventeenth birthday, the girl had been dismissed through the agency of Pook's mother, who felt the girl was too familiar with her son.

Edmund Pook proved to be a spoiled, swaggering, altogether unpleasant young man. He flatly denied any intimacy with Jane Clouson, and said she was dirty. But he was unable to explain bloodstains on the cuff of his shirt, or on his clothes.

Fifty years later, it would have been a simple matter to test his later assertion that the blood was his own – he was subject to epileptic fits and nosebleeds. It is possible, of course, that his blood and Jane Clouson's were of the same group; but then, he certainly left fingerprints on the hammer. As it was, all the evidence was against Pook. The shopkeeper from whom he bought the hammer identified him. He had no alibi for the evening of the crime. Jane Clouson had told her landlady that she was going out to meet 'her Edmund' shortly before the murder, and she told a cousin at length of how Edmund wanted her to run away with him and marry him secretly, and then promise not to communicate with relatives or friends for several months. The same cousin also stated that Jane had received a letter, which she immediately burnt, after telling her cousin that she meant to meet Edmund shortly. It seems fairly plain that the letter contained instructions to burn it. This also explains why, when the police inspector asked him if he had written Jane a letter, Edmund told him arrogantly that if he thought so, he had better produce the letter and prove it was in his handwriting

He knew it had been burned, and it was no doubt the first question he asked the girl when he met her.

Pook was acquitted, largely because so much confusion surrounded the case, and his solicitor, Henry Pook (no relative), managed to throw up even more dust. Every possible contradiction of witnesses was endlessly pursued, and evidence of police incompetency was made to sound at least as shocking as the crime itself. When the prosecution pointed out that a hair that matched Jane Clouson's was found on Edmund Pook's trousers, his solicitor leapt to his feet to say that if that was all the evidence they could present, then the case against Edmund was hanging by a single hair. Today, it would be possible to state definitely whether the hair belonged to Jane Clouson or not. And there are few writers on the case who feel any doubt about it.

I am inclined to doubt whether modern forensic methods would throw any light on the classic American murder mystery, the Lizzie Borden case. However, modern research has now thrown so much light on the case that it may be regarded as solved.

At 11.15, on the morning of 4th August 1892 – the hottest day of the year – Lizzie Borden called the maid Bridget Sullivan and told her that someone had killed her father. The seventy-year-old banker was found on the divan in the parlour, his face unrecognisable; someone had struck him several blows with a hatchet. Borden's second wife, Abby, was believed to be out visiting a sick friend – according to Lizzie – but she was later found upstairs in the guest room, lying face downwards. She had also been killed with blows from a hatchet – much heavier, more savage blows than those that had killed Andrew Borden. Lizzie's story was that she had been out in the barn, and had heard a cry from the house; she rushed back to find her father dead.

It soon became clear that Lizzie had much to hide. Her mother had died when she was two; two years later her father remarried; Abby Gray was six years his junior, twenty-two years older than Lizzie's sister Emma. Two days before the murder, Lizzie had tried to buy prussic acid.[1] Lizzie's father and stepmother had been experiencing stomach pains for some time before the murder. Lizzie hated her stepmother.

Moreover, medical evidence proved that Abby Borden had died shortly after 9 am, while her husband was not killed until about two hours later. It was just within the bounds of possibility that an unknown assassin had entered the house and murdered the couple – but not that he had remained concealed for two hours, in a small house in which there were two women. (Lizzie's sister was away staying with friends.)

Lizzie was arrested and tried. The evidence against her was purely circumstantial; the prosecution merely attempted to demonstrate that she was the likeliest person to have committed the murders. But she was a respectable girl of unblemished reputation, and the jury found her not guilty. She lived on until 1927.[2] During her lifetime it was impossible for writers to speculate about whether she killed her father and stepmother. But after her death, Edmund Pearson lost no time in publishing his opinion that she was the killer. (Even during her lifetime, the local newspaper in Fall River, Massachusetts, printed sarcastic articles on the anniversary of the murder – one of which concluded that the Bordens had not been murdered at all, but had died of the heat.) His *Trial of Lizzie Borden* in the Great American Trial series came out in 1937, and the book is dedicated to the district attorney who built up the case against Lizzie Borden. In 1959, a new piece of evidence turned up. In a book called *Murder and Mutiny*, published in 1959, E R Snow tells how he received a letter from an elderly gentleman named Thomas Owens, who had listened to a broadcast about the Borden case by Snow. Owens had a strange story to tell. In 1896, four years after the murder, Lizzie Borden went into the art gallery and shop of Tilden-Thurber in Providence, Rhode Island, and when she left, the assistant found that two expensive paintings on porcelain were missing. The following February, a lady went into the shop with one of the two

---

[1] But was not successful – as was mistakenly asserted in the *Encyclopedia of Murder*. Mrs. Borden's age was also mis-stated there.
[2] Not 1944, as is stated in the *Encyclopedia of Murder*.

paintings, and asked if a crack could be repaired. The manager was told, and he asked the lady where she had obtained the painting. 'From Miss Lizzie Borden of Fall River.' As a result of this, a headline 'Lizzie Again' appeared in the *Providence Journal*, which stated that a warrant for her arrest had been issued for the theft of two paintings. What had happened, said Owens, was that the owners of the gallery had put a proposition to Lizzie: sign a confession to the murders, or we prosecute. Lizzie refused, and the item was published in the newspaper. This caused Lizzie to change her mind. After promises that the confession would not be used, Lizzie typed on a sheet of paper: 'Unfair means force my signature here admitting the act of August 4, 1892, as mine alone, Lizbeth A Borden.' The store decided to have the document photographed in case of accident, and Owens was asked to do it. He did; but he also made a second copy – or, he said, decided that the first copy was indistinct, and made another one for the store, without mentioning that he had the other. As the four principals in the episode died – there were two other men besides the store owners – he expected it to be publicised. And now, Owens was willing to sell the photograph of Lizzie's confessions for one hundred dollars. Snow persuaded him to take fifty, and printed the story in his book.

Another crime writer, Edward Radin, decided to look into the matter, and he soon established that Snow had been the victim of a swindler. It was Lizzie's signature, and the type face was that of a machine of the period, but the signature had been traced from Lizzie's will. It would be interesting to know whether Mr Snow demanded his fifty dollars back.

But obviously, the first part of the story was true. Lizzie *had* stolen the paintings, and the item really appeared in the *Providence Journal* in February 1897. Lizzie was a kleptomaniac. Although she had plenty of money (she left over a million dollars), she was a compulsive stealer. Oddly enough, she was also capable of great generosity.

Radin's book *Lizzie Borden, The Untold Story* asserts that Lizzie was innocent. The killer was Bridget Sullivan, the servant girl. It is known that Bridget was feeling ill on the morning of 4th August; yet Mrs Borden had her cleaning all the outside windows at 7.30 in the morning. Later that morning, Bridget vomited. Certainly, she had a motive of sorts – sheer resentment at her employer. Radin tells how he was completely convinced by Pearson's view of the case until he read the actual trial reports for himself and discovered that Pearson had suppressed many pieces of evidence in Lizzie's favour.

In 1964, Gerald Gross edited a volume of selections from Edmund Pearson's articles on murder, and wrote a postscript to Pearson's 'final word' on the Borden case. Gross says, very fairly, that Radin has distorted the evidence for Lizzie's innocence as carefully as Pearson distorted that for her guilt, and he points out that Pearson had to do a great deal of omitting anyway, to pack the trial into one fair-sized volume. But Gross's theory is that Lizzie killed her parents aided and abetted by Bridget. There is a persistent story that Bridget returned to Ireland after the trial, with a great deal of money given to her by Lizzie. Radin points out, quite correctly, that Bridget could certainly not be said to have testified in Lizzie's favour at the trial; on the contrary, most of her evidence told against her employer. If, however, she was an accomplice – or an accessory after the fact – perhaps to helping Lizzie conceal the murder weapon or the bloodstained dress (which Lizzie burnt) – then Lizzie would certainly have a motive for giving her money.

In 1967 there appeared in America Victoria Lincoln's *A Private Disgrace*. When Foster Damon – another expert on the Borden case – sent me a copy, he enclosed a card which said: 'I think this is the final word on Lizzie.' I am inclined to think he is right.

Victoria Lincoln was born in Fall River, so her insight into the town is obviously authentic. She was able to uncover some facts that suddenly make the whole case quite clear. There is only one point in Miss Lincoln's account that might be described as 'speculation'; from accounts of the periodic fainting illness that Lizzie suffered from, she arrives at the conclusion that Lizzie suffered from epilepsy of the temporal lobe of the brain. Psychomotor epilepsy is distinguished by seizures of automatic activity. Miss Lincoln cites a case from a medical textbook in which a man woke from a seizure, to find that the boss had raised his salary, impressed by the lucid and forceful way in which the man had asked for a raise. Lizzie undoubtedly had strange attacks about four times a year, always at the time of her menstrual period. The evidence about these attacks points to psychomotor epilepsy. And Lizzie was menstruating at the time of the murders.

But Miss Lincoln's theory is not an attempt to prove that Lizzie committed the murders in a trance-like state. She intended to kill her stepmother – but by poison. She hated her and was violently jealous of her. A year before the murders, her stepmother's room had been broken into and robbed when Lizzie was in the house. The thief was supposed to have flitted in silently, without alerting Lizzie, Emma and the maid Bridget, broken into the room, taken money and jewellery, and flitted out via the cellar door. Andrew Borden soon asked the police to drop the investigation. He had a fairly shrewd idea of the identity of the thief.

Lizzie felt she had reason for hating her stepmother. First of all, it was a quarrel about a house. Mrs Borden's sister had not married so well, and she lived in half a house, the other half of which belonged to her mother. Her mother wanted to sell, but could hardly turn her own daughter out. So Andrew Borden came to the rescue, and quietly bought the whole house, giving half to the sister, and half to his own wife Abby. He did this with great secrecy, knowing the feelings of his children about their stepmother and her family, but the news leaked. Lizzie was furious. She told her father that charity should begin at home. She ceased to call Abby 'mother', and from then on, addressed her – when she had to – as Mrs Borden. Andrew Borden tried to restore peace in the home by giving Lizzie and her sister another house, which had belonged to their grandfather. Lizzie was placated; but she never forgave her stepmother, and continued to address her as 'Mrs Borden' after twenty-three years of calling her 'mother'.

The trouble that led directly to the murder was an identical situation, which took place five years later – just before the murder. Uncle John Vinnicum Morse was a mid-westerner, and he decided that he would like to move closer to his brother-in-law's home (he was the brother of Borden's first wife). Borden owned a farm at nearby Swansea, and Morse asked if he could rent it. Borden said yes – and decided to do again what he had already done over the business of his sister-in-law's house – to transfer the farm to his wife's name. Miss Lincoln dug up this curious transaction, the immediate motive of the murder; Pearson and the other writers on the case were unaware of it. Lizzie already disliked Uncle John because he had aided and abetted her father in the previous house transaction. So now he moved into their house again as a guest, she felt distinctly edgy. Miss Lincoln does not produce a convincing explanation why Borden decided to transfer the farm to Abby; perhaps he wanted to give her a present – he had recently bought back the other house from his daughters for two thousand more than its value, thus making them a present of a thousand dollars each. But Borden was seventy; no doubt he wanted to leave his wife well provided for in the event of his death. This was also why Lizzie was so bitterly opposed to these property deals. And it did not take long for the news about the Swansea property to leak back to her. This is when she started trying to buy poison. And although she was unsuccessful in her attempts to buy prussic acid ('for cleaning a fur'), she presumably bought *something*, for that evening Mr and Mrs Borden were very sick indeed. Lizzie said she had been sick too, but we have only her word for this.

There was another factor that has been largely ignored by Pearson and Radin. Lizzie had a deep love of animals, and she owned some pigeons, which lived in the barn roost. Borden kept everything locked up – he was capable of obsessive meanness – and when the barn was broken into twice by youths who wanted pigeon pie for supper, he chopped off the heads of all the pigeons with a hatchet. It was not exactly unkindness; in those days, America was still close to the pioneers, and most people killed their own chickens and butchered their own hogs. But he failed to calculate the effect on Lizzie.

This, in summary, is the new evidence dug up by Victoria Lincoln, and it certainly makes the case in every way more straightforward. The transfer of the deeds on the Swansea property was to take place on the day of the murder. Borden had thought up a stratagem to do this without arousing Lizzie's suspicions – a carriage would be sent to the door, and a note requesting that Mrs Borden visit a sick neighbour. The note arrived – or so Miss Lincoln believes – but by then, Mrs Borden was already dead, or about to die. She was working in the guest room, on all fours, when Lizzie came in behind her with the hatchet, and sliced into her skull with blow after blow. At this point, Miss Lincoln embarks on a speculation that I find difficult to accept. John Morse had left the house much earlier. He had no alibi for the time of the first murder, but an extremely detailed one for the second. Miss Lincoln believes that Morse went along to the house just to make sure that all went according to plan – after all, the affair of the farm was of immediate interest to him. He watched the boy deliver the note, and observed Lizzie's very abrupt manner as she took it, followed by her slamming of the door. Obviously, she was having one of her queer spells. Ever since Morse had been in the Bordens' house, there had been a brooding tension, and Mrs Borden probably suspected Lizzie of wanting to poison her. So Morse listened with more than usual attention to what followed, and rightly interpreted the heavy thud from the upstairs room – its window was wide open on the hot August morning – followed by a succession of squelching noises. Probably Mrs Borden groaned the first time – Bridget was out at the other side of the house cleaning windows, so she would not hear. And Morse, realising what had happened, knew that an uncle from the mid-west would be a far more likely suspect for a murder than the respectable daughter of the house. So he hurried away and started establishing an alibi.

This *could* have happened, but there is no evidence that it did. All that seems moderately certain is that, with the stifling heat of the August morning, and the irritation of her menstrual period, Lizzie had one of her queer spells, and decided that she could not stand her stepmother a moment longer. Miss Lincoln may well be right; it may have been committed in a dream-like state, and the dream may have involved the headless pigeons.

Miss Lincoln could be wrong in her diagnosis of psychomotor epilepsy; but it is hard to doubt that all kinds of factors – the knowledge of another property deal, her hatred of her stepmother and determination to kill her, the heat, menstrual irritation – suddenly decided her to use violence. Earlier writers on the case were not aware of just *how much* violence and tension there was in the air in the Borden house in the weeks before the murder; it was a storm that had to break. Borden broke his usual habit of reticence to tell a business associate that he was having a lot of trouble at home at the moment.

What Lizzie did about her bloodstained dress after this first murder is rather a mystery. Presumably she took it off. At 10.45, Andrew Borden arrived home unexpectedly, no doubt puzzled by his wife's non-appearance at the bank. His daughter was on the point of leaving the house – to establish an alibi. The doors were locked – as usual – and Bridget had to let him in. Lizzie was heard to give a strange laugh as her father came in. She told her father that Mrs Borden had been called away to see a sick neighbour. Possibly Andrew Borden accepted this story; possibly he supposed Mrs Borden and Uncle John were now signing papers that he had already signed. At all events, he went into the sitting room and fell asleep. Bridget Sullivan testified that he was carrying 'something like a book'. Miss Lincoln is inclined to believe that this 'something' wrapped in white paper was the deeds to the Swansea property, and the agreement to transfer it. Lizzie was later seen burning something in the kitchen stove.

What happened next? Miss Lincoln believes that Lizzie genuinely loved her father, but that seeing him asleep was tempted to spare him the horror of seeing his wife's body, and knowing that Lizzie was the killer. (For he *would* have known, just as he knew that Lizzie was the invisible thief of a year earlier.) Undoubtedly, he loved her, and he would cease to do so when the body was discovered. And so, according to Miss Lincoln, she regretfully raised the hatchet. . . .

I find this hard to accept. Andrew Borden was killed with nine blows, one of which sliced down through his eye. Lizzie must have gone back upstairs to change her dress before the murder – unless she disposed of two bloodstained dresses – and then gone to get the hatchet from the basement. (It is true that she may have kept the dress in the basement too.) Two days before, her father had suffered from the same serious stomach complaint as her stepmother. She had made up her mind to kill him too. She did it less violently than in the case of her stepmother – nine blows instead of seventeen – but unflinchingly. Then she went to the barn and washed the hatchet, smashed off its bloodstained handle in a vice – which she burnt – and rubbed the blade in ashes. She removed the dress and folded it into a bundle. Or she may have simply hung it in her closet among her other dresses, as Miss Lincoln suggests, simply putting it inside another. By the time Bridget came in from cleaning the windows, and went to her room to lie down for a moment, Lizzie had changed and was ready to give the alarm.

There is some evidence for the epilepsy theory. Lizzie's mother suffered from severe migraines and sudden violent seizures of unmotivated rage. The evening before the murder, Lizzie called on a friend, Alice Russell, and said: 'I'm afraid someone will do something. I don't know but what someone will do something.' The heat wave had started the day before; she was experiencing the sense of brooding depression that Dostoievsky has described as preceding epileptic fits. 'I feel depressed,' she told Miss Russell, 'I feel as if something was hanging over me that I can't shake off.' Only that morning there had been a strange scene; her stepmother had approached a Doctor Bowen who lived opposite, and told him that her husband had received a letter threatening to poison him, and that they had been sick all the previous night. Doctor Bowen finally agreed to come to the house – and was met by a furious Andrew Borden, who told him to mind his own business and go away. And meanwhile the heat was tremendous, oppressive – it was one of the hottest days recorded in Fall River in living memory – and Lizzie's abdomen was aching in a way that indicated the approach of a menstrual period. . . . She may well have foreboding.

No, forensic medicine would have made no difference to the Borden case. It might have established blood on the blade of the ash-coated hatchet, and drawn the net of circumstantial evidence a little tighter. And if someone had had Miss Lincoln's shrewdness, the forensic laboratories might have examined the *inside* of all Lizzie Borden's dresses for bloodstains that proved that a bloodstained dress had been hung up inside one of them. For what Lizzie did with the bloodstained dress between the day of the murder – Thursday – and Sunday morning, when she burnt it, is the chief unsolved mystery of the case. Emma and Alice Russell walked into the kitchen, and interrupted Lizzie, who was holding the Bedford cord dress. 'I'm going to burn this old thing,' said Lizzie. 'It's all covered up with paint.' Alice and Emma must have exchanged a horrified glance. It was their moment of decision. If they snatched it from Lizzie, or casually asked to look at it, it would undoubtedly send Lizzie to the scaffold. But what was the point? The Bordens were dead, and both Emma and her friend Alice knew about Lizzie's 'queer spells'. Alice merely said: 'I wouldn't let anyone see you doing that if I were you,' and then conveniently forgot the incident for four months. When Alice was questioned about Lizzie's dresses the next day, she went in to Lizzie and told her she really ought not to have burnt the dress. Lizzie simulated concern, and said: 'Why did you let me do it?' Quite.

Perhaps I might be forgiven for dwelling on the Borden case with a certain nostalgia. I have never visited Fall River, but I have spent some time in nearby Providence, with its clapboard houses, which look exactly like the photograph of the Borden house, and its streets ankle deep in leaves in the autumn. The old part of the town, around Brown University, is full of memories of H P Lovecraft and his horror stories, and there is something timeless about it; there may be television aerials, but apart from that, you feel that the place is exactly as it was in the 1890s. You can still find parts of the sea-front that are straight out of *The Shadow Over Innmouth*. But I think it is safe to say that crimes like the Borden mystery are a thing of the past; not because emotional stepdaughters will cease to take choppers to their parents, but because when they do, the crime will be solved within hours. Fall River was a sleepy, quiet community, in which everyone knew everyone else. Uncle John Morse did not come home and say reproachfully: 'Lizzie, why did you do it?' – as he obviously knew she had. Emma and Alice did not say: 'Could I see that dress a moment?' Murder or no murder, one's upbringing made such an approach impossible. It would simply not have been tactful. Nowadays, the police would be grilling Lizzie at the station within hours, while a squad of detectives went over the house with the 'murder bag', examining the soles of Lizzie's shoes for samples of dust from the barn, wondering about the burnt papers in the kitchen stove, noting the minute splinter of bloodstained wood clinging to the inside of the vice. . . . Lizzie would not go to the gas chamber, of course. A good psychiatrist would soon get the secret of the 'queer spells' from her, or from Emma; the charge would be reduced to one of second degree murder; or the case might not even come to trial. Lizzie would vanish into the violent ward of the Providence mental institution.

A few miles from where I now live in Cornwall, a crime very similar to the Borden murder took place in 1953. No one will ever write books about it because it was solved within hours. It has only one interesting aspect – the psychological aspect – which makes it a convenient bridge to the last chapter of this book.

On the evening of 7th November 1953, the maid at Carrick-owl, Porthpean, near St Austell, came back home and went to bed without noticing anything unusual in the kitchen. As she went in, she noticed the car belonging to her employer, Mrs Giffard, being driven away. Obviously, their twenty-six-year-old son Miles was on his way somewhere, perhaps to a party. The next morning, she woke up and was surprised by the silence in the house. The place was empty. And in the garage there were heavy bloodstains. She sent for the police. Superintendent Ken Julian followed a trail of blood across the back garden, through a copse, to the edge of the cliff. Lying on the rocks, two hundred feet below, lay the body of Giffard, with a wheelbarrow beside him. There was no sign of Mrs Giffard – she was found later in the day, when the tide washed her in. Examination of the bodies and the scene of the crime by the Cornish pathologist, Dr Denis Hocking, left no doubt what had happened. Giffard – who was a solicitor and the local Clerk of the Court – had been struck down in the garage with something heavy, probably an iron bar. He had seen the blow coming and raised his hand to defend himself. Mrs Giffard had been struck down in the kitchen. The murderer had wheeled them both to the cliff edge, pausing to rifle Charles Giffard's pockets, and thrown them over. Mrs Giffard had been alive when thrown over; the impact on the rocks had killed her.

The only suspect was their son Miles. The only puzzling thing was that he had made no attempt to cover up his trail. This could only be explained by the assumption that the murders had been committed when his balance of mind was disturbed. An examination of Giffard's case history made it clear that this was the only explanation. He had always been a difficult child, lying, stealing and subject to nightmares. A lady psychiatrist who had treated him during his teens believed that the trouble may have started when a sadistic nurse beat him and shut him in a dark cupboard as a baby. At his public school – Rugby – Giffard was impossible. He lied for no reason at all, wet the bed and chewed holes in the bedsheets. His father was having a mental breakdown at the same time, so the home background was hardly as secure as it might have been. His parents were asked to remove him; they sent him to Blundell's, but he was no better there. Oddly enough, when called into the Navy to do his National Service, there was an immediate improvement; he became tidy, well-adjusted and responsible. But back home he drank too much, quarrelled with his father – who was disliked in the area because his manner was overbearing – and stole money. When he had a legacy of five hundred pounds, he went to London and spent it within weeks. The only thing he seemed to be good at was sport; he was chosen to play cricket for Cornwall. He spent the summer of 1953 in London, drinking too much and occasionally bouncing cheques. He also met a girl, Gabrielle Vallance – seven years his junior – and decided he

195

wanted to marry her. At the end of the summer, moneyless, he hitch-hiked back home. His father was furious – no doubt he had had to make good the dishonoured cheques – and told Miles he could stay at home and work in the office. He was given a daily allowance for beer and cigarettes. He wrote Gabrielle long letters, and in one of them told her that he had just had a serious row with his father – 'he is right, as usual' – and that 'short of doing him in, I can see no future . . . at all'. He asked his father if he could borrow his car to go and see Gabrielle – he was jealous of a sixteen-year-old schoolboy she knew – and received an angry refusal.

On the Friday of the murder, his parents went out all afternoon, and he sat at home reading a morbid murder story about a soldier who murders his unfaithful wife. He had a headache and took four aspirins, then made the mistake of drinking half a bottle of whisky on top of them. By five-thirty he had already decided to kill his father – he rang Gabrielle and told her he expected to come to London that evening. His parents arrived home – in separate cars – simultaneously. (If they had not gone out in two cars, he would probably have simply taken one and driven to London.) It was 7.30. He went out to the garage, spoke to his mother, and then stood watching his father as he bent over the engine of his mother's car, looking for some minor fault. When his mother was in the house, Miles raised the iron bar that he had pulled up from the garden, and hit him. It took only a few seconds to batter him unconscious. Then he went to the kitchen, and struck his mother on the back of the head several times. Now, with both parents unconscious, he rang Gabrielle to tell her he would definitely be coming to London. On returning to the garage, he found his father coming round. Several more blows shattered his skull. Giffard then put his mother in the wheelbarrow, took her to the point, and threw her over. He did the same with his father, pausing to empty his pockets. He then cleaned up the bloodstains in the house, and took all the jewellery he could find in his mother's room. Outside Okehampton, he paused to change into a suit he had thrown into the car before driving off. He stopped again at Fenny Bridges to throw his bloodstained clothes and the iron pipe into the stream there, then picked up two hitch-hikers, and drove on to London. They noticed nothing strange about him. 'He seemed a decent type,' said one of them later. In London, he slept for three hours in the car, close to Gabrielle's house in Tite Street, and knocked on her door – rather to the disgust of her parents – at 8 am. Later that morning, he sold his mother's jewellery for fifty pounds. In the afternoon, he took Gabrielle and her mother to the cinema to see Chaplin's *Limelight*. Afterwards, he and Gabrielle went on a round of pubs. During the course of this pub-crawl, he asked her to marry him, and then told her he had killed his parents. She said later that she thought he was joking – although he was still wearing the bloodstained tie he had worn twenty-four hours earlier. When they arrived back home in a taxi, the police were waiting for them.

Nothing is more plain than that Giffard was not thinking ahead when he committed the murder. He had obviously planned it at 5.30, two hours before his parents returned home, when he rang Gabrielle to tell her to expect him in London. But how could he expect to escape? He must have known that the bodies would be discovered in a matter of hours, and that he was the only possible suspect. If he had really wanted to avoid detection, he would have tried to establish an alibi, perhaps going out to the pub immediately after the murders, burning his bloodstained clothes first. Throwing the bodies over the cliff argues that he may have hoped they would be carried out to sea, but in that case, why did he not clean up all the bloodstains?

The defence argued very reasonably that he was obviously not sane, that he had a long history of mental disturbance, and that a psychiatrist had told Charles Giffard years earlier: 'The doors are closing on his sanity.' The same psychiatrist had told Giffard that his son was suffering from a form of schizophrenia that sometimes afflicts young persons, and that is more or less incurable. But the jury of Cornish farmers and tradesmen were suspicious of psychiatric jargon. Giffard threw away his only chance of escape when he decided not to appear in the box. He might at least have given the impression of a troubled human being, and allowed the court some slight insight into what sort of a person he was and why he did it. The judge commented with obvious annoyance on this decision not to stand in the witness box, and his summary was very much against Giffard. He was sentenced to death.

Dr Hocking is of the opinion that if the case had taken place ten years later, Giffard would have been found guilty but insane, and sent to Broadmoor; understanding of mental illness had grown in ten years. A London jury would certainly have found him insane.

I find the most significant statement in the defence testimony the evidence that Giffard improved so markedly in the Navy, when he had no kind of responsibility – that is, no *freedom*. He was not called upon to think, as he had been at school; he was simply subjected to physical discipline. And he had never had any trouble with physical discipline – he was a good sportsman. The trouble with his home was that it combined permissiveness – he was an only child – with harshness. He was allowed to do what he liked most of the time, and then quite abruptly brought up with a jerk.

This question of freedom becomes the fundamental question of the most typical murders of the twentieth century. I believe that the basic thesis of Pamela Hansford Johnson's book *On Iniquity* is sound: murder should not be explained away in deterministic language. Millen Brand, in his interesting novel *Savage Sleep*, has pointed out that, even in the most violent psychotic, there is a small observer who is not insane, sitting in the corner of the mind and witnessing everything.

What must be understood is that our freedom is never very great. Gilbert Ryle's phrase 'the ghost in the machine' is, in a way, a highly appropriate description of man. This body of mine is a machine, over which I have a limited control. But like my car or my typewriter, it has rigid limitations that no amount of will-power can alter. But my body is not the only machine. My whole *personality* is a kind of Frankenstein monster that is not really 'me'. It has been built up by years of response to experience. I have pointed out elsewhere that in the few authenticated cases in which human babies have been stolen and brought up by animals, the child remains an animal for the rest of its life, even if it is rescued and brought back after a year or so.[1] From the earliest age, we learn to live, to act, to *be*, by watching and imitating other people. Just like the body, the personality is a shell that contains the living being. It is our link with the world, our telephone line to other people.

Miles Giffard showed a definite tendency to 'autism' when he was psychoanalysed in his early teens: withdrawal, indifference, total failure to establish a relation with the psychiatrist. A shy, nervous person, he had always been dominated by his father; his personality was passive, feminine. Personality is built up through habit. A child who is born into an aristocratic background becomes accustomed to giving orders to the servants, to being obeyed – a pattern that will later be repeated if he enters the Army. He feels he knows who he is, and in his relations with other people, he presents a 'united front'. Giffard never established this feeling; trapped in his personality, he was like a man sitting in a car he cannot drive. The confident boy who goes to an expensive public school is prepared to adopt a new role: the upper-crust English boy who will become a member of his country's ruling class one day. But in Giffard there was no foundation to receive these new layers. It was his father who was a member of the ruling class, the representative of the law, and this school was his father's agent, a disguised version of his father. It was not until he entered the Navy that he could establish a regular behaviour pattern into which he fitted easily and begin to create a personality with which to establish contact with the world. A few more years in the Navy would almost certainly have left him free of his basic anxieties, his feeling of being a nobody, a sort of ghost. But he left after his National Service, and was thrown back into the old, pointless life that acted as a solvent for his personality. He had no shell. And unfortunately, his only serious sexual involvement was with a girl much younger than himself, as irresponsible as he was. If he had been more of an 'intellectual', he might have rationalised his feelings of inadequacy by telling himself that

[1] The psychologist Bruno Bettelheim cites such a case in his study of autistic children, *The Empty Fortress*.

brilliant and sensitive people are always misfits; but he was sensitive without being brilliant; he had no outlet.

It can be seen that the talk at his trial of incurable schizophrenia and spontaneous hypo-glycaemia may have been completely beside the point. He was a snail without a shell; he was the sort of person who could look into a mirror and experience delusions that he wasn't there. His only link to the normal world was his desire to stay with Gabrielle and start his own life with her. With her, *he* was the father-figure, nearly eight years her senior. As soon as he got home, his father's glare reduced him to the cringing schoolboy. His father's greatest mistake was to keep him away from her. The murder was a frantic effort at self-assertion, an attempt to write off his old life and start afresh as a man in his own right. But did he not realise that the murders would destroy all chance of starting again? Not completely; the feeling of being a ghost, a nonentity, made it somehow unreal. There is a scene in O'Neill's *Hairy Ape* where the 'ape' goes berserk and batters at the faces of the businessmen walking down Broadway; they walk on, completely oblivious. Giffard felt like that about his father's world. It is hardly surprising that he struck the two hitch-hikers as completely normal; with the murder behind him, he *was* normal, for the first time in years.

The Giffard case is typical of the 'new age in murder' that started with Jack the Ripper. The most typical murders of the twentieth century are not 'murder for business' or even murder for pleasure; they are 'murder for freedom'.

Six: Chamber of Horrors

INEVITABLY, THIS CHAPTER on murder in the twentieth century will be one of the longest and most gruesome in the book. The pattern of twentieth-century murder is extremely complex. In previous centuries, a single murder case can give us the feeling of the whole age – Sawney Bean, Arden of Faversham, Catherine Hayes, Maria Marten, Lacenaire, Neill Cream. But there is no typical case of the twentieth century; all reflect different aspects of its chaos and complexity. Some of the most famous cases really belong to the previous age: Crippen, Smith (The Brides in the Bath case), Seddon (the poisoner who killed an old lady for the sake of her annuity of 65s a week),[1] Rouse, the burning-car murderer.

Of this latter, executed in the year of my birth, I have a story to tell. Sometime in the early autumn of 1930 my mother – who then worked in a hosiery factory in Leicester – made the acquaintance of a good-looking commercial traveller in his mid-thirties, who pressed her to go out with him. This was Alfred Arthur Rouse, who was not, as he told my mother, a widower. She agreed to see him next time he came to Leicester. But before that date, Rouse was arrested for murder – this was on 7th November. Since he received a skull injury in the First World War, Rouse had changed from a quiet teetotaller to a liar with an obsessive Casanova complex. After seducing more than eighty women, and fathering a flock of illegitimate children – several of whom he had to maintain – he decided to 'die' one day. His idea was to pick up a hitch-hiker of about the same

---

[1] Seddon was almost certainly guilty, but he was convicted on evidence that would not be regarded as adequate today. The only source of poison the prosecution could unearth was fly-papers.

build as himself, knock him unconscious, then burn him in his car, so that the body would be identified as his own. He did this on 6th November 1930; but he was seen by two rustics as he ran away from the scene of the murder. Their description of the running man led to a general alert for Rouse. He was arrested two days later. His story was that the fire was an accident, started by his companion; but circumstantial evidence was too strong, and he was sentenced to death. He was executed a few months before I was born; it is a disquieting thought that under slightly different circumstances Rouse might have become my father.

The first and most obvious thing about crime in the twentieth century is that there is so much more of it. We have no crime statistics for earlier centuries except the few I have been able to quote, but it is fairly clear that the *Lives of the Most Remarkable Criminals* and *Newgate Calendar* provide a representative cross section of crimes of the period, including so many minor crimes that it is hard to believe that many murder cases have gone unrecorded. If a panel of crime-writers tried to produce a yearly *Newgate Calendar* for modern America, it would run to about twenty thousand-page volumes; America has nearly ten thousand murders a year. With a population of nearly two hundred million, this means that about one person in every twenty thousand gets murdered. (In England, with one hundred and fifty murders a year and a population of about sixty million, this amounts to one person in every four hundred thousand.) The rape rate is more than twice this: and since this does not include men, this means that one girl in every nine thousand is raped in America per year. In the United Kingdom there are about five and a half thousand rapes a year.[1] This reveals the disturbing fact that although the English murder rate is one-twentieth of the American rate, our rape rate is approximately the same. If it is any comfort, the murder statistics in England have remained almost completely unchanged since 1900; in fact,

[1] It is true that the English figures are for 'sexual offences' – not necessarily rape; a large proportion are connected with homosexuality, offences against minors, etc.

they have shown a slight drop. The high rate of crime in America is largely due to poverty; nearly three-quarters of all murderers in America belong to the class of 'socially dispossessed' or sub-average incomes, a very high proportion of murderers and victims being Negroes. In other words, America is still in the midst of the problem that caused the high metropolitan crime rate in England at the time of Burke and Hare. But poverty is not always the explanation. Southern Ireland is a poor country and has a low murder rate. Finland is a prosperous country with a high murder rate.

But the statistics tell us less than individual cases. In England, the Jack the Ripper murders might be regarded as the beginning of the 'modern period'. In America, the incredible crimes of Jesse Pomeroy took place eight years before the Ripper murders. The name of Pomeroy is surprisingly unknown – no doubt because his insane mutilation murders of children have none of the interesting features of the Ripper case. Pomeroy was a tall, gangling boy with a hare lip; one of his eyes was completely white. His extreme ugliness seems to have made him anti-social and cruel, particularly towards younger children. Even at the age of thirteen, he seems to have been a sexual pervert. After various minor offences against children, he was placed in a mental home for a year, then released as cured. For a year he worked in his father's shop in Boston, subdued and apparently sane enough. Then children began to disappear, and others were found strangled or stabbed; all those who were found had been badly beaten. Suspicion slowly settled on Pomeroy, now in his mid-teens. It began to build up to something like certainty after the disappearance of a boy named Albert Pratt. Pratt's father hired an armed escort to take him to school. One day, he received an anonymous letter telling him that his precautions were useless, because 'the gang' would get the twelve-year-old boy. A few days later, Harry Pomeroy, the twelve-year-old brother of Jesse, went to his schoolmaster, William Barnes, and told him that Albert Pratt's father was outside and wanted to see his son. Barnes allowed him to go. Albert Pratt disappeared, and some days later, his mutilated body was found in the marshes near the Bigelow school. Harry Pomeroy's story was that a tall man in a business suit had identified himself as the boy's father and asked to see him. But the schoolmaster was suspicious. Eventually, the inevitable happened; one of Pomeroy's victims got away. It was a boy named William Barton, who was attacked by Pomeroy and tied to a telegraph pole; somehow, he broke loose. His description of his attacker left no doubt of his identity. Police dug in the rubbish dump behind the Pomeroy house, and found the bodies of a dozen children, girls as well as boys. Pomeroy had killed twenty-seven children in all.

A witness at his trial said: 'He seems to emanate a concentrated ferocity of mind and purpose. . . .' In 1881, Pomeroy was sentenced to death for murder, but after eighteen months of appeals, this was commuted to life imprisonment.

Pomeroy made two attempts to escape from prison by means of tools smuggled in to him by his mother. Finally, he devised an incredible plan of escape. By means of certain small tools that he was allowed – because they seemed useless for breaking out of a jail – he managed to loosen a stone in the wall and get access to a gas pipe. He released the gas, waited until it almost overcame him, then struck a match he had managed to save. The explosion blew him out of the door of his cell, and when the panic died down, he was found there, unconscious. Three convicts had burned to death. After this – it took place when he had already been in prison nine years – he was moved to the new Charleston jail on the north bank of the river. There he spent forty-one years in solitary confinement in a special cell, until, as an old man, he was removed to the Bridgewater State Farm for the criminally insane. (Albert de Salvo, the Boston Strangler, was later to escape from there.) He died in his late sixties.[1]

[1] I regret that I am unable to offer more detail about this case. I have only seen two accounts of it; a brief one in *Boston Murders*, edited by John N Makris (Duell, Sloan and Pierce, 1948), and a longer, but obviously less reliable one in Guy B H Logan's *Rope, Knife and Chair* (Rich and Cowan, no date). Logan's account states that Pomeroy killed the twenty-seven children *before* his term in the asylum, and that when he was released, he killed more; this is obviously impossible.

Why was such a case not reported in every American newspaper and written about as fully as the murder of Dr Parkman by Dr Webster, or the murders of the Bender family some ten years earlier? Partly because of the horrifying nature of the mutilations to the children; partly because the crime must have struck his contemporaries as unexplainable, except by saying, 'He was obviously insane'. If the crime had occurred today, a psychologist would write a lengthy book about it, exploring the roots of Pomeroy's hatred of children. As it is, the Bridgewater hospital records may one day provide a fuller account of the first murder case that had a distinctively twentieth-century flavour.

I have often regretted that the science of criminal psychology had not developed sufficiently by the mid-1890s to justify a careful study of one of the most interesting mass murderers produced by America – Herman Webster Mudgett, alias H H Holmes, whose arrest in 1894 came about through the discovery of an insurance fraud. When his 'castle' – a huge house he had had built on 63rd Street, in Chicago's Englewood section – was examined, it was found to be a maze of trapdoors and secret rooms; and a large number of bones, skulls and teeth were found buried in the basement. It soon became clear that America had produced its most spectacular mass murderer. Newspapers spoke of two hundred victims, but the sum is probably about twenty – exceeded, so far as America is concerned, only by Pomeroy.

Harry Howard Holmes – as he came to call himself – is a paradoxical character. Born in 1860 in Gilmanton, a small town in New Hampshire, he came of a secure middle-class background – his father was postmaster. He graduated at a school in Vermont, was a schoolteacher for a while, then went on to medical school at Ann Arbor, Michigan (a town that deserves a chapter to itself in the history of murder – it has had several remarkable cases). John Bartlow Martin[1] believes that it was

[1] In an article 'The Master of Murder Castle' that appeared in *Harper's* in 1943, and is reprinted in the *Viking Murder Book*. There is a full-length book on Holmes, *The Girls in Nightmare House*, by Charles Boswell and Lewis Thompson (Frederick Muller, 1955).

at medical school that Holmes practised his first swindle, an insurance fraud involving the theft of a body on its way to the dissecting room, and the faked death of a patient whom Holmes had insured. Presumably he and the patient split the proceeds. He had married at eighteen, but deserted his wife and child eight years later, after he had graduated from medical school. He combined the natural temperament of a swindler with a curious interest in hypnotism and the occult – Martin suggests that his later murders were an attempt to put into practice certain 'theories about human nature' that he does not specify. It is typical of him that, having deserted his wife, he arranged for her to hear indirectly that he had been in a train wreck and was probably suffering from amnesia.

Under his true name – of Mudgett – he practised medicine briefly in Mooers Forks, NY, but when he moved to Chicago in 1886, he had decided to call himself Holmes – presumably so as to be untraceable by his wife, Clara Lovering. In Wilmette, a northern suburb of Chicago, he met a pretty girl named Myrta Belknap, whose family was well-to-do, and married her bigamously in early 1887. The family broke with Holmes after he had forged the signature of her uncle John Belknap on a note, and it is recorded that he invited Uncle John up to the roof of his new house to discuss the matter. Some instinct told Uncle John not to go.

His only venture in legitimate business failing – it was a duplicating company – he discovered an interesting possibility on the south side: a Mrs Holden, who ran a drugstore on 63rd Street, Englewood, needed an assistant. With his medical knowledge, Holmes was the ideal man. Three years later, in 1890, Holmes had become a partner in the store, and Mrs Holden talked about rigged books and prosecution. Then Mrs Holden vanished, and Holmes owned the store. No one knows what happened to her, and Holmes never told.

Soon he was doing so well in business that he built another house opposite the store – his 'murder castle'. His method here was to quarrel with the gangs of workmen every few weeks and pay them off – so that no one knew too much about the place. He apparently raised the money for the building by the sale of patent medicines for which he made spectacular claims. It was three storeys high; the ground floor contained shops, the next floor contained Holmes' 'chambers', the top floor consisted of apartments. The reason he gave for building the castle was that it was intended as a hotel for visitors to the Chicago World Fair of 1893. But he had gas pipes installed so that he could flood any room with gas – recalling Marcel Petiot – and secret peep-holes into every room.

Now, with his second 'wife' safely at home in Wilmette, Holmes began to go in for seduction and murder. A jeweller named Conner moved into the drugstore – it was agreed that he should have a corner of the store for his watch-repairing business, while his wife Julia helped Holmes as a clerk. When Conner realised that Holmes and Julia were lovers, he moved out, leaving his wife and her sister Gertie – aged eighteen – behind. Both of them became his mistresses. Then Gertie became pregnant, and disappeared. Holmes took her in to a business acquaintance to say goodbye, and then told him some weeks later that Gertie had died. The business friend said, 'Holmes, you've killed her.' Holmes said: 'Pooh! what makes you think that?' and nothing more was said.

Holmes was attracted by a sixteen-year-old blonde named Emily van Tassel, who came to the ice-cream parlour, usually with her mother. When Emily disappeared one day, Holmes denied all knowledge of her whereabouts. She was never seen again.

In spite of now owning two drugstores and a 'hotel', Holmes preferred to live by various forms of confidence trickery. There was a machine which, he claimed, could make inflammable gas out of water by splitting up its hydrogen and oxygen. Actually, the machine was connected to the gas supply; but it was sold to a Canadian for two thousand dollars. Holmes discovered that the gaseous water was a mild stimulant (alcoholics still use gas bubbled into water when they can get nothing else), and sold it in the shop, claiming he had discovered a medicinal spring. The gas company found out and threatened to sue. He furnished the 'castle' on credit. When he failed to pay, the company tried to reclaim its property, but found the house empty. A porter who was bribed with twenty-five dollars told them that the furniture had all been put into a room whose door had been bricked up and then wallpapered; the company recovered its furniture. Huge quantities of crockery were found in a space in the roof, and repossessed. Holmes met a thief named Pitezel, who became a partner in his swindles. When Pitezel was arrested in Terre Haute for a dud cheque, Holmes posed as an Indiana congressman and bailed him out with another dud cheque.

Holmes' career as a seducer and murderer was also going forward swiftly. A new blonde secretary, Emily Cigrand, moved into the store. Julia showed signs of jealousy, and would tiptoe from her upstairs apartment to listen outside Holmes' door. Holmes had a buzzer installed under one of the steps to warn him. Finally he got tired of her jealousy; Julia and her eight-year-old daughter disappeared in early autumn, 1892. Miss Cigrand also vanished in December. The reason seems to have been that he had met a girl named Minnie Williams, who had inherited property to the value of twenty thousand dollars. Minnie, a pretty but brainless girl, lived with Holmes throughout the World Fair, which started on 1st May 1893. The upper apartments were kept permanently filled, and at least two of Holmes' female guests simply vanished; there may have been more. In June, Minnie's sister Annie came to stay with them. Like Minnie, she believed Holmes to be a wealthy businessman. In July, she wrote to the aunt who had brought them up : 'Brother Harry says you need never trouble any more about me, financially or otherwise.' She was going to Germany to study art. She vanished. Minnie continued to live with Holmes as his wife, and Pitezel often lived with them. (He also had a wife and five children.)

It should be clear by now that Holmes was not a successful confidence swindler; something always seemed to go wrong with his plans. But he had now got himself so far into debt that he could see no alternative. When the castle was empty again – the Fair being over – Holmes set fire to it, and tried to collect sixty thousand dollars from an insurance company for damage to its upper storeys. They were suspicious, and soon uncovered something of Holmes' past. Holmes was living in a small hotel with Minnie and Pitezel in November, when the insurance company lured him to their office to talk it over. Then a police inspector named Cowrie called on Minnie and sternly told her that the fraud had been discovered. She believed him, and confessed. Cowrie left with the policy, and the insurance company decided not to sue for attempted fraud. But Holmes' other creditors heard about it – no doubt Cowrie took care that they should – and presented Holmes with bills totalling fifty thousand dollars. On 22nd November, Holmes and Minnie fled from Chicago. By this time, she had transferred all her property to Holmes. It was time for her to disappear, and she did. Holmes was later to accuse her of murdering Annie by hitting her with a stool in a jealous rage.

Holmes had met a blonde girl with immense blue eyes during the Exposition; her name was Georgiana Yoke, and she demanded marriage if she was to surrender her virginity. It made no difference to Holmes – he already had two wives; so he married her in Denver in January 1894. Martin adds the astonishing detail that Minnie was a witness, and that she did not 'disappear' until some months later, which raises the possibility that Minnie knew more of Holmes' affairs than his previous mistresses had, and was an accomplice – perhaps even in her sister's murder. With Minnie out of the way, Holmes and Pitezel went to Fort Worth to realise her property. They used it to raise a loan of sixteen thousand dollars, and also as collateral for the purchase of a large number of horses. In June, Holmes and Pitezel moved to Saint Louis, where Holmes bought another drugstore, mortgaged the stock, then let Pitezel remove it all. This fraud led to his only period in jail; he was arrested on 19th July 1894, and bailed out by Georgiana on 31st.

It was in jail in St Louis that Holmes met the celebrated train robber, Marion Hedgepeth, of whom the detective Pinkerton said, 'He was one of the worst characters I ever heard of. He was bad all through.' Hedgepeth dressed like a banker, but was reputed to have the fastest draw in the West; he once killed a man whose gun was already out of its holster when Hedgepeth started to draw. Women fought to get into the courtroom when the good-looking Hedgepeth was tried.

Holmes told Hedgepeth that he had worked out a perfect insurance swindle. It involved insuring a man's life, getting him killed in an apparently accidental explosion, and substituting another body for the 'victim'. (It will be recalled that Holmes started his career with a similar swindle.) He asked Hedgepeth if he knew of a suitable crooked lawyer to deal with the insurance company. Hedgepeth put him on to one Jephta D Howe. Pitezel was to be the 'victim', who would be insured for ten thousand dollars. In the event of a successful swindle, Hedgepeth would get five hundred dollars, Howe two thousand five hundred dollars, and Pitezel and Holmes would share the rest.

What Pitezel did not know was that Holmes had no intention of finding a corpse to substitute for his own. Holmes had a much simpler method. Kill Pitezel, and take his share of the money.

For the purpose of the fraud, Holmes and Pitezel moved to Philadelphia, and rented a house at 1316 Callowhill Street, which backed on to the morgue. No doubt Holmes told Pitezel he intended to get the body from the morgue. Under the name of B F Perry, Pitezel moved into the house, and erected a sign that claimed he was a dealer in patents. He moved in on 17th August. A carpenter named Eugene Smith brought him a device for setting saws. Pitezel told him to leave it. On 3rd September, Smith called in to find how the sale of his patent was going, and found the place empty, with the door open. After waiting for a while, he looked upstairs – and found Pitezel's swollen and decomposing corpse. The police were called in, and soon decided that Pitezel had been conducting some experiment using chloroform, and had made the mistake of trying to light his pipe too close to it. The inquest found that his death was accidental. Five days later, the Fidelity Mutual Life Insurance Company on Walnut Street received a telegram from their St Louis branch declaring that B F Perry was actually Benjamin Fuller Pitezel, and that he was insured by them. A few days later, the company received a letter from the lawyer Jephta D Howe saying that he represented Pitezel's widow Carrie and would be calling on them. The insurance company tried to trace Pitezel's former address in Chicago, and found their way to Myrta Belknap, the second Mrs Holmes. Holmes apparently kept in touch with her, for she agreed to send him a message – he was on a 'business trip' – and in due course, Holmes contacted the insurance company. By this time, Pitezel was buried. Eventually, Holmes arrived in Philadelphia, and offered to identify the body. Jephta D Howe also arrived with Pitezel's second eldest daughter, Alice, and the body was exhumed and quickly identified. The insurance company paid up without hesitation. But Holmes was less willing to part with the five hundred dollars he had promised Hedgepeth, not to mention the two thousand five hundred dollars for Howe. Howe told his elder brother about his grievance, and since the elder brother was Hedgepeth's lawyer, he advised the train robber to make some capital out of it by denouncing 'Howard' (Holmes' alias) and trying to get his sentence reduced for his public spiritedness. This did not work – he was still sentenced to twelve years – but the insurance company suddenly realised they had been defrauded. The alarm went out for Holmes. But he had returned to St Louis, and taken away two of the remaining four children – Nellie, aged eleven, and Howard, nine – claiming that they were on their way to rejoin Pitezel. Alice had been left in Indianapolis – no doubt Holmes was afraid that she would reveal that the body *was* that of her father after all – and Holmes then rejoined her.

For the next week or so, Holmes was nowhere to be found. It was later established that he visited his family in New Hampshire, and even his first wife. He defrauded his brother of three hundred dollars, then went back to Burlington, Vermont, where Pinkerton detectives finally traced him. He was living with Georgiana, and Mrs Pitezel, with two remaining children – a girl of sixteen and a baby – were living nearby. The detectives traced Holmes by following the trail of Mrs Pitezel from St Louis to Detroit and Toronto. When the fugitives moved to Boston, and Holmes began making the round of steamship offices, the police decided it was time to pounce, and Holmes was finally arrested on 17th November 1894. His career of murder had been brief – from 1890 to 1894 – but eventful.

On the way back to Philadelphia (with Mrs Pitezel), Holmes lied fluently and involvedly, and offered the guard five hundred dollars if he would allow him to hypnotise him. (This raises an interesting possibility about why Minnie Williams and so many other women were so completely in his power.) When he arrived in Philadelphia, it was to find that Pitezel's body had been exhumed again, and that it had now been discovered that he died of chloroform poisoning, not of the explosion. It must have begun to dawn slowly on Mrs Pitezel about now that her husband was dead and the three children had vanished. Holmes had told her he had no idea what Pitezel had done with them, and suggested that the eldest girl Dessie should be sent to join him.

A detective named Geyer did a remarkable piece of work in tracing what had become of the children. Geyer plodded from hotel to hotel in Cincinnati – where Mrs Pitezel thought Holmes had taken the children – until he found one where a man had stayed with three children. Holmes had used an alias, of course. After weeks of checking hotels and houses, he had the photographs of Holmes and the children published in the press, and this led him to a house in Toronto where a man and two girls had arrived in late October. Holmes had borrowed a spade from the old gentleman next door. The bodies of the girls were found in the cellar, buried under a few feet of earth. The boy Howard was more difficult to trace. Evidence showed that he had never even reached Toronto. Accordingly, Geyer returned to Indianapolis, and began patiently checking hotels in every outlying town. At last there was only one left – Irvington; and it was in Irvington that Geyer at last discovered that Holmes had arrived at a rented house with a nine-year-old boy and a large stove. The boy had watched two workmen erect the stove; later in the day, he ended up in it. Geyer found a few charred bones and teeth in the kitchen chimney.

In his *Book of Remarkable Criminals* (1918), H B Irving has quoted from the letters the children wrote to their mother on that last trip from town to town, bringing home their misery and home-sickness so sharply that they are almost unbearable to read. And suddenly, it becomes very hard to understand how

Holmes can have gone through with it, or why he did it. He was covering up his trail; he had killed Pitezel, now he had to kill the rest of the family to escape detection. All for a few thousand dollars. Mrs Pitezel, Dessie and the baby Wharton were next on the list.

Police now opened Holmes' 'castle' and examined it from cellar to roof. There was a large stove in the cellar with charred human bones in it. More bones were buried under the floor. A dissecting table in the corner was heavily stained with blood. Greased chutes ran from the second and third floor down to the cellar. A handyman who had worked for Holmes now gave the information that Holmes had once given him a male skeleton to mount, and on another occasion, asked him to finish removing the flesh from another skeleton. He said he assumed Holmes was engaged in surgical work. The skeletons were then sold to medical schools. Holmes did not believe in wasting anything.

Holmes lied on to the end. He kept a diary in which he recorded his sense of shock at the discovery of the children's bodies, and how he recalls the 'innocent child's kiss so timidly given' before they waved him goodbye. He accused Minnie Williams of hiring someone to do the murder to spite him. When condemned to death – as he inevitably was – he wrote a long confession for the newspapers in which he admitted to twenty-seven murders, then, after selling it for seven thousand five hundred dollars, he repudiated the whole thing and again declared himself innocent. He conducted his own defence and did it well; but it made no difference. He was hanged on 7th May 1895, at Moyamensing Prison.

It is true that, to a very large degree, Holmes was merely a confidence swindler. It is surprising how many mass murderers began as confidence swindlers – Landru, Joseph Smith, Petiot, Fernandez and Beck. But if he was only a confidence swindler, then his case would rightly belong to the chapter of this book dealing with the nineteenth century. There is reason to think that he was a man who was fascinated by crime, as Lacenaire was. Martin talks about his 'lifelong preoccupation with cadavers', and one can sense this in reading the full account of the case. One might add: his lifelong preoccupation with sex. The wife of Arthur Rouse referred to him in a letter as a 'sex maniac' – meaning by that a man who needed all the sex he could get, rather than a rapist. Holmes was a sex maniac in this sense. A short, well-dressed, dapper man – he was five feet seven inches tall – with a large droopy moustache and a pink complexion, he had exactly the same kind of sexual vanity as Rouse. Writers on the case who talk about his baleful power over women are talking romantic nonsense – as are the writers who talk in the same way about Landru and Joseph Smith. Any fairly presentable man with a glib tongue can spend his life in seduction if he wants to. Most men over twenty-five are married; most unmarried girls are anxious to marry, and prefer the security of a father-figure, particularly a property owner who claims to be wealthy. But it must also be remembered that Holmes was not living in the mid-twentieth century when very few girls are virgins when they marry. He was living in America – basically a Puritan country anyway – at the end of the nineteenth century, when fiction was full of the awful fate of girls who rashly surrendered their virginity. A girl who did so felt like a criminal.

The business partner Frederick Nind, to whom Gertie Conner came to say goodbye – and who later accused Holmes of killing her – described how Holmes had come into the office one day, and described how he had been out with Gertie the night before and 'committed an indiscretion'. It may be that Holmes was preparing his partner for his later admission that Gertie was pregnant; but the fact that he thought it worthy of remark demonstrates that he was not seducing women every other day. And why did the sixteen-year-old Emily van Tassel vanish? She had no money, she was not living in the castle. It is fairly obvious that Holmes managed to get her into the castle one night, chloroformed and raped her, then put her body into the chute to the basement. The larger number of his victims were women; from what we know of his sexual appetite, it is probable that he violated most of them either before or after death; if Martin is correct about his 'lifelong preoccupation with cadavers', the probability is that it was after death. What was his aim in building a house with peepholes into every room and secret passageways? That he intended to use it, to some extent,

214

for confidence trickery cannot be doubted; but not *every* room. He was a voyeur; and unlike most voyeurs, he wanted to do more than look. A solitary girl could be rendered unconscious by gas piped into the room after she was asleep, then chloroformed to keep her unconscious, and later disposed of in the stove. What of the two male skeletons the caretaker mentioned? Were they the husbands of women Holmes particularly wanted? It is true that they might just as well have been men he had killed for their money. But in that case, why this odd touch of selling the skeletons instead of disposing of them in the normal way? They could not have brought in all that much money – a medical student can buy his own skeleton for a few dollars – and they were a considerable risk. But Holmes was a strange kind of power maniac, a man who enjoyed the feeling of being a wolf preying on society. It would have increased his pleasure in possessing the wife to think that her husband had not been able to protect her – that, in fact, he would soon be an exhibit in a medical school, murdered by Holmes, the super-criminal and super-ravisher.

It is true that, as a super-criminal, Holmes is disappointingly unlike Conan Doyle's Professor Moriarty; no 'Napoleon of crime', but a bungling confidence man. But real super-criminals are like that; if they had the brains and imagination to turn them into Moriartys they wouldn't be criminals. At worst, they might write obscene books, like Sade.

It is a disquieting thought that Holmes could have killed off the Pitezel family and continued his career of murder for years if it had not been for the denunciation by Hedgepeth. Martin professes himself baffled by Holmes's motive in telling Hedgepeth about his scheme of collecting insurance – for obviously, he could have asked Hedgepeth about a crooked lawyer without telling him everything. But there is really no problem about the motive. Hedgepeth was the 'handsomest outlaw in the West', one of the most famous criminals of his day. Holmes no doubt looked at him with involuntary respect, and then told himself that *he* was a far more successful criminal and lady's man than Hedgepeth. He wanted to boast to Hedgepeth about the superiority of his own methods. I am not now drawing the usual moral that all criminals are trapped by their vanity; Holmes was no more vain than the rest of us. The desire to boast to 'the handsomest outlaw in the West' was natural, if incautious.

I have written about the Holmes case at such length because there is something about his 'murder castle' that catches the essence of murder in the twentieth century. We have grown up too fast; villages expand into towns, and then into cities, in the space of a few years. The result is 'civilisation neurosis', the fear and hatred of civilisation as such. The Elizabethans were always writing nostalgically about 'the shepherd's sweet lot', but Shakespeare had only to stroll a mile to be in the fields. A century later, the killers of John Hayes walked a hundred yards north of Oxford Street and threw his body into Marylebone pond. But by the second half of the nineteenth century, there were children in the slums of London and New York who had never seen a green field and never would. The men who build houses feel that they are playing a small part in the battle of order against chaos; but the people who live in them fifty years later may feel that brick and mortar surround them like some creeping fungus.

The same is true of attitudes to sex. For the Elizabethan or the Jacobean, sex was an experience of the same order as getting pleasantly drunk. It could be romantic, as with Romeo and Juliet, or healthily physical. Sir John Suckling ends a poem on the wedding of a friend:

> *'At length the candle's out, and now*
> *All that they had not done they do.*
> *What that is, who can tell?*
> *But I believe it was no more*
> *Than thou and I have done before*
> *With Bridget and with Nell.'*

This attitude is still present in Fielding. Then comes the age of Jane Austen and the age of Dickens, and suddenly, young ladies are hedged around with a glass barrier. There, under those skirts that trail on the ground, are hidden mysteries. In the year in which H H Holmes was hanged, a Sunday school superintendent named Theodore Durrant asked a pretty girl named Blanche Lamont into the Emanuel Baptist Church in Bartlett Street, San Francisco. Then he choked her, dragged the body up to the belfry, removed all the clothes, and violated the corpse. He carefully placed a block of wood under her head. How many visits he paid to the corpse during the next week is not known, but on 12th April he lured a friend of his victim – named, oddly enough, Minnie Williams – into the church. In the course of a struggle he raised her dress above her head and jammed some of it down her throat, choking her. He then took a table knife and carefully cut both her wrists and her forehead, then drove it into each of her breasts. After this he violated Minnie. The body was discovered the next morning by ladies holding a church social. Theodore Durrant had been seen with both girls shortly before killing them, so there was no difficulty in pinning the murder on him. Legal appeals occupied three years, but he was executed in January 1898.

Theodore Durrant experienced exactly the same desires as H H Holmes – the desire to remove those frustrating Victorian dresses. But Durrant approached the problem without calculation. Holmes brooded on it, and decided that what he needed was a house with secret rooms and peepholes. He ruined himself building it, but he built it. And now he was king of the castle; he had found his own answer to the problem of civilisation neurosis and sexual underprivilege. It has to be recognised that, in his ghoulish way, Holmes was as much the exponent of the American dream as Henry Ford or Horatio Alger.

This explains why the sex crime is the typical crime of the twentieth century. A large book could be written on the varieties of sex crime; but I shall have to confine myself to a fairly small number. I shall not write about Heath, Christie and the Birmingham YWCA case, which have been discussed *ad nauseam* by other writers, but speak of some of the lesser known cases.

A typical case, that does not involve murder, is recounted by Frederick Oughton in his history of private detection, *Ten Guineas a Day* (chapter 5). An American businessman named

Weckler was travelling in England with his beautiful wife, an ex-model. She decided she would like to take a trip on British Railways, and agreed to meet her husband in a certain hotel. When she failed to arrive, he went to the station. There had been a train crash, and his wife's body was in the morgue with the other victims. But one thing puzzled the husband. Her suspender belt was torn – one of the suspenders was almost detached. How would a train crash tear a suspender belt? Weckler had the body examined by a surgeon friend, who pronounced that Mrs Weckler had been sexually assaulted. Weckler approached a private detective agency. The detective assigned to the case went about it in the traditional manner, plodding from house to house, speaking to hundreds of people. His suspicions finally fixed on a neurotic young workman who lived in a railway cottage with his wife and child. By pretending to be friendly, the detective got an admission from the man that he travelled alone in the same compartment as the ex-model. The boss of the agency now took over the case; he fired some harsh questions, and the neurotic suspect broke down and confessed that the sight of the model's legs in sheer nylons had excited him so much that he ended by raping her. After this came the crash which broke her neck; the suspect had survived with a few bruises. Weckler was handed the man's confession, but he apparently decided to take no action; it was enough to have his suspicions confirmed.

Or is the case as straightforward as this? A woman being violently raped – the vagina was badly torn – puts up a fight, and probably scratches her attacker. She gets skin under her nails, and he gets distinctive nail scratches. The suspect's wife did not mention such scratches. No, the far more probable order of events was that Creel (the suspect) was fascinated by the woman – he admitted that he could not take his eyes off her stockings – but made no attempt to assault her; after all, she would call the guard at the next station, or pull the communication cord. It was more probably after the crash, when he found himself lying on the floor of the carriage with an unconscious woman, that he decided to snatch the opportunity he had been daydreaming about for the past half-hour. The owner of the nylon clad legs lay still; perhaps he assumed she was dead. Patrick Byrne, the YWCA murderer, said that when his victim lay dead on the floor 'I wanted to do everything at once'. So did Creel – hence the extreme violence that caused the crime to be discovered.

This atmosphere of sexual desire hangs over the twentieth century in a way that would have baffled an Elizabethan. Repression explodes into irrational violence. In her book *Le Couple*,[1] Suzanne Lilar recounts the strange story of Jan and Ada, a fifteen-year-old boy and girl. She does not give their full names or the name of the town in Holland where it took place, but the date was 19th November 1948. The girl, Ada, was found attached in an upright position to two iron bars in the form of a cross. The boy Jan gave himself up a few days later. The story he had to tell was confirmed by Ada's diaries and their love letters. They were lovers, although both remained virgins. He used to dream of undressing her, tying her up, and pricking her with a knife. When they bathed together naked, he sometimes slapped her breasts, and she enjoyed it. She wrote : 'Have a good rest, brute of brutes. I am mad on you . . . Even if you do kill me, I shan't say anything. . . . Love is a hard thing to understand.' (It recalls what Peter Kürten said to a girl he had hurt as he had intercourse with her: 'Love is like that.') He would fire notes at her with a bow and arrow, with such messages as, 'This evening Ada will be assassinated. The Serpent.' One day he saw a scout-knife in a shop and bought it, after some preliminary resistance. Ada went with him to a shooting range, and allowed him to tie her in a crucified position to the bars. Then, as he gagged her, she got frightened, and began to struggle. He became excited and tore off her clothes. Then he pricked her several times, bound her eyes, and ended by stabbing her and cutting her throat. The game of sadist and victim had suddenly become reality. He did not rape her, for the incredible reason that he had no idea of what to do to make love to her. They were both children of respectable middle-class families, and in the rather puritanical little town, children did not come by their sexual knowledge early. Instinct

[1] Translated as *Aspects of Love in Western Society*, 1965.

told him that the man 'did something' to the girl; instinct told her that the girl remained passive while the man did things to her. It was unfortunate for both that this was as far as their knowledge went.

The story raises a fundamental point. The sexual act has a close affinity with murder, and this may well be the basis of the human interest in murder. Murderer and victim are in the same sort of relation as the male penetrating the female. Does this explain the steep rise in murder in our century? For most animals, sex occurs only when the female is on heat; for human beings, it can occur any time. But in past centuries, men and women worked so hard that sex was something that happened on weekends. Industrialisation has brought leisure, and leisure means sex at any time. And an immense amount of the energy that was once entirely absorbed by work flows into sex. It is also a disturbing factor that many criminals are above average intelligence, and may feel that their intelligence places them above society and its laws.

The most famous case of this type is the murder of Bobby Franks by Nathan Leopold and Richard Loeb, the two Chicago college boys. Both were the sons of rich parents, and their relation was homosexual. Significantly enough, their first idea was to kidnap a girl and kill her. Then they thought it would be a good idea to kidnap Loeb's younger brother. Finally, they fixed on a pupil at a nearby boys' school. They did not see the boy on the afternoon of the murder – 21st May 1924 – but Loeb's cousin Bobby Franks, aged fourteen, was offered a lift instead. Loeb knocked him unconscious with blows of a chisel in the back; then they drove through Chicago while the boy bled to death. They then carried him to a culvert, undressed him, and poured sulphuric acid over his face to disfigure him. After this, they rang the Franks' home and demanded money, claiming the boy was still alive. Unfortunately for them, the body was found, and Leopold's glasses were also found nearby. The two youths soon confessed, and were sentenced to life imprisonment.

Here again, the murder was motivated by the strange relationship between them. Loeb was the 'Master', Leopold the 'Devoted Slave'. Both read Nietzsche and absorbed the gospel of the superman. But if it is asked exactly why they committed murder, the only valid answer is: because they *chose* to. They were free; they were intelligent; they were rich. Life offered them no sense of resistance, of goals worth striving for, so they set up an imaginary goal and played a game; then the game turned to reality. As Leopold looked over his shoulder in the car and saw the blood spurting, he said: 'Oh God, I didn't know it would be like this.' Meyer Levin called his excellent novel about the case *Compulsion*, but the title misses the point. It was not a matter of compulsion, but of free choice. The crimes of Jack the Ripper were a compulsion. So were the crimes of that other Chicago murderer, William Heirens (another student at the University of Chicago), who began by stealing pairs of women's panties, and ended by murdering two women and a child; he was sentenced to life imprisonment in 1946. The crime of Leopold and Loeb was not compulsive; it was a crime of freedom, a crime of boredom. The first writer to make a study of the psychology of this type of criminal was Dostoievsky, whose Nicholas Stavrogin, in *The Possessed*, is rich, handsome and spoilt, and deliberately commits crimes to try to rouse himself from his moral stagnation. No writer before Dostoievsky could have grasped the possibility of such a motive for crime – with the possible exception of Goethe.

One of the grimmest cases of compulsion on record is the murder of Alice Porter by Donald Fearn near Pueblo, Colorado, in 1942. Fearn was a railway mechanic, twenty-three years old; he was married, and had two children. But, like Patrick Byrne, he dreamed of torturing women. He was particularly fascinated by the practices of a sect of Pueblo Indians called the Penitentes. During Holy Week, they held religious ceremonies involving torture, and crucified one of their own members. This kind of thing was not unusual among Indians, who judged a man's bravery by his ability to bear pain; early travellers have described incredible torments that Indians bore willingly to prove their manhood. This aspect of it did not interest Fearn. He began to spend time in an old adobe 'church', fifty miles from Pueblo, in which there was a bloodstained altar; it had been one of the last strongholds of the Penitentes' religion.

In April 1942, Fearn's wife was in hospital having her second baby, and Fearn's sexual desires, starved for many months, reached a point where he decided to put his dreams of torture into practice. 'Ever since I was a young boy I have wanted to torture a beautiful young girl.' On several occasions he had succeeded in luring girls into his car, but always lost his nerve. Then, a week before the murder, he saw Alice Porter, a seventeen-year-old student nurse, and something about her convinced him that she was his victim. He followed her for several days, establishing her routine. On 22nd April, there was a storm, and Alice Porter walked home from classes alone at about 9.30. Fearn pulled his car up near her, pointed a gun at her, and ordered her into the car. Before she climbed in, she screamed, and a man in a nearby house went to his door, in time to see the car driving away. Fearn took her to the adobe church, bound her hands and feet, and took off her clothes. Then he built a fire and proceeded to torture her, binding her with red-hot wires, and whipping her with a heated wire whip. He brought out his torture kit – an awl and various other instruments – and tortured her in a manner that has never been reported fully. Finally, he placed her on the altar and raped her. She was still alive, but he was afraid she might identify him, so he killed her with a hammer, and threw her body down a well.

He had spent the night torturing her; in the morning, driving back, his car skidded into mud and would not move. He had to pay a local farmer to haul it out. Then he drove back to Pueblo, to go and visit his wife in hospital; the baby had been born the day before.

It took the police several days to think of searching in the adobe church, but when they got there, they found the burnt remains of the girl's clothes, the smoke-blackened wires, and the 'torture kit'. They looked down the well outside, and found the body. There were fingerprints on the awl, but not of any known sexual offender. But routine questioning led them to the farmer who had hauled the car out of the mud. He described it as a blue Ford sedan, old and battered. The detectives visited every garage in Pueblo asking if the proprietor knew of such a car. One of them did – in fact, he had it in there at the moment. It was a blue car, but the mud on it would explain why the man who heard Alice Porter's scream thought it was brown. When Donald Fearn came in for it, the police were waiting for him. The fingerprints found in his car matched the prints on the awl; the case against him was complete.

When details of the murder came out, mobs collected and there was talk of lynching. Fearn was taken away to the jail in Canon City. On October 22nd 1942, he was executed in the gas chamber there.[1]

Since the Second World War, the crime rate has slowly increased, and the number of murder cases involving perversions and fantasies has become enormous. The 'classic' murder case – involving the uncovering of motives, the accumulation of clues – has become a rarity. At the time I write this, in December 1968, two small girls from Newcastle, Norma Bell and Mary Bell (not related), aged thirteen and eleven, are on trial for killing two three-year-old boys 'for pleasure'. The boys were both strangled, and the children later broke into a nursery and left notes boasting about the murders. Mary Bell knocked on the door of the parents of Martin Brown, whose body had been found four days before in a derelict house, and asked to see him. 'I'm sorry, pet,' the mother said, 'Martin is dead.' 'I know he's dead. I want to see him lying in his coffin.' The case obviously sets a precedent for England[2] – although there are American cases in which children have shot their parents or other children – and it emphasises that the murders of the twentieth century are of a new and horrible kind. Let us look at some typical cases since the war – and observe how often they are 'firsts'.

On 11th May 1961, a schoolteacher driving through Peter

---

[1] A bizarre aspect of this case is that Alice Porter was the daughter of Detective Marvin Porter who, ten years before, had solved the rape-murder of Dorothy Drain, daughter of Under-Sheriff Riley Drain, Frank Aguilar and Joe Arridy were executed for this crime. It was Under-Sheriff Drain who solved the murder of Marvin Porter's daughter.
[2] Norma Bell was acquitted; Mary Bell – the younger of the two – sentenced to life detention (Dec 1968).

Skene Ogden Park, Oregon, decided to stop at a scenic spot above Crooked River Canyon. Far down in the Canyon, at the base of the sheer cliff, she saw two small figures that looked like dolls, lying at the side of the river. A man to whom she pointed them out said they were obviously dolls, and walked on. But that evening, the schoolteacher reported it to a local ranger, who went to investigate. The 'dolls' proved to be the naked bodies of a girl, aged four, and a boy, aged six, both badly battered. Their genitals had been mutilated with a knife. The boy had been dead when he was thrown over, but the girl had been alive.

The publicity given to the story brought the investigating sheriff a call from Eugene, West Oregon, from a woman who said she thought the murdered children must be the son and daughter of a neighbour. The neighbour was Mrs Gertrude Jackson, and she had moved into the area early that year with her children and a young girl who was a baby-sitter. Later on, they were joined by a mannish young woman. The neighbourhood gossip had it that the three women were lesbians. On 9th May, two days before the children were found, the baby-sitter went to her home in Lebanon, and the other two had gone off with the children. The lesbian girl was called Jeannace June Freeman, aged twenty-one. The housewife was able to describe their car – a red Mercury – so accurately that within twenty-four hours, it was located in a used car lot in Oakland, California. The dealer was able to give the address of the woman who sold it to him – a Mrs Gertrude Jackson. The apartment manager told the police the women had left, but that they would have to return for some clothes they had left behind. The police waited until the two women walked in. One was thin, bespectacled, with shoulder-length hair; this was the mother of the children. The other was squarely built, pretty, in a tough sort of way, with her short hair in tight curls; this was Jeannace Freeman, who admitted frankly: 'I'm the butch.' Mrs Jackson, aged thirty-three, broke down and confessed almost immediately. Her husband had left her, and she met Jeannace Freeman, who seduced her. 'Jeannace was boss. Her word was law.' 'She wanted me to walk around the house naked all the time, but I couldn't do it in front of the children.' As to Jeannace Freeman, she had been in trouble since childhood. It had begun when she was four, and her mother left her in charge of a young boy while she went shopping. The mother returned to find Jeannace in hysterics; the boy had raped her. (Nothing was done about him; he was later caught trying to rape another child, and sentenced to thirty days in jail.) From then on, Jeannace had become an exceptionally tough child, who was in trouble with the police so often that she was soon sent to a girls' reformatory.

Jeannace dominated Gertrude Jackson, and used to fly into a rage if she wanted to make love to her and the children came in. On the morning of 10th May, they had driven to the cliff above Crooked River Canyon. Jeannace told Mrs Jackson to take a walk. Then she strangled the boy Larry, undressed him, and mutilated his genitals – possibly to make it look like sexual assault. Mrs Jackson came back, and helped Jeannace to undress her four-year-old daughter. They then mutilated her genitals, and tossed her, still alive, over the cliff. The prosecutor asked Mrs Jackson, 'Didn't you feel anything?' 'No, I didn't feel anything.' After both children had been thrown over, Mrs Jackson pointed to some blood on Jeannace's hand; Jeannace said 'Yum yum,' and licked it off. They then hugged and kissed in the car.

Jeannace Freeman let her hair grow, and wore a dress, for the trial, in an attempt to counteract the jury's prejudice. (She was quoted as saying: 'I'd vomit if a man kissed me.') Both women were sentenced to death; but their appeals were still going on in November 1964, when Oregon abolished capital punishment. Their sentence was commuted to life imprisonment, so that both women may be out of prison by 1971.

Truman Capote, whose overrated novel *In Cold Blood*[1] deals with the murder of a Kansas family by two burglars, is quoted as having said that he was tempted to use the Jackson murder as the basis of a novel, before deciding definitely on the Clutter case (which took place two years earlier). It is hard to see how such a novel could have been made bearable for the

[1] Michael Joseph, 1965.

sexually normal reader; which is no doubt why Capote dropped the idea.

Capote's novel deserves some passing comment, in view of its success, if not of its inherent interest. The two killers, Richard Hickock and Perry Smith, broke into the house of Herbert William Clutter on the night of 15th November 1959, in the mistaken belief that he kept large sums of money on the premises. They tied up Clutter and his wife, and also the daughter Nancy, sixteen, and the son Kenyon, fifteen, and later shot them all. They were caught without difficulty – another ex-convict gave them away – and hanged in April 1965. At some point in the novel it is remarked that killers such as Hickock and Smith 'had shallow emotions regarding their own fate and that of their victims', and it is this lack of motivation that robs the case of interest. It is significant, though, that during the five years he was awaiting the sentence of death, Perry Smith suddenly developed an interest in literature and ideas. The emotional shallowness that made the murders possible vanished in the face of death. If it had happened earlier, the murders would never have happened. Which raises an interesting question for sociologists and psychologists, as well as underlining the real purpose of the study of murder: to teach the human imagination to create crisis situations without the physical need to act them out.

One of the strangest cases to come out of America since the war received almost no publicity in England. We had just moved to Cornwall in 1957, and were living in a cottage in the middle of nowhere during the rainy winter of 1957. The *Daily Express* carried a small paragraph stating that out in the wilds of Wisconsin, police had entered a farm, and found a headless woman hanging upside down from the ceiling. The farmer, Ed Gein, lived alone, and admitted that he had an uncontrollable impulse to rob cemeteries of newly buried women. Listening to the wind howling around our tin-roofed cottage, I experienced a sudden flash of sympathy for this sex-starved man, living alone with his obsession. And then, although I searched other newspapers for further items on Gein, I was unable to learn anything more. Presumably newspapers felt the case to be too gruesome to describe. It was only a couple of years ago that I was able to find a short account of the murders. My old friend August Derleth has not even included it in his volume *Wisconsin Murders*.

On 16th November 1957, Frank Worden, a deputy sheriff, returned to the hardware store that he operated with his mother, Mrs Bernice Worden, and found it locked. He got inside, and found a pool of blood on the floor, but no sign of his fifty-eight-year-old mother. The sheriff hurried over, and they checked the receipts to see who had been in the store that day. The last customer had been Ed Gein, a mild, peaceable little man, who lived alone on his one-hundred-and-ninety-acre farm near Plainfield. Gein was such a timid person that it seemed clear that he could know nothing about Mrs Worden's disappearance, but since he might have seen the killer, they went out to his farm. Gein was out, having supper with neighbours, who liked to offer the lonely man a little family life. The house was locked, but they looked into the woodshed. Hanging upside down from a hook in the ceiling was a naked, headless woman, whose body had been opened up like a carcass in a butcher's shop. In a room next to the woodshed, they found a woman's heart in a dish: significantly, this was Gein's dining room. The head and intestines were found in a box. Gein was arrested at his neighbour's, and when he learned that the sheriff had found the .22 calibre rifle with which he had shot Mrs Worden, he admitted the murder, but claimed he had been in a daze all the time. Police searched his farm house – which was filthy and full of every kind of rubbish – and found ten skins from human heads, and a box containing noses. Skin had been used to repair leather chairs and to make a belt. The skin of the complete upper half of a woman was found rolled up under the floor. They discovered eleven heads altogether, one of them of a woman named Mary Hogan, aged fifty-four, a tavern keeper from nearby Bancroft, who had disappeared in 1953. The other nine, Gein said, came from graveyards.

Slowly, his story emerged. His mother, Augusta Gein, had been crankily religious. Every time it rained heavily, she would read him the story of Noah from the Bible and prophesy the end of the world. She was convinced that the modern world was so full of sin that God would destroy it at any minute – women wearing lipstick and short skirts. . . . Ed Gein was the younger of two brothers, and he became a mother's boy. His father died in 1940, and his brother Henry two years later. Henry had also been a bachelor – their mother's upbringing had made both men very nervous of women – and he died in 1944, the same year in which Augusta Gein also suffered a stroke. Her son nursed her until she died in the following year. Ed was then thirty-eight, a small, thin man with a pleasant smile, well liked by everyone. Admittedly, there was an odd story about him. His nearest neighbours, the Bankses, had invited him to their house in 1942 when a female relative was in the house; she was wearing shorts, and Gein clearly found it hard to keep his eyes off her legs. That night, a man broke into the woman's house and seized her small son by the throat, asking him where his mother had gone. The man fled before he found out, but the boy thought he recognised Gein. Ever since then, the Bankses had had reservations about their quiet, pleasant neighbour.

What happened seems fairly clear. Gein was a sexually normal man – his mother's undivided attention had not turned him into a homosexual – but he was frightened of women, and not very attractive to them. He had a woman friend, with whom he went out for twenty years, but she finally decided against marrying him. She said his conversation was all about murder. Alone in the farmhouse, he thought endlessly about sex, until one day he saw a newspaper report of a woman who had been buried that day. In the middle of the night, he set off with his pick-up truck and a spade. He dug up the woman, unscrewed the coffin, and put her into the truck; then replaced the coffin and carefully remade the grave. Then he took the corpse home, feeling happier than ever before. At last he had a woman all to himself. Like Patrick Byrne, he was probably so enthusiastic that he didn't know how to start. But he had plenty of time. . . . He explained: 'It gave me a lot of satisfaction.'

Gein's graveyard excursions were not very frequent. Over

ten years there were only nine. He suffered from remorse, and decided every time never to do it again. The craving was so strong that it went beyond the desire to perform normal acts of love. He ate parts of the bodies, and made waistcoats of the skin, which he wore next to his flesh. His gravedigging expeditions – and murders – were always at the time of the full moon.

Gein understood himself well enough to realise that his mother was the root of all the trouble. Consciously, he loved her, unconsciously, hated her: hence his choice of elderly women as the only two victims he actually murdered.

At Christmas, 1957, it was decided that Gein was insane, and he was committed to Waupan State Hospital for life. No doubt some of the people of Plainfield for whom he acted as a baby-sitter think about their narrow escape; but there is no evidence that Gein was violently inclined towards young women or children.

The Gein case is horrible, but somehow not at all incomprehensible. Any man who has ever looked with interest at the legs of a woman in shorts can gain some insight into it. It will be even more comprehensible to anyone who knows Wisconsin, with its level fields and open spaces; it is all good farmland, but it seems to go on forever. In England, there is never that sense of emptiness. Every year in America, dozens of murders are committed in these open spaces – the deserts of Nevada or California, the snowy deserts of Alaska – and the bodies can lay there for weeks or years without any chance of discovery. In England, most murders are committed in towns – as often as not, in slums. And the lonely places of America conduce not only to murder, but to the states of mind that add the nightmare quality to so many American murders – the Texarcana moonlight murderer, the Donald Fearn case. Added to this is the fact that a country as large as America has difficulty in keeping any kind of check on its sexual deviates. A sex murder in New Mexico may be committed by a tramp whose last crime took place several thousand miles away in Michigan. In other cases, a man who is known to be a dangerous sexual offender may be released as 'cured' because the hospital can see no purpose in keeping him there for the rest of his life.

This is what happened in one of New Mexico's worst cases since the war. In 1949, a seventeen-year-old girl answered an advertisement in an Albuquerque newspaper for a domestic; the enormous, white-haired man who met her seemed harmless enough, so she got into his car. He drove her to a lonely stretch of road and ordered her out; then he tore off her clothes, tied her to a tree, and proceeded to rape and beat her several times. The girl was found some hours later. She had noted the number of the car, and the police were about to arrest Carl J Folk, the owner of a travelling carnival stationed in Albuquerque. By the time he finally came to trial, his victim had had a mental breakdown and was in a hospital. Folk spent three years in the same mental home, and was then released. One year later, a couple named Allen set out to drive from Pennsylvania to a new home in San José, California. They had an aluminium caravan in which they slept at night. On the morning of 1st December 1953, Carl Folk drove up to the petrol station where they were parked, and struck up a conversation. He liked the look of twenty-two-year-old Betty Allen, who was holding her ten-month-old baby. Several times later in the day, the Allens saw Folk, who was apparently also driving west. Late that night, they stopped in a caravan site in Arizona. Raymond Allen woke up to find a flashlight on his face, and received a tremendous blow on the chin. When he recovered consciousness, he was tied up, and Carl Folk asked him to tell him where the money was kept. When Folk threatened to mutilate his wife with a knife, Allen told him. Folk then climbed into Allen's car, and drove on for several miles. Then he stopped the caravan – which half overturned in a ditch – and carefully carried Raymond Allen into the other room. For the next hour or so, Allen listened to his wife's cries as Folk beat her and raped her. The cries eventually ceased. Finally, Allen managed to free his legs. He staggered out of the caravan – unheard by Folk, who may have been sleeping after his orgy – and ran down the road. A car stopped for him, and the driver untied his hands. Allen was shouting 'I'll kill him!' as he rushed back to his car and found the revolver he kept under the seat. Folk was now pouring petrol over the wife and baby – the latter was still alive – and went into the other compartment to pour some on Allen – to discover that he had gone. Folk looked outside, saw Allen, and said with mild surprise: 'What are you doing there?' Allen fired six shots at him, only one of which hit him – in the stomach. Allen found the baby crying loudly, and his wife dead, with a sheet tied tightly round her neck. The autopsy the next day reported that Folk had tortured her for seven hours, burning her with matches and cigarettes and biting her all over, before he strangled her. This time, with a certain lack of logic, the state found Folk sane and guilty of murder, and he died in the gas chamber in March 1955.

Arizona also provided one of the most widely publicised murder trials of 1966; I was doing a lecture tour in America at the time, and discovered that most local newspapers kept the trial covered. The defendant was twenty-three-year-old Charles Schmid, of Tucson.[1] Tucson is a teenagers' town, since the University of Arizona is situated there; in the evenings, its restaurants and drive-ins are crowded with teenagers in blue jeans. The town has a high proportion of runaways from other parts of the state, mostly girls who have eloped with boyfriends. It is a place with a great deal of 'action' for young people. Charles Schmid, known as 'Smitty', was well known among this set; in fact, he was a founder member of a teenage sex club that included a number of girls from the Palo Verde High School. Smitty was a youth who liked to be known. His five feet three inches worried him, so he wore cowboy boots with high heels, and added another half-inch or so by stuffing them with paper. He also painted a large beauty spot on his left cheek and wore pancake makeup. He talked a great deal about sex and claimed that he had taught his girlfriends 'a hundred different ways to make love'. His parents were well-to-do and allowed him complete freedom; he even had a small house of his own at the end of their garden.

On 15th May 1964, a pretty fifteen-year-old girl named

[1] For the benefit of English readers, this is pronounced Tuson.

231

Alleen Rowe was alone in the house when a friend called; her mother had gone out to do some night work. The friend was Mary Rae French, four years her senior, and she asked Alleen to go out with her and two male friends on a date. Alleen left with them. The two males were Charles Schmid and John Saunders, aged nineteen. They drove to a desert area by the golf links, and Alleen was dragged out of the car. She had been invited to join the high school 'sex club', and the youths were apparently determined to initiate her in the quickest way. Mary French sat and listened to her screams. Then 'Smitty' returned to the car, took a shovel from the boot – obviously, he had come prepared for this contingency – and told Mary to follow him. Alleen Rowe lay face down, her head battered with rocks. The three of them took turns digging a shallow grave, then rolled her into it.

While the police were searching for Alleen Rowe, a great many teenagers heard the rumour that Schmid had killed her; but none of them bothered to repeat this to the police, or their parents.

In mid-August of the following year, 1965, two daughters of a Tucson doctor disappeared; they were Wendy Fritz, aged thirteen, and her neurotic but beautiful sister Gretchen, seventeen. Gretchen had been having an affair with Schmid for some time, and he told a friend, Richard Bruns, that he was getting sick of her because she was too possessive. He invited her to his 'pad' one night; she brought her thirteen-year-old sister. So Schmid strangled them both, then took the bodies out into the desert, and dumped them. He then confided in Richard Bruns, and even took him to show him the spot where they were buried. Once again, Tucson's teenagers knew all about the murders, but none of them went to the police. Rumours of Smitty's part in the disappearance of his daughters reached Dr Fritz's ears, and he took the unusual step of hiring two gangsters to go and frighten Smitty. Smitty told them he had no idea where the girl was, and he frightened his girlfriends with lurid stories about the 'mob' that was out to get him.

It was Bruns who decided to go to the police; he was involved in an unhappy love affair, and somehow got the idea that the girl would be the next victim on Schmid's list. He was able to take the police to the spot in the desert where the girls lay. The skeletons were plainly visible from a distance – the Arizona sun and the buzzards had stripped them bare, and they lay exposed on a hilltop. The search for Alleen Rowe's body was less successful; Saunders and Mary French could not remember exactly where they had buried it.

Schmid had been married three weeks – a fifteen-year-old girl he had met on a blind date – when he was arrested.

The police began questioning Tucson's teenage set, and the case hit the headlines as the parents of Tucson suddenly became fully aware of some of the things that went on – for example, of sex parties at Smitty's pad with alcohol and drugs. It was also discovered that Smitty had boasted openly that he intended to kill Gretchen Fritz *before* the murder – and, moreover, in front of the mother of a teenage girl. He told the girl that Gretchen had stolen a diary of his, containing details of previous murders, including a man whose hands had been cut off and buried separately. The police also suspected him of being concerned in the disappearance of Sandra Hughes, a fourteen-year-old who vanished from her home a few days before Smitty was arrested. The police estimated that about thirty teenagers knew that he had killed Alleen Rowe, and kept the secret for eighteen months, before Richard Bruns decided to talk. It was disturbing proof of the teenage axiom 'Nobody over thirty can be trusted'. Schmid was tried separately and sentenced to die in the gas-chamber, but at the time of writing his appeals continue.

As far as I know, the case of Lloyd Higdon and Lucille Brumit is also a 'first'.[1] Higdon was a rapist whose methods were

[1] There have been others since. In January 1969, the *News of the World* reported that the police were hunting for a middle-aged man and a young woman driving an Austin A40 car. A fourteen-year-old girl waiting at a bus stop on the outskirts of Southend was offered a lift; she was driven to a back road, where the woman held a knife to her throat and the man raped her. The following night, the same couple picked up a Dutch *au pair* girl who was also assaulted. After a newspaper report of these attacks, fifteen teenage girls came forward to report that they had been through the same experience. The couple were later arrested.

altogether peculiar. He found girlfriends who wanted to see a girl raped, and on 4th July 1963, he and his wife picked up the fourteen-year-old daughter of a neighbour, offering to take her for a ride. The girl accepted, and was driven to Higdon's house, where she was ordered to get undressed. When she cried and protested, she was told that if she refused, she would be sold into white slavery and never see her parents again. Finally, she removed her own clothes in a bedroom, and allowed Higdon to have intercourse with her. After this, he allowed her to dress, and drove her home, warning her never to mention it. She told her parents, and Higdon was arrested and convicted of statutory rape. (The fact that the girl had finally allowed Higdon to rape her apparently decided the court to treat it as statutory rather than as actual rape.) He was out of prison again two years later. And on the afternoon of 17th July 1967, Higdon, together with Lucille Brumit, aged twenty-eight, picked up another girl in Lansing, near Ypsilanti; she was thirteen-year-old Roxanne Sandbrook. Like his first victim, Roxanne was already acquainted with Higdon, and thought it safe enough to accept a ride with a man and a woman. She was driven to a rubbish dump five miles north of Jackson, Michigan. Perhaps she refused to be convinced that she had better remove her clothes quietly; she was strangled and raped, then left on the rubbish dump. When her body was found a month later, it was badly decomposed.[1] As a known sex offender, Higdon immediately came under suspicion, but he had left the district. When he returned, he claimed to have been in Grand Rapids on the day of Roxanne's disappearance, and was immediately held in

[1] It is typical of this area – which has figured in spectacular murder trials since August 1931, when three men killed four teenagers in a car and set it on fire – that a second body was found on the same day. This was identified as Mary Fleszar, aged nineteen, who had vanished a week before Roxanne Sandbrook. She was naked and her hands and feet had been removed. At the time this book goes to press, it is clear that the murder of Mary Fleszar was the first in the series of a new Ann Arbor Jack the Ripper, who sometimes mutilates, stabs and shoots his victims as well as sexually assaulting them. There have been five other cases since then: Joan Schell (5th July 1968), age 22, Jane Mixer (21st March 1969), age 23, Maralynn Skelton (25th March 1969), age 16, Dawn Basom (16th April 1969), age 13, and finally, Alice Kalom (9th June 1969), age 21. The police admit that so far they have no lead of any kind.

jail, since his parole did not allow him to leave Lansing. Under questioning, Higdon confessed to the murder, and implicated Lucille Brumit. Higdon received life imprisonment.

The method here brings to mind another 'first' that received far more publicity – England's Moors murder case. This has been written about at such length that I shall not try to summarise it in any great detail. The two accused were Ian Brady, twenty-seven at the time of his arrest in October 1965, and Myra Hindley, his mistress, twenty-three. Brady, an illegitimate child, was born in a slum district of Glasgow's Clydeside; his mother was at work, and he was brought up by a neighbour with three children of her own. At the age of eleven, he got a scholarship to Shawland Academy, a school where most of the students were from middle-class homes, and he seems to have developed his attitude of resentment from this period. He began committing thefts and burglaries, and from the age of thirteen to seventeen he was on probation for a series of such offences. He moved to Manchester with his mother in 1945, and was soon sent to a correctional school for a year. He was of above average intelligence, introverted, bad-tempered, and with a well-developed sadistic streak. In 1959 he became a stock clerk in a chemical company in Manchester. A great deal of his wages went on cheap Spanish wine and pornographic literature. By the time Myra Hindley joined the firm as a typist in 1961, Brady's tendencies were well-developed; he was interested in obscene photographs – in taking them as well as buying them – and in torture; he felt that modern society was totally decadent and corrupt, and that in such a society any healthy-minded person would inevitably be an outcast and a criminal. Hitler was his ideal, and he owned a great many books about concentration camps and tortures.

When Myra Hindley became infatuated with him, Brady was not interested; perhaps he felt she looked too healthy. She was a perfectly normal girl with religious tendencies, who had been brought up in an affectionate family; she loved children and animals. But when he began to realise that she possessed masochistic tendencies, his interest grew. At the trial, no evidence was offered about the development of their relationship, but the police uncovered a great deal. She became his mistress, then joined him in posing for pornographic pictures taken with a camera with a timing device. Brady soon convinced her that religion was a sign of weak mindedness. In 1963, Brady moved into the house in which Myra lived with her grandmother. One month later, a sixteen-year-old girl named Pauline Reade vanished; she lived close to them. Although her body has never been found, and Brady never confessed to the murder, it seems probable that Pauline Reade was the first victim of this strange duo. Six months later, in November 1963, twelve-year-old John Kilbride vanished on a Saturday afternoon. He was last seen in a busy marketplace at Ashton-under-Lyne. That day, Myra Hindley hired a mini.

Six months later, Keith Bennett, aged twelve, disappeared on his way to see his grandmother. This was in the Longsight district, where Brady had lived for many years with his mother. And six months after this, on Boxing Day, 1964, a ten-year-old girl named Lesley Ann Downey left her home to go to a nearby fair, and vanished. By this time, Brady, Myra Hindley and the grandmother had moved to a house in Wardle Brook Avenue, Hattersley, closer to the moors where certain bodies were buried. . . .

In August 1964, Myra's sister Maureen had married a youth with a police record, sixteen-year-old David Smith. When Brady learned about the police record he suddenly became very interested in Smith, and was soon proposing that they should rob a bank. He invited Smith and Maureen to the house a great deal, gave them wine, and preached the doctrines of the Marquis de Sade – that society has made laws for the protection of the law-givers and the oppression of people stupid enough to accept them. Smith was soon writing in his diary such sentences as, 'Murder is a hobby and a supreme pleasure'; 'God is a superstition, a cancer which eats in the brain'; 'People are like maggots; small, blind and worthless'. The sentiments themselves are hardly more extreme than those held by Swift; but Brady was soon explaining to Smith that he had put them into practice – that he had killed 'three or four people' and buried

236

their bodies on the moors. It was his first major mistake. On 5th October 1965, Brady told Smith to bring his own library of murder and pornography to Wardle Brook Avenue; he and Myra took two suitcases to Manchester Central Station. They intended to stage a murder to initiate Smith into the pleasures of crimes of violence. In a pub in Manchester, they picked up Edward Evans, aged seventeen, whom Brady later alleged to be a homosexual. Evans agreed to go home with him, and when Evans and Brady were comfortably installed in the living-room with a bottle of cheap wine, Myra hurried off to fetch David Smith, who lived nearby. Almost as soon as Smith arrived, there was a loud scream, and Smith rushed into the sitting-room to see Brady attacking Evans with a hatchet. Brady hit him fourteen times before he stopped moving. Then he poured two glasses of wine and offered one to Smith. The latter was afraid for his own life, and took a drink. Brady told him to feel the weight of the hatchet – no doubt with the intention of getting Smith's fingerprints on it. Then Smith helped him carry the body upstairs. Myra's grandmother, who had heard the scream, was told that Myra had dropped the tape recorder on her toe. Smith finally said: 'Well, I'd better be getting along now,' and to his surprise, Brady agreed. He rushed home to tell his wife the story. The following morning they hurried to the phone and the police closed in on the house in Wardle Brook Avenue, and discovered the body of Edward Evans wrapped in a blanket in a bedroom. Evans had kicked Brady on the ankle as he writhed on the floor; it was this that decided Brady not to bury him for another twenty-four hours.

The suitcases in Manchester Central Station were discovered through the cloakroom ticket; they proved to contain pornographic books and photographs, and two tapes. Some of the photographs showed Lesley Ann Downey, with a scarf around her eyes, posing naked for the camera; one of the tapes had her voice on it, begging her kidnappers to allow her to go home, and asking them not to hurt her.

The photographs led the police to an area of the moors between Lancashire and Yorkshire, where they finally uncovered two bodies that were identified as Lesley Ann Downey

237

and John Kilbride. Both bodies were too far decomposed for the pathologist to determine how they had died, but the boy's trousers had been pulled down, suggesting that some form of sexual assault had occurred.

In May 1966, Brady and Myra Hindley were both sentenced to life imprisonment, and a few months later, a paragraph appeared in the newspapers stating that Myra Hindley had been moved into solitary confinement for her own safety.

It has never been ascertained whether they killed Pauline Reade and Keith Bennett. It is also highly probable that there is another victim whose name is still unknown. It will be noticed that the murders occurred roughly every six months – and in fact, Brady told David Smith as much. Lesley Downey was killed on 26th December 1964, and Edward Evans on 6th October 1965. Yet Brady told Smith he was 'not really ready for another one yet'. Was there another victim in June or July, 1965?

Although the Moors case has already been the subject of four books (the best of which[1] is by Emlyn Williams), it still presents many mysteries, the chief one of which concerns the relationship between Brady and Hindley. Was this another 'master and slave' relationship, like Leopold and Loeb? Was Brady also homosexual? Were the murders genuinely sadistic, or were they a sort of anarchistic gesture, like Ravachol's? The only thing that can be said is that there is no precedent for this type of murder – that is, for an intellectually unbalanced male to persuade a perfectly normal and affectionate girl to take part in child murder. The couple even spent Christmas Eve of 1964 sleeping out on John Kilbride's grave, and Brady took a photograph of Myra Hindley holding her dog and looking down at it. The couple will probably spend the remainder of their lives in prison; but it would be more to the point if a psychologist could get them to explain exactly why they committed the murders. For the crimes may be a portent.

Burke and Hare, Voirbo, Lacenaire, Palmer, all killed for money. Jack the Ripper and Jesse Pomeroy mark the beginning

[1] *Beyond Belief*, 1967.

of a new era in which money gives way to sex as a motive for murder. What is more, as we have seen in the case of Brady and Kürten, there is a tendency in the twentieth century for the worst criminals to be slightly above the average in intelligence. It must be emphasised that when I say 'slightly above' I do not mean greatly above. He is clever enough to feel a misfit and resent the society that has no place for him; not clever enough to view his situation objectively, and plan how to get society to accept him on his own terms. He is a man with the capacity for action, but without the long-range foresight to use it to best advantage. And so, like Brady, he plans bank robberies, or, like Holmes, petty swindles, failing to recognise that these can probably only bring short-term advantages. A slightly more cunning type of criminal might set up in some more or less legal profession like casting horoscopes or contacting the dead. If the same mentality advances another step, the swindler might become an abstract painter or a non-tonal composer, and he then ceases to be in any sense outside the law. He may still be as basically irresponsible and self-centred as the true criminal, and the anger he arouses when he exhibits his strange pieces of functional sculpture is actually a recognition that he is a kind of confidence swindler who is not attempting to deepen human experience. But at least he has ceased to be socially harmful.

It may therefore be a sign of the evolution of our society that we are producing more types who fall into this penumbral area between the socially irresponsible and the criminal. And if such a person happens to have a dominant personality and strong sexual urges, it is not at all improbable that he will be closer to the criminal than the pseudo-artist. And it has to be accepted that the number of such people will increase steadily before the end of the century.

The mentality behind the Moors case can also be seen, for example, in the case of Melvin Rees, a jazz musician and multiple sex killer, whom a friend quoted as saying: 'You can't say it's wrong to kill. Only individual standards make it right or wrong' – the de Sade argument. And even stranger, when the same friend suspected Rees, 'I asked him point-blank if he had killed those people. He evaded the question. He didn't deny it.' H H Holmes would have cast up his eyes to heaven and said: 'My dear fellow, what a *horrible* idea. . . .' Rees was capable of murder, but he couldn't be bothered to lie.

The murders for which Rees was convicted took place on Sunday, 11th January 1959, near Apple Grove, Eastern Virginia. A middle-aged lady driving along a lonely stretch of road saw a car which she recognised as belonging to her niece, Mildred Jackson; its front wheels were off the road. The Jackson family – twenty-nine-year-old Carrol Jackson, his wife Mildred and their two children, Susan, aged five, and the eighteen-month-old baby Janet – had vanished completely. There was no blood, no sign of a struggle. And for two months, the most careful search failed to reveal any clues. Carrol Jackson had been a truck driver who had just changed his job – he was now a bank clerk. He was a non-smoker and teetotaller who had met his wife at the Baptist church; she was president of the women's missionary society. They paid regular instalments on their house and car. Clearly, they had not disappeared voluntarily. The only indication of what might have happened to them came from another couple, who had been driving nearby on the same day; an old blue Chevrolet had forced them off the road, and a man had walked back from it towards their car. The husband had quickly reversed and drove off; the Chevrolet did not attempt to follow them.

Two months later, on 4th March, two of the missing family were found. A man pulling a dead branch to gain traction for his car uncovered the body of a man lying face downwards, his hands tied behind him. Carrol Jackson had been shot and beaten with a blunt instrument. Underneath him was the eighteen-month-old baby. She had been thrown there alive, and suffocated with her father's body.

On 21st March, boys hunting squirrels near Annapolis, Maryland, saw a human foot sticking out of the ground. The bodies of Mildred Jackson and five-year-old Susan were soon uncovered. Mildred Jackson had a stocking tied round her neck; Susan had been beaten to death with a blunt instrument.

Although the bodies were badly decomposed, there could be little doubt that Mildred Jackson had been sexually assaulted.

The police wondered whether these murders could be connected to a case that had taken place two years earlier. An army sergeant had gone out for a drive with a thirty-six-year-old woman, Margaret Harold. They had stopped in a lonely spot, and were approached by a man who told them he was the caretaker of the property. He asked for a cigarette, then for a lift back to the road. On the way, he pulled a gun and demanded money. Margaret Harold said, 'Don't give it to him,' and the man immediately shot her through the head. The sergeant leapt out of the car and ran away, but the killer was not interested in him, but in the body. Police later described the killer as 'a sexual degenerate'. The murderer had gone by the time the police returned, some hours later, but they found a deserted shack nearby with pornographic pictures on the walls, and Press cuttings about sex crimes. Witnesses in the area described a tall man driving a battered blue Chevrolet. There was also a photograph of a pretty girl, torn from a University of Maryland yearbook, in the shack. Police traced the girl, but a check through her long list of dates led nowhere. Unfortunately, she omitted to mention one of her dates because he was married. . . .

In May 1959, the police received the anonymous letter that quoted Melvin Davis Rees as saying that he thought murder was not wrong. The police tried to locate Rees, but without result. Then, early in 1960, the writer of the letter went to the police and identified himself as Glenn L Moser, a salesman and a friend of Rees. He had received a letter from Rees, who was working as a salesman in a music shop in west Memphis, Arkansas. The police picked him up, and the sergeant identified him as the killer of Margaret Harold.

It was at this point that the clairvoyant Peter Hurkos entered the case. Dr F Reisenman, a psychiatrist, was so disturbed by the case that he decided to lay out three thousand dollars on the famous 'psychic', who lived in Florida. Hurkos flew to Virginia, went to the churchyard where the Jackson family were buried, and described the killer. His first description was wrong

– he described a man the police had already cleared, apparently because he unconsciously read the mind of a police officer. His next attempt was an accurate description of Melvin Rees: slightly over six feet tall, left-handed, tattooed on the arm, with a walk like a duck, and ape-like arms. Hurkos also went to the scene of the murder of Margaret Harold, and went straight to a bush, from which he plucked the woman's torn skirt – it had hung there unnoticed for three years, since the killer flung it out of the car. Hurkos added that the man had committed nine murders altogether.

A search of the home of Rees' parents in Hyattsville revealed a .38 revolver – with which Carrol Jackson had been shot – and a number of sheets of paper describing sadistic acts. One of them was what they were looking for: a photograph of Mildred Jackson clipped from a newspaper, with an account of the murder. 'Caught on a lonely road. . . . Drove to a select area and killed the husband and baby. Now the mother and daughter were all mine. . . .' The letter made it clear that both mother and daughter had been kidnapped for sexual purposes. The details of the assault have not been released, but it was apparently not a normal sex act. (The details of the assault on Margaret Harold have also been suppressed.) Rees was a sadist of the same type as Donald Fearn; he tortured the mother to death.

The papers apparently also connected Rees with four more sex murders: a double murder of Marie Shomette and Ann Ryan, teenagers, who were shot to death, and of Mary Elizabeth Fellers, eighteen, and Shelby Jean Venable, sixteen, found floating in Maryland rivers. Rees was sentenced to death for the murder of the Jacksons. People who worked with him were startled when he was accused, and described him as mild-mannered and intelligent. He had been a student at the University of Maryland and had dated the girl whose photograph was found in the hut – where he had later tortured Mildred Jackson. If the girl had mentioned Rees – whom she gave up because he was married – the Jacksons would never have been killed. Rees had also been arrested once for dragging a woman into his car and assaulting her, but the woman later decided to drop the charge. Moser said that on the night before the Jackson killings, Rees was 'on a benzedrine kick', and 'he told me that he wanted to experience everything – love, hate, life, death'.

It is worth noting that Rees, like so many other sex killers, was an itinerant. He played piano, guitar, saxophone and clarinet, and moved around with jazz bands.

The case makes another point worth noting: that the killing of the Jackson family had been preceded by five other murders. A mass murderer seldom *starts* by killing several people (although, of course, there are exceptions – Jean Baptiste Troppmann, for example, the twenty-year-old homosexual who murdered a family of eight people for money in 1869; even so, Troppmann had earlier killed a man in a brawl by throwing him into a river).

The same thing can be noted in the case of Richard Speck, the killer of the eight Chicago nurses, another tramp. Towards midnight on 13th July 1966, Speck entered a nurse's hostel at Jeffrey Manor, in Chicago's south side, and went upstairs. He knocked on the door of a Philippine nurse, Corazon Amurao, twenty-three, who was asleep. The nurse opened the door, and saw the rather goodlooking, pockmarked young man who wore his hair swept straight back, and who smelt of alcohol. He was holding a small black gun. When he saw her room was empty, he ordered the nurse down the hall to another bedroom, where three girls were sleeping, then made all four go to yet another room, where there were two more. He told them, speaking softly, that he did not intend to harm them, but that he needed enough money to get to New Orleans. He tied up and gagged six of them with strips cut off sheets, and collected the money of each. At 12.30, three more nurses rushed into the dormitory. Speck pointed the gun at them too, assured them that no harm would come to them, and tied them up. Then he began to take them out of the room, one by one. The girls probably assumed that his intention was rape; when Corazon Amurao suggested getting free and attacking the man, one of the nurses told her that they hadn't better start anything, in case they provoked him. Corazon Amurao decided to roll under the bed. She stayed there all night as the man came in and took the girls out one by one. At five o'clock, when the killer had not reappeared for a long time, she crept from under the bed, and looked outside. What she saw there sent her screaming to a balcony, where she attracted the attention of neighbours. When the police arrived, they found the eight nurses, all dead. They were scattered all over the house. Gloria Davy, twenty-two, was the only one who had been ravished; she was one of the nurses who came in late. She lay naked, face down, on the living-room couch; she had been strangled and savagely slashed. Mary Ann Jordan, twenty, was stabbed in the heart, neck and left eye. Susan Farris, twenty-one, had been mutilated before she was strangled. The other five had been strangled and stabbed. Six of them were still tied up. But the killer had lost count – he thought he had killed every girl in the dormitory, and he had left one alive to describe him.

Miss Amurao remembered one thing clearly about the killer – a tattoo 'Born to raise hell' on his upper left arm. Apart from this, the police had two clues: the knots were tied in a manner that suggested a seaman, and the girls' hands had been tied with the palms together, in the way that a policeman handcuffs suspects; this suggested an ex-convict. And he had mentioned wanting to get back to New Orleans several times. With these clues, it proved remarkably easy to identify the killer. Half a block from the hostel there was a seamen's employment bureau. There, the police discovered that a man had been asking about a ship to New Orleans. His application form had a photograph clipped to it; he was Richard F Speck, aged twenty-five. The surviving nurse identified the photograph as that of the killer, and the alarm went out for Speck. When he saw his photograph in the newspaper, he realised that his chances of escape were nil. He slashed both his wrists with a razor. On Sunday the 17th, four days after the murders, a doctor in Cook County Hospital recognised the 'Born to raise hell' tattoo, and Speck wearily admitted his identity. It emerged that he had spent the day before the murders – Wednesday – drinking beer near the nurses' hostel, and trying to catch a glimpse of the nursing staff sunbathing from the park behind the hostel. He also took drugs

– 'yellow jackets' and 'red birds' – sodium amytal and sodium seconal – and was last seen at eleven o'clock. He claimed he could remember nothing of the murders. When he left the hostel, in the early hours of the morning, he went into a bar, and seemed in a cheerful mood; he told a fellow customer that his knife had come from Vietnam and had killed several people, and he put one arm round the bartender's neck and pretended to cut his throat. He had been drunk all day, and spent a few hours with a prostitute, whom he paid thirty dollars. Later, he went off with another prostitute and paid her five dollars. Obviously, drink had the effect of awakening his sexual appetites. This prostitute went back to his room in a cheap hotel on Dearborn Street, and later told the manager that Speck had a gun. The manager notified the police, who called on him. Speck said the gun belonged to the prostitute. And when the police moved out, he also moved out quickly; the police were notified half an hour later that the man wanted for the murder of the nurses was Richard Speck, and they rushed back to the hotel; Speck had already gone. By Saturday night, Speck was broke again, and was in the Starr Hotel on West Madison Street. He asked a man in the next room for a drink, but the man told him to go to hell. At midnight, Speck knocked on the man's door and fell into the room with his wrists slashed.

Investigation of Speck's background revealed that he was born in Kirkwood, Illinois, on 6th December 1941. At twenty, he married a fifteen-year-old girl, Shirley Malone, and they had a daughter. The marriage was not a success and – for reasons that have not yet been made public – Speck had a passionate hatred for his wife; he told friends that he was going back to Texas to kill her if it was the last thing he did. Significantly, the only nurse who was sodomised, Gloria Davy, bore a close resemblance to his wife. While he was still living with his wife, Speck had been arrested in Dallas, Texas, for pressing the blade of a knife against the throat of a young woman who was parking her car. He was sentenced to eighteen months in jail, but was released a few months later. Authorities at Huntsville, Texas, wanted him as a parole violator, but he moved on before they could catch him. There seems to be some reason for believing that after his release from jail, Speck went on a murder rampage that culminated in the killing of the eight nurses. On 10th April 1966, a pretty divorcee, Mary Pierce, vanished from the tavern in Monmouth, Illinois, where she worked. Her naked body was found three days later in the pigsty behind the tavern. Speck, who was in Monmouth staying with his brother and working as a carpenter, had asked the divorcee for a date and been refused. A week later, a sixty-five-year-old woman was raped and robbed; but by the time the police arrived to question him, Speck had left town. He took a job on an ore boat on the Great Lakes, but was dismissed on 2nd July, in Indiana Harbour. That day, in the nearby Indiana Dunes Park, three girls vanished, leaving their clothes behind them in a car.

These were the crimes of which Speck was suspected by the police; there had also been four attacks on women in Benton Harbour, near Indiana Harbour, in February 1966; the ages of the women ranged from seven to sixty, and all were strangled and stabbed, like the eight nurses.

The theory of the psychiatrist who examined Speck in prison, Dr Marvin Ziporyn, is that Speck was in a trance-like state due to drugs on the night of the murder of the nurses, and that the sight of the girl who resembled his wife – whom he had sworn to kill – triggered some mechanism of violence. He believes that Speck may have wandered around Chicago after the murders completely oblivious of what he had done. If, in fact, Speck had committed any of the crimes mentioned above, this theory would cease to fit the facts. Speck was a neurotic, and had been since childhood; once, in a fit of frustration with his father, he had hit himself on the head with a hammer and caused an injury; later, he suffered more head injuries in a barroom brawl. In compiling the *Encyclopedia of Murder*, I observed that many 'insane' killers had suffered head injuries – Earle Nelson (the 'gorilla murderer') and Lock Ah Tam, for example. But, above all, his personality was quiet and pleasant (I spoke to a man who knew him in Chicago, who described him as a 'charmer'), and his sexual desires were violent. This is always a dangerous combination – as can be seen in the case of

246

Christie, and of so many murderers discussed in this book – Gein, Rees, Kürten. A nurse who went out with him in Hancock, Michigan (where Speck had an emergency operation to remove his appendix) described him as very gentle, but with an enormous amount of hatred in him.

Speck was sentenced to death; but at the time of writing, he is still appealing against the sentence. A few months after his murders, on 12th November 1966, eighteen-year-old Robert Benjamin Smith walked into a beauty parlour in Mesa, Arizona – where he was a high school student – and forced five women and two little girls to lie face down on the floor; then he went around and shot them one by one in the back of the head. (He explained later, 'I wanted to be known'. When Speck heard of the crimes, he remarked: 'Boy, I'd like to get my hands on that guy. I'd kill him.' Psychologists found it hard to understand Smith's motives; he was an excellent student, and had no hostility towards his parents.

To speak of 'motiveless murder' would obviously be inaccurate, particularly in the case of sex crime; but what we are facing in the twentieth century is a type of murder in which the motive seems wholly inadequate. In April 1959, a man called Norman Smith had been watching a television programme called 'The Sniper'. He loaded his pistol and went out looking for someone to shoot. He saw Mrs Hazel Woodward watching the television with her window open, and shot her. He had never seen her before. Smith was a bachelor, who lived alone in his caravan in Sarasota County, Florida; so we have a repetition of the motive of loneliness; but this crime was less an explosion of frustration than an explosion of boredom.

On 4th July 1967, Klaus Gosmann came to trial, and told the judge who asked him if other people did not have a right to live: 'No, people are no more than things to me. Inanimate. Ciphers. I am a pragmatist.' Gosmann was the infamous 'Midday murderer' of Hersbruck, near Nuremberg. His first murder had taken place seven years before, when he was nineteen, and still a student. He was fascinated by guns – his father had been a captain in the German army, who had been shot by Americans at the end of the war, and Gosmann treasured his memory. He decided one day to commit a murder at exactly midday, when the town's churchbells were making such a noise that no one would hear the shot. Timing it exactly, he walked into a house on the Tuchergarten Strasse ninety seconds before midday. He listened outside doors for a noise that might tell him that someone was at home. And in one of the flats, Valeska Eder was entertaining her fiancé Ernst Hering to lunch. Gosmann knocked at the door and Hering opened it. Gosmann had half a minute to go, so he said carefully: 'Sir, I wish to ask you a question, and I shall not repeat it.' Hering asked 'What?' and Gosmann said: 'Your money or your lives?' But it was not their money he wanted, for as the bells chimed midday, Gosmann carefully shot Hering through the heart with his Walther P-38. Then, as the bells drowned the screams of Valeska Eder, he shot her through the head. Then the killer walked home for lunch, and went back to his studies afterwards – he was deeply interested in mystical theology and had a daydream of a quiet little church somewhere in the country, and a life of dedicated service.

Later in the day, Klaus Gosmann wrote up the story of the murder with careful detail in his diary. Obviously, it gave him a great feeling of power and self-respect that he had committed the murder so stylishly, without the slightest nervous tremor.

Two years later, Gosmann decided to try again. This time, the victim was the director of the Deutsches Bank at Ochenbruch, fifty-year-old Erich Hallbauer. Again, Gosmann shot him as the bells pealed midday, and this time he took 3,060 marks from a tray in the office. This time, he used a Mauser pistol.

Two months later, the murder at another bank hold-up was almost accidental. The robber walked into the Neuhaus-Pegnitz branch of the Deutsches Bank, and held it up at exactly midday, when there was only one customer present. As he was leaving, with money in a briefcase, the porter reached for his pocket to put on his glasses – he had not noticed the hold-up. Gosmann shot him twice.

On 29th March 1963, Gosmann entered a gun shop in the Spittlertorgraben district of Nuremberg, and shot down the widow who kept it, Frau Korola Hannwakker, and her twenty-nine-year-old son, Helmut. His motive this time was presumably to add to his armoury. The police discovered that the gun used to kill the two was the same as the one used in the first bank hold-up.

In December 1964, Gosmann enlisted in the German army, but the discipline was too much for him, and he absented himself without leave in April of the following year.

For his next – and last – crime, Gosmann made the mistake of choosing a big store. He snatched a woman's handbag on the first floor of Brenninkmeyer's, in Nuremberg. The woman screamed, and Gosmann was chased. He fired at the woman and missed, fired at a store official, and hit his briefcase. 'I kept thinking: "How ridiculous, it can't be happening".' Finally, he was beaten to the ground – but he managed to claim one more victim, Hermann Thieman, the man whose briefcase had stopped his first bullet.

In prison, Gosmann continued to keep his diaries, which are highly literate: 'I would say there is a great difference between me and Raskolnikov [of Dostoievsky's *Crime and Punishment*]. Just as long as I don't get it in the neck from the judge, I don't have to consider myself as the perpetrator. Raskolnikov always thought of himself as the perpetrator. . . .' One of his guns had 'Elke' carved on the handle, and he admitted that he had intended to kidnap the film star Elke Sommer next time she came to Nuremberg to visit her family. None of his other crimes show any sexual motive.

Gosmann was sentenced to life imprisonment, with no chance of release. Gosmann's diary admits that he has done wrong, but goes on: 'But now, to play the role of a broken man, to beg for understanding – or for sympathy – that I am not going to do.'

The chief point to note about the case is Gosmann's alienation: 'How ridiculous, it can't be happening.' Like so many other murderers, he was playing a game; in spite of his interest in mysticism, he could not feel that life was serious. Albert Camus was the first to write at length of such a man in his novel *L'Etranger,* although it might be argued that Dostoievsky's Stavrogin anticipated him by seventy years.

The next point to note is the purely practical one: that Gosmann was caught because he went on committing his crimes. If he had stopped before the last one, he would have been safe enough. Moreover, the crimes became steadily more careless – as if there was a subconscious compulsion to be caught. Many sex killers have continued until they were actually caught in the act – like the French Ripper Joseph Vacher – or were forced to flee, leaving behind some vital clue, like Joseph Phillipe, a killer of prostitutes, who was caught by the great Claude in 1866;[1] or Gordon Cummins, who had a brief but spectacular rampage of murder and rape during the blackouts in 1942. Rather less frequently, such a criminal ends by making a slip that gives the clue to his identity. This latter was the case of Lucian Staniak, the 'Red Spider', whose series of sadistic sex murders in Poland between 1964 and 1967 can be compared only with those of Jack the Ripper or the Boston Strangler. Since these murders have never received the publicity given to the Boston Strangler – due to the reluctance of the Red authorities to publicise crime – it may be instructive to consider them here in some detail.

In July 1964, the communist régime in Poland was getting prepared to celebrate the twentieth anniversary of the liberation of Warsaw by Russian troops; a great parade was due to take place in Warsaw on the 22nd. On the 4th July the editor of *Przeglad Polityczny,* the Polish equivalent of *Pravda,* received an anonymous letter in spidery red handwriting: 'There is no happiness without tears, no life without death. Beware! I am going to make you cry.' Marian Starzynski thought the anonymous writer had him in mind, and requested police protection.

[1] Phillipe strangled and cut the throat of a prostitute in 1861, another in 1862, and another in February 1864. In this year he killed five girls altogether, including a child of seven. On 8th January 1866, he killed another prostitute, but on the 11th, he was interrupted in the course of an attack. His victim had noticed the tattoo 'Born under an unlucky star'. Caught as he fled, he was identified by Claude, and was executed in July. He was charged with eight murders, but is believed to have committed seventeen. Resemblance to the Speck case will be noted.

But on the day of the big parade, a seventeen-year-old blonde, Danka Maciejowitz, failed to arrive home from a parade organised by the School of Choreography and Folklore in Olsztyn, one hundred and sixty miles north of Warsaw. The next day, a gardener in the Olsztyn Park of Polish Heroes discovered the girl's body in some shrubbery. She had been stripped naked and raped, and the lower part of her body was covered with Jack-the-Ripper-type mutilations. And the following day, the 24th, another red-ink letter was delivered to *Kulisy*, a Warsaw newspaper: 'I picked a juicy flower in Olsztyn and I shall do it again somewhere else, for there is no holiday without a funeral.' Analysis of the ink showed that it had been made by dissolving red art paint in turpentine.

On 16th January 1965, the Warsaw newspaper *Zycie Warsawy* published the picture of a pretty sixteen-year-old girl, Aniuta Kaliniak, who had been chosen to lead a parade of students in another celebration rally the following day. She left her home in Praga, an eastern suburb of Warsaw, and crossed the river Vistula to reach the parade. Later, she thumbed a lift from a lorry driver, who dropped her close to her home at a crossroads. (The fact that a sixteen-year-old girl would thumb a lift like this indicates that the level of sex crime in Poland must be a great deal lower than in England or the US.) The day after the parade, her body was found in a basement in a leather factory opposite her home. The killer had removed a grating to get in. The crime had obviously been carefully planned. He had waited in the shadows of the wall, and cut off her cry with a wire noose dropped over her head. In the basement, he had raped her, and left a six-inch spike sticking in her sexual organs (an echo of the Boston Strangler). While the search went on another red-ink letter advised the police where to look for her body.

Olsztyn and Warsaw are one hundred and sixty miles apart; this modern Ripper differed from his predecessor in not sticking to the same area. Moreover, like Klaus Gosmann, he was a man with a strong dramatic sense: the selection of national holidays for his crimes, the letters philosophising about life and death.

The Red Spider – as he had come to be known, from his spidery writing – chose All Saints day, 1st November, for his next murder, and Poznan, two hundred kilometres west of Warsaw, as the site. A young, blonde hotel receptionist Janka Popielski, was on her way to look for a lift to a nearby village, where she meant to meet her boyfriend. Since it was her holiday, the freight terminal was almost deserted. Her killer pressed a chloroform-soaked bandage over her nose and mouth. Then he removed her skirt, stockings and panties, and raped her behind a packing shed. After this, he killed her with a screwdriver. The mutilations were so thorough and revolting that the authorities suppressed all details. The Red Spider differed from many sex killers in apparently being totally uninterested in the upper half of his victims. Janka was stuffed into a packing case, where she was discovered an hour later. The police swooped on all trains and buses leaving Poznan, looking for a man with bloodstained clothes; but they failed to find one. The next day, the Poznan newspaper *Courier Zachodni* received one of the now-notorious letters in red ink, containing a quotation from Stefan Zeromsky's national epic *Popioly* (1928): 'Only tears of sorrow can wash out the stain of shame; only pangs of suffering can blot out the fires of lust.'

May Day, 1966, was both a communist and a national holiday. Marysia Galazka, seventeen, went out to look for her cat in the quiet suburb of Zoliborz, in northern Warsaw. When she did not return, her father went out to look for her. He found her lying in the typical rape position, with her entrails forming an abstract pattern over her thighs, in a tool shed behind the house. Medical evidence revealed that the killer had raped her before disembowelling her.

Major Ciznek, of the Warsaw Homicide Squad, was in charge of the case, and he made a series of deductions. The first was that the Red Spider was unlikely to confine himself to his well-publicised murders on national holidays. Such killers seek victims when their sexual desire is at maximum tension, not according to some preconceived timetable. Ciznek examined evidence of some fourteen other murders that had taken place since the first one in April 1964, one each in Lublin, Radom,

Kielce, Lodz, Bialystock, Lomza, two in Bydgoszcz, five in the Poznan district. All places were easily reached by railway; the *modus operandi* was always the same. Every major district of Poland within four hundred kilometres of Warsaw was covered. Ciznek stuck pins in a map and examined the result. It looked as if Warsaw might be the home of the killer, since the murders took place all round it. But one thing was noticeable. The murders extended much farther south than north, and there were also more of them to the south. It rather looked as if the killer had gone to Bialystock, Lomza and Olsztyn as a token gesture of extending his boundaries. Assuming, then, that the killer lived somewhere south of Warsaw, where would this be most likely to be? There were five murders in the Poznan district, to the west of Warsaw. Poznan is, of course, easily reached from Warsaw. But where in the south could it be reached from just as easily? Cracow was an obvious choice. So was Katowice, twenty miles or so from Cracow. This town was also at the centre of a network of railway lines.

On Christmas Eve, 1966, Cracow was suddenly ruled out as a possibility. Three service men getting on a train between Cracow and Warsaw looked into a reserved compartment and found the half naked and mutilated corpse of a girl on the floor. The leather miniskirt had been slashed to pieces; so had her abdomen and thighs. The servicemen notified the guard, and a message was quickly sent to Warsaw, who instructed the train-driver to go straight through to Warsaw, non-stop, in case the killer managed to escape at one of the intervening stations. A careful check of passengers at Warsaw revealed no one stained with blood or in any way suspicious. But the police were able to locate the latest letter from the killer, dropped into the post slot of the mail van on top of all the others. It merely said: 'I have done it again,' and was addressed to *Zycie Warsawy*. It looked as if the Red Spider had got off the train in Cracow, after killing the girl, and dropped the letter into the slot.

The girl was identified as Janina Kozielska, of Cracow. And the police recalled something else: another girl named Koziel-ska had been murdered in Warsaw in 1964. This proved to be Janina's sister Aniela. For Ciznek, this ruled out Cracow as the possible home of the killer. For he would be likely to avoid his home territory. Moreover, there surely had to be some connection between the murders of the two sisters. . . . The compartment on the Cracow-Warsaw train had been booked over the telephone by a man who said his name was Stanislav Kozielski, and that his wife would pick up the tickets. Janina had paid 1,422 zloty for them – about twenty-five pounds. Janina had come to the train alone and been shown to her compartment by the ticket inspector. She said that her husband would be joining her shortly. The inspector had also checked a man's ticket a few moments later, but could not recall the man. It was fairly clear, then, that the Red Spider knew the girl well enough to persuade her to travel with him as his wife, and had probably paid for the ticket. He had murdered her in ten minutes or so, and then hurried off the train.

Ciznek questioned the dead girl's family. They could not suggest who might have killed their daughter, but they mentioned that she sometimes worked as a model – as her sister had. She worked at the School of Plastic Arts and at a club called The Art Lovers Club.

Ciznek recollected that the red ink was made of artist's paint dissolved in turpentine and water; this looked like a lead.

The Art Lovers Club proved to have one hundred and eighteen members. For an Iron Curtain country, its principles were remarkably liberal; many of its members painted abstract, tachiste and pop-art pictures. Most of them were respectable professional men – doctors, dentists, officials, newspapermen. And one of them came from Katowice. His name was Lucian Staniak, and he was a twenty-six-year-old translator who worked for the official Polish publishing house. Staniak's business caused him to travel a great deal – in fact, he had bought an *ulgowy bilet,* a train ticket that enabled him to travel anywhere in Poland.

Ciznek asked if he could see Staniak's locker. It confirmed his increasing hope that he had found the killer. It was full of knives – used for painting, the club manager explained. Staniak daubed the paint on with a knife blade. He liked to use red paint. And one of his paintings, called 'The Circle of Life', showed a flower being eaten by a cow, the cow being eaten by a wolf, the wolf being shot by a hunter, the hunter being killed by a car driven by a woman, and the woman lying with her stomach ripped open in a field, with flowers sprouting from her body.

Ciznek now knew he had his man, and he telephoned the Katowice police. They went to Staniak's address at 117 Aleje Wyzwolenia, but found no one at home. In fact, Staniak was out committing another murder – his last. It was a mere month after the train murder – 31st January 1967 – but he was impatient at the total lack of publicity given to the previous murder. So he took Bozhena Raczkiewicz, an eighteen-year-old student from the Lodz Institute of Cinematographic Arts, to a shelter built at the railway station for the use of stranded overnight travellers, and there stunned her with a vodka bottle. In accordance with his method when in a hurry, he cut off her skirt and panties with his knife. He had killed her in a few minutes between six o'clock and six twenty-five. The neck of the broken bottle had a clear fingerprint on it.

Staniak was picked up at dawn the next day; he had spent the night getting drunk. His fingerprints matched those on the bottle. He was a good-looking young man of twenty-six. And when he realised that there was no chance of escape, he confessed fully to twenty murders. He told the police that his parents and his sister had been crossing an icy road when they were hit by a skidding car, being driven too fast by the young wife of a Polish Air Force pilot. The girl had been acquitted of careless driving. Staniak had seen the picture of his first victim in a newspaper, and thought she looked like the wife of the pilot; this was his motive in killing her. He had decided against killing the wife of the pilot because it would be traced back to him.

Sentenced to death for six of the murders – the six described here – Staniak was later reprieved and sent to the Katowice asylum for the criminally insane.

The Red Spider murders are certainly a great deal easier to understand than those of Speck or Klaus Gosmann. The death

'break open' very fast indeed. The police traced six university students who had been friendly with Weinstein at some time, and had then broken with him. Their stories were always the same. Weinstein had invited them to the shop after hours, and offered them food and drink. Ham sandwiches with thick mustard was his speciality. The boys became unexpectedly drowsy, then fell asleep. When they came to, they were bruised and naked. They had been driven home by one of Weinstein's helpers in the shop.

The helper was traced; he was fourteen-year-old Clark Vestry, tall and powerful for his age. He decided to tell the police all he knew, and the story was incredible. Weinstein had been pursuing his hobby of raping college boys for at least a year. When he had finished with them, he would order Vestry to kill them. Vestry would agree, and then drive the student home, warning him to stay away from Weinstein. (One of the youths told the police that he woke up and found a man standing over him who told him he had been hired to throw him in the river, but that he didn't propose to do this.) Vestry's confession was amazingly casual:

'Then there was another guy named Bill. He was also a Penn student. In July he came to the shop and when I got there I saw he was drowsy and staggering around. He wanted me to strangle this kid and I told him no – that another fellow had seen me with the kid. I made up that excuse and I took the kid home by cab.

'Another guy named Bill was there in either late September or October. "Strangle him," Steve told me, handing me a rope. . . . When Steve was through with him we took him to the dormitory and afterwards Steve gave me twenty-five dollars.'

John Green, the murdered youth, was just unlucky. Weinstein was unable to bring him round – although he was still alive. They poured ammonia down the youth's throat and he went into convulsions. The next day, Weinstein phoned Vestry to say: 'I couldn't bring him round so I strangled him. . . . Come on over. We'll get rid of the body.' Two of Vestry's friends, aged fifteen and sixteen, also knew about Weinstein's sexual burglaries, and they came over to help get rid of the body – which was beginning to smell, four days after the murder. It was put into a sleeping-bag, then the trunk, and lifted into the boot of the car. Vestry said he had an appointment, so the other three drove out to an area near Hamburg, Berks County, and tried burying the body. The earth was too hard. They drove back to Philadelphia, and Weinstein told them to put some gravel in the trunk while he kept watch. The youths were lazy and only put a few shovelfuls in. They then threw the trunk off the pier, where it promptly bobbed up again. Weinstein told them not to worry – it would soon sink – and they went home.

The search was now on for Weinstein, and his photograph was published in the newspapers. He was recognised in a Times Square theatrical booking agency four days after the body had been discovered. The young man who recognised him worked for a Philadelphia ticket agency, and Weinstein had invited him back to his shop after hours – the offer had luckily been refused. When the booking clerk recognised Weinstein, the latter hastened out of the agency; the young man followed, and told a policeman on traffic duty that the short, fat man crossing the street was a wanted murderer. At this, Weinstein began to run, and was soon overtaken by the policeman. The twenty-nine-year-old Weinstein made a full confession to the murder. His three helpers were arraigned as accessories after the fact. On 16th May 1968, Weinstein was sentenced to life imprisonment.

Inevitably, Ypsilanti has its homosexual murder case. On Sunday, 16th October 1966, a good-looking youth of seventeen, Arland Withrow, returned home at 11.15 pm from a date with his girlfriend. The phone rang and he talked into it briefly. Then he said that he was going out to move his car out of the driveway. His parents did not see him alive again. His naked body was found in a creek near Port Huron four days later; he had been strangled and sexually abused.

No one seemed to be able to throw any light on the disappearance. But the detective in charge of the case was intrigued about why certain of Arland Withrow's male friends should blush and look embarrassed when questioned about older males who might be acquainted with Arland. The detectives had learned that although Arland was dating a girl and talked about getting married, he seemed to have an obsession about immaturity. He had left school to go to work in a Ford plant, saying that work was more important than education. He had given his age as eighteen, instead of seventeen. The detectives wondered whether, in his attempts to feel 'grown up', he might not have involved himself with a homosexual.

On 24th October, eight days after Arland Withrow's disappearance, police at Toledo, Ohio – forty miles away – found another naked, battered body of a man; once again, it was in a creek. He was identified from fingerprints as Robert Pugh, a thirty-two-year-old schoolteacher from Virginia.

Some of the teenagers who belonged to Arland Withrow's group eventually admitted that they had received indecent proposals from a man of about thirty. He was known as Don Russell. Finally, one of them admitted that a man called Ralph had taken him out in a car, and had forced him to do things 'that disgusted me'. He thought that Ralph – who was very strong – was connected with prisons.

The detectives asked the sheriff of Ypsilanti if he knew of a man named Ralph connected with prisons. The sheriff suggested they try the Federal Correctional Institution fifteen miles south of Ypsilanti. And the governor there immediately recognised the description as that of Ralph Nuss, a social and psychiatric worker whose position in the institution was one of great responsibility. He was working on a scheme for getting prisoners gradually rehabilitated by letting them out to do part-time work. He was regarded as brilliant at his job.

Picked up by the police later in the day, Nuss made no attempt to deny the murder, although the police declined to publish his statement of the motive – presumably for reasons of public decency, and to avoid upsetting his family. Nuss also admitted to a second murder – not that of the thirty-two-year-old schoolteacher, but a Canadian named Thomas Brown, an eighteen-year-old truck driver who had vanished from his lodgings, where he lived with another male friend. They owed rent, and Brown suddenly told his friend that he was going out 'on business'. The nature of his business may be surmised; Nuss was known to be generous with his money. But Nuss shot the youth through the head, and dumped his naked body in a creek. He led the police to the body. The motives for the murders has never been uncovered – although it may be that Nuss enjoyed beating his bedfellows, and they sometimes objected. Nuss has never been tied to the murder of the thirty-two-year-old schoolteacher. In court, Nuss wept, but he explained that this was because there were women in court, and he did not want them to see his humiliation.

In December 1966, two homosexuals went on a murder rampage that claimed six victims before they were caught. Six days before Christmas, at Salt Lake City, Utah, the town that was founded by Mormons was electrified to hear that the body of an eighteen-year-old petrol station attendant had been found on a lonely road; he had been stabbed five times and sexually assaulted. The naked youth proved to be Stephen Shea, and he had vanished the night before, 18th December. $147 was missing, so sex had not been the only motive of the killer or killers.

The following day, another naked youth was found east of the city. He had been killed by a stiletto thrust to the heart, and there was also evidence of a beating and sexual assault. It seemed to be the same knife that had killed Stephen Shea. He was identified as another petrol station attendant, Michael Holtz. The police requested all petrol stations to either close at dusk, or to make sure that older men were in charge – if possible, downright ugly as well.

On 21st December, the killers decided to go on a rampage – no reason has ever been established. A twenty-nine-year-old taxi driver stopped at the office of his company and reported that he was just about to take a fare out to the airport, but that he didn't like the look of him. He told the man at the radio transmitter: 'If I get into trouble, I'll click my microphone twice.' A few minutes later, the microphone clicked; police and other taxis rushed to the assistance of Grant Strong; but when they arrived, they found him dead, shot in the back of the head. He had been robbed.

In Lally's Tavern, near the airport, there were only five customers. At 11.15 pm, half an hour after the death of the taxi driver, two men strolled in. One of them put money in the one-armed-bandit, the other wandered over to the conter, produced a gun, and shot one of the customers in the back of the head. Then he told the bartender: 'This is a stick-up.' The bartender handed over three hundred dollars. The man then began shooting, as if to see if he could kill every witness. The four remaining customers dropped to the ground. One was pretending to be hit; the other three were wounded, and two of them later died. As the two men ran out, the bartender snatched up his gun and fired at them. He missed.

The alarm went out within minutes, and roadblocks were set up. Two hours later, a car approaching a roadblock at high speed braked to a halt and tried to turn. Deputies with guns quickly surrounded it. The two men inside were identified as Myron Lance, twenty-five, and Walter Kelbach, twenty-eight, both ex-convicts. The dead taxi driver's wallet was found in the car. In Kelbach's room were found articles of clothing belonging to the two murdered petrol station attendants. Kelbach – a raw-boned, blue-chinned man – was identified as the killer in the tavern hold-up. His companion, Myron Lance, looked altogether milder, with receding hair, and the studious look that seems to be typical of certain American college boys. The two of them showed no remorse about the murders, and smiled contemptuously throughout the hearing.

This note – of indifference and contempt – has been sounded repeatedly throughout this chapter. It seems to be typical of twentieth-century murder. Lance and Kelbach must have known that they hardly stood a chance after the tavern robbery; that the whole countryside would be up in arms looking for them. It was a sudden explosion of violence, as absurd as if a man driving along a mountain road should suddenly twist the steering wheel and plunge over a ravine. There have been many other cases of similar murder rampages – the case of Charles Starkweather is the best known – but there had usually been some immediately identifiable reason behind them: parents announcing that a young couple must stop seeing one another, a violent quarrel. Lance and Kelbach seem to have simply decided they were tired of conforming to social rules.

There is an aspect of murder that I have hardly touched upon in this book: what Louis Blom Cooper calls 'victimology'. It is a matter that will need to be carefully studied in the future. Arden of Faversham and John Hayes were fairly obvious victims – Arden was even aware that his wife wanted to kill him. And we can note repeatedly in this book that victims fall into certain categories: misers, husbands who allow their wives to take younger lovers (the recent Max Garvie case being an example), middle-aged sex-starved ladies, and so on. In the twentieth century, women have become murder victims more often than men. Donald Fearn chose his victim when he saw her walking along the pavement; she was pretty, but there must also have been something about her that made him want to torture her, a passivity, a hint of masochism. One gets a similar feeling about the murders of the Jackson family and the Clutter family. Herbert Clutter was such a strict teetotaller that he would not hire a man who drank; Mildred Jackson was president of the women's missionary guild. There can be no doubt that Herbert Clutter and Carrol Jackson were good men; but it was a passive, unadventurous kind of goodness. In the case of the eight nurses, one cannot help wondering what kind of passivity kept them from getting to a window the moment Speck left the room, and screaming the place down, or accepting Corazon Amurao's suggestion to attack him.

But in a case like the bar-room shooting by Walter Kelbach, even this rough attempt at victim-classification breaks down. It may be true that a man petting with his girlfriend in a car is more likely to end up dead than a man kissing her in the front room at home; but a man quietly drinking his beer at a bar can hardly expect to be shot in the back of the head. What murders such as this indicate is that some of the basic rules of civilisation are being broken by people who – without really considering the question at length – suddenly say: 'I don't wish to be a part of your civilisation any more.' We have come a complete circle from Wells' nomads, huddling together in river valleys for protection, whose killings were an attempt to establish a more secure foothold in the society. This pattern held true up to the time of Burke and Hare – and then slowly began to change. In a century, the old pattern has almost ceased to be discernible. We are in an age of murders committed out of frustration, sadism, revolt – or simply boredom.

But it would be a pity to close a book such as this on such a disquieting note. To begin with, we might bear in mind that, given the size of the population, murder has not risen appreciably. And in America, the murder rate has probably fallen since the old lawless days of the Wild West. And if the American murder rate is still so much higher than the English rate, this is because, as a country, America is still almost as lawless as many of the poorer and more backward nations. Most murders in America are committed with guns; and yet there is at present no sign that Congress will simply ban all firearms except shotguns. Such a measure would reduce the murder rate by a half within years.

At the time of writing, I have just finished reading John Hersey's *Algiers Motel Incident*, describing how, on the fourth day of the Negro riots in Detroit in 1967, a group of 'rogue policemen' went to a motel where there had been reports (false, it turned out) of a sniper, and shot three of the Negro guests; they beat up several others, including two white girls, who were also stripped of their clothes. Such incidents as this become possible in times of racial tension. (It should be borne in mind that Speck's murders took place after days of rioting in Chicago, following a policeman's refusal to allow Negro children to turn on fire hydrants on the hottest day of the year.) Many of the victims of murder in America might almost be regarded as war casualties.

Even in this century of irrational violence, there are still murder cases that conform to the old 'classic' pattern. And what is a 'classic murder'? Perhaps the simplest definition is: the kind of murder that appeals to mystery writers, the kind of murder that might almost have been invented by a mystery writer. Most

264

murders are messy, straightforward and pointless; they could not be invented because there is nothing to invent. This raises the interesting point that many of the murders described in this chapter might have been invented by a writer – the Red Spider, Klaus Gosmann, H H Holmes; which suggests that even psychopathic criminals are capable of 'classic' murders. The year 1967 provided two murder cases that might be regarded as models of the classic pattern.

The mayor of Escalles, M Jean Boutroy, was sleeping after a hard day's work in the strawberry fields, when the braying of a motor horn woke everyone in the farmhouse. It went on until M Boutroy reached the car – a CV Camionette – and found a half-naked man collapsed against the steering wheel, his chest pressing the horn button. He recognised the man as Armand Rohart, mayor of the nearby village of Peuplinges, and the richest man in the place. Forty-seven-year-old Rohart had been elected mayor in 1947, at the age of twenty; he employed forty villagers on his farm, and he was the most important man for many miles around.

Rohart was still breathing, but no amount of shaking could rouse him. He was clad only in wet swimming trunks. Boutroy drove him to the Lille hospital, where the doctor decided that he was suffering from some form of nervous shock. Boutroy then proceeded to Rohart's farm, La Bien Batie (well built), where Rohart's brother Jules told them that the farmer had driven off with his wife after lunch; their destination was the beach at Escalles. A search of the beach soon revealed the body of Jacqueline Rohart, dressed in a pink bikini and wreathed with sea-weed. It looked as if she had drowned. And this was the story told by Armand Rohart to Police Commissioner Henault when the farmer regained consciousness. He and Jacqueline – aged forty-five – had decided to go for a swim in the sea, to remind them of their courting days. They had walked in up to the neck – although neither could swim. And then, quite suddenly, a big wave struck them; Rohart lost his grip on his wife's hand, and eventually struggled back to the shore. He had been unconscious for several hours, and then staggered up to the car.

But what made a married couple in their forties decide to go bathing in the English Channel on a chilly June day? Rohart was quite frank with Henault. He admitted that he had been unfaithful to his wife a few years before – the girl was a fourteen-year-old children's nursemaid. When she became pregnant, he sent her back to her parents and settled money on her. Then he decided that he had been a fool to alienate his wife; he did his best to make her forget what had happened, buying her presents, treating her with the attention of a lover. It had been a whim of hers to revive their early days with a swim at Escalles.

Henault found the story convincing and touching; until the post mortem revealed that Jacqueline Rohart had no water in her lungs. She had not died of drowning. And yet Rohart's grief at his wife's funeral seemed so genuine that it was hard to believe that he was responsible for her death. Could she not have died of shock as the wave struck her?

Henault's men searched the beach for weeks, upturning every stone. The more they discovered, the less they were able to believe in the shock theory. Two weeks after the tragedy, the sea uncovered two bottles: one contained some sleeping capsules, the other was labelled 'ether', and still had a strong smell of the liquid. They also discovered a face mask of the type used by farm workers using a poison spray on vegetables and fruits. It could have been used as a pad to soak up the ether before it was applied to Jacqueline Rohart's face. Witnesses were found who had seen a man and a woman entering the sea at about four o'clock that afternoon; others had passed by much later, when a fog had come down, and saw a man at the foot of the cliff wrapped in a car blanket.

And at this point, the final piece of evidence appeared. An ex-legionnaire, Jacob Karbahay, approached the presiding judge, M Vergez, and told him that Rohart had asked him to kill his wife for him. Karbahay had occasionally had a little trouble with the local police – which may have made Rohart decide that he was the man for the job. When Karbahay saw what Rohart had in mind, he decided to tape-record him for his own protection. Rohart's first scheme was that the legionnaire should get him a deadly poison like curare – the alkaloid used by pygmies on their darts – which Rohart would smear on a needle hidden in the seat of his wife's car. The poison would take effect while she was driving; she would crash the car and die. Death would be due to the impact.

Even Karbahay could see the flaws in this. Suppose she simply stopped the car? Suppose she felt the needle scratch and simply got out to examine it? Suppose the police found the needle?

Karbahay set up his tape recorder on the shelf. The next time Rohart called on him, he got up casually and turned it on. Rohart noticed it, but Karbahay told him it was recording music from the radio, and played it back for a moment – on another track. It went on to record Rohart's proposal that Karbahay should murder his wife. Karbahay had kept quiet about the recording until he read in an account of the case that Rohart's lawyer declared that a 'second man' might be involved. If they intended to try shifting some of the blame to him, he was ready for them.

Henault went on probing Rohart's background. He soon discovered that Rohart's story of the love affair with the nursemaid was untrue in one particular: he had not broken off with her. They had been seen lying on a blanket together, embracing, long after the baby was born. But the girl decided she wanted to marry a younger man. Rohart was frantic with jealousy. The day before the murder, he went to the store in Calais where she worked, and asked her to sit in his car with him. There he told her that 'things might change' soon.

The final twist was given by Jacqueline Rohart's hairdresser. On the day before her death, he had cut her hair in a new style – to make her more attractive to her husband – and set it with an Italian fixative. If she had been in the sea long, the fixative would have been washed out. Jacqueline Rohart's body was exhumed, and it was seen that the hair was still firmly in place. A second post mortem established that the bruises on her face and neck were made by a man's fists, not by the sea.

Rohart's murder was almost perfect. If it had gone according to plan, all would have been well. The ether would have rendered Jacqueline unconscious; she would then have been drowned in the sea. As it was, she fought him, scratching his chest – he had showed the scratches as evidence that his wife tried to cling to him as the waves swept them apart. He had pounded her into unconsciousness with his fists and then smothered her with a car blanket or a cushion. He decided to drag her into the sea all the same, but did not stay in long enough to wash the hair fixative out. . . . He was sentenced to life imprisonment.

I am reminded of the equally 'neat' solution of the Ivy Giberson case in Lakehurst, New Jersey. Ivy Giberson was a thirty-eight-year-old widow. She became a widow when, according to her own account, two burglars shot her husband with his own gun. She explained that she was a lighter sleeper than her husband Bill – who was fifteen years her senior. She heard a noise from the kitchen and went to investigate. One of the two burglars clapped his hand over her mouth and proceeded to gag her, while the other ransacked the place. Then the sound of a shot came from the bedroom, and the man binding her called : 'Why did you shoot?' She believed that her husband had awakened and grabbed for the gun under his pillow, and that the burglar wrested it from him and shot him. The gun was found on a rubbish heap nearby.

Detective Chief Ellis Parker instantly saw two flaws in her story. He decided to look more closely into her background. Checking at the local telephone company, he discovered that she had made many long-distance calls to a New York number. It proved to be that of a young man who admitted that he and Ivy Giberson were lovers, and that she had been speaking about marriage recently.

Parker revealed the two flaws in her account to the jury at her trial. No woman with an able-bodied husband beside her would herself get up to investigate a strange noise in the kitchen. Secondly, no burglar, hearing a shot from the bedroom, would yell 'Why did you shoot?' Because, for all he knew, it might be his companion who had been shot by the husband, and he would be next. Ivy was found guilty on 14th August 1922. She died in 1957, after serving a life sentence.

But the most determined attempt at a perfect murder I can think of was made in May 1967; the scene was the Cliffs of Moher, on the west coast of Ireland. On the morning of 24th May 1967, a fisherman noticed a body wedged between two rocks, the hair floating in the tide. It proved to be the body of a young girl, naked except for a pair of black panties. When the body was hauled on to the beach, it was seen that there was little left of her face. Her ribs were fractured, and she had apparently been in the water for about three days. It was the pathologist's opinion that she had died of a fall from a great height.

Some locals were certain that she was an American girl from San Diego who had been in the area recently; this seemed very likely, since the panties had an American maker's tag inside. But this girl was traced to Aberdeen, and proved to be alive and well. There seemed to be no other clues. The girl's hands indicated that she was not a manual worker, and the fillings in her teeth were expensive. She was buried in Dromcliffe, Ennis, and the case marked time.

Three months later, in August, the Dublin police received a letter from the FBI. They had finally managed to trace the dead girl's prints. She was Maria Virginia Domenech, aged twenty-eight, a social worker from New York. The enclosed photograph showed that she was exceptionally beautiful – in fact, she had been a beauty queen.

Another letter, from the girl's uncle, the Assistant Attorney General in the Department of Justice in Puerto Rico, mentioned that Maria Domenech's mother, Mrs Virginia Domenech, fifty-one, had also disappeared on 30th May, a week after her daughter's death; she had disappeared from the apartment in which she lived with her daughter. The New York police were also able to tell the Irish Gardai that Maria Domenech had had an unfortunate love affair, and had gone for a holiday in Europe to get over it. The pretty social worker had money of her own as well as her salary. Her disappointment in love had been made worse by the fact that the man – a travel agent – had become very friendly with her mother, who, at fifty-one, was still an attractive woman. She had withdrawn $6,000 in traveller's cheques from the bank, and flown off to Paris.

The detective forces of three nations were now working on the case. And it was the French police who eventually found some clues to the mystery. Maria Domenech had not been alone in Paris; she had been with an American whose description matched that of the travel agent.

The New York police interviewed every male friend Maria Domenech had ever had, including a man named Patrick D'Arcy, who was, in fact, a travel agent. He told them that he had not been abroad for a long time, and they accepted his word.

A postcard sent to a relative on 22nd May stated that Maria intended to remain in Paris for a while. Then, later in the day, she sent another card – from Orly Airport – to another friend, saying that she intended to fly to Ireland for a day or two and would send him a sweater. It began to look as if her male friend had persuaded her to take a quick trip with him – with every intention of killing her.

Now the pieces began to fall into place. A member of the Immigration Department was going through hotel slips for the weekend of 22nd-23rd May, when he came across one in the name of 'A Young'. He had booked a room in the International Hotel on Shannon Airport for four hours. This was not unusual; passengers in transit often did that. But 'A Young' was not a passenger in transit, for his name did not appear on any airline list for that day. So he had come by car. Then why spend only four hours in a hotel?

A check with the hotel not only verified that 'A Young' had come by car, but that he had arrived at eight in the morning and left at midday. The number of the car had been noted. It proved to be from a Dublin rental agency. They were able to verify that A Young had rented the car at eleven on Saturday night, and returned it at six the following evening. He had driven three hundred and twenty miles in that time, the milometer revealed.

Checks at Orly and London Airports revealed that a man in his forties had travelled to London with a girl who signed her name as 'M Young'. Miss M Young had booked a room at the Grosvenor Hotel in London overnight, but had apparently changed her mind. Her companion had persuaded her to go on to Ireland.

A shoe found near the Cliffs of Moher, across the bay from the spot where Maria Domenech was found, led to the discovery of a cache of the girl's jewellery and some of her clothes. Now it was clear that this is the spot she had fallen from, and the incredible story became clear. Her murderer had arrived at the Paris hotel on 21st May. Later that day, her murderer came to the hotel, and she spent the evening with him. She had told the desk clerk she intended to stay for some time, but, instead, she checked out the next morning, and drove to Orly Airport with her male friend. She was at London Airport by 3.30, and had cashed all her traveller's cheques there. They arrived together in Dublin a few hours later. They hired a car, and drove through the night – the one hundred and fifty miles or so to the west of Ireland. At about four or five in the morning, they arrived at the spot he had selected for the murder – O'Brien's Tower, on the Cliffs of Moher. There he probably knocked her unconscious with a blow from some blunt instrument, and took off her clothes to prevent identification. Some odd feeling for decency made him leave her panties on – his first mistake. For it was the tag inside that turned the search to America. However, the man could not guess that her fingerprints would be in a file in Washington, since she was a native of Puerto Rico, as well as being a city employee.

He drove to the Shannon hotel, twenty or so miles away – one wonders if he was acquainted with the story of the Colleen Bawn who died close by – and slept for four hours. Then he drove back to Dublin, handed the car over at six o'clock, and flew out of Ireland at seven-thirty. It had been a crowded thirty hours since he left Paris with Maria Domenech.

But there was still the fear that Maria might have written

letters to her mother, mentioning that she intended to see him in Paris – after all, their meeting at the hotel was no accident. He hurried back to America, and called on Mrs Virginia Domenech. And Mrs Domenech vanished. She is presumed to be dead, but so far, her body has not been found.

All the evidence pointed towards Patrick J D'Arcy. He was the son of Irish immigrants who had lived near Galway before they sailed for America. Undoubtedly, the widely travelled D'Arcy had visited his old home, and had noted the height of the Cliffs of Moher. Perhaps he persuaded Maria Domenech to go with him on a sentimental pilgrimage to his family home. D'Arcy's description certainly corresponded with that of 'A Young'. Investigation of his affairs revealed that he was a free-lance travel agent whose business had been doing badly lately. His business was not entirely legal, for he carried identification papers for 'A Young' as well as 'John J Quinn'. He was married, and had a six-year-old son and a twelve-year-old daughter who was a polio victim. In January 1967, he had taken her to Rome to receive the Pope's blessing. A check on his passport revealed that he had been out of the country on the weekend of Maria Domenech's disappearance, and back just before Mrs Virginia Domenech's.

D'Arcy was questioned by the New York police, but he flatly denied everything, even though his handwriting and the handwriting of 'A Young' were pronounced identical by experts. The Irish applied to have him extradited. But before that could happen, he vanished from New York. Police traced him to Miami, Florida, where he had made certain 'business trips' recently. They found the signature 'John J Quinn', who gave his address in Roanoke, Virginia, in the register of the McAllister Hotel. The manager said he had not seen the man who booked the room for days. They opened his room with a pass key. Patrick D'Arcy, alias John J Quinn, was lying dead on the bed. The autopsy revealed that his death was due to a lethal mixture of whisky and barbiturates. D'Arcy's priest in New York later told the police that he was suffering from a serious heart condition. He added that he believed that D'Arcy was involved in some illegal activity that was much 'bigger' than his murder of

Maria Domenech. Miami is a centre of drug-smuggling and gambling rackets, as well as of espionage. But there is hardly a need to assume anything 'bigger' behind the murder of Maria Domenech. It was done for money – about five thousand dollars; and if it had not been for a pair of black panties, it would have been a perfect murder.

But to end this book by talking about 'perfect murders' would be misleading. I have already quoted Shaw's remark that we judge an artist by his highest moments, a criminal by his lowest. And it is certainly true that just as a great poem or symphony gives us a sense of the endless potentialities of human life, so murder makes us clearly aware of what might be called 'original sin'. All men live in a limited and short-sighted way, but the great artist and the saint reject the limitation that their senses and their lives impose upon them; they refuse to be defeated by the limitations of everyday consciousness, to betray the god in them by behaving like dwarfs. The murderer formally signs a pact with triviality as black magicians once signed a pact with the Devil. And his pledge of allegiance is the ultimate crime – ultimate because it cannot be undone.

The problem raised by murder in the twentieth century is no longer a social problem; the murders in an affluent society seem to become more violent and cruel than ever before. On a practical level, the solution lies in a more efficient police system, and in a massive psychiatric study of crime and its causes in which every nation in the world co-operates. On the more ultimate level, there is only one solution: that man should advance to a new stage, in which the Shavian antimony of artist and criminal ceases to exist.

The evolution of crime, as traced in this book, is disturbing; but, as far as I can see, it is no cause for despair. The irrational crime of the twentieth century is the price we pay for our civilisation. Two centuries hence, the Red Spider murders or the Moors case will strike our descendants as strangely old-fashioned, quite typical of this present quaint era, the transition between the machine age and the space age.

Let me repeat the point I made in the Introduction. Crime is a valuable and important study because of its implications in terms of social evolution. Whenever I read William Roughead or one of his followers, I am reminded of the story of the poet Laurent Tailhade, who hailed Vaillant's bomb outrage in the French Chamber of Deputies with the comment, 'What do the victims matter if it's a fine gesture?' (*'Qu'importe les victimes si le geste est beau?'*) Five months later, in April 1894, an anarchist who wished to avenge Vaillant placed a bomb in the fashionable Restaurant Foyot, which fortunately killed no one. But it put out the eye of Laurent Tailhade, who was dining there. The moral of the tale should be taken to heart by the idiots who speak lyrically about 'the fine art of murder'. It is the ability to discount the victim that distinguishes the murderer from the rest of us.

Select Bibliography

Bayer, Oliver Weld, ed. *Cleveland Murders,* Duell, Sloan and Pearce, 1947

Berg, Dr Karl, *The Sadist,* Heinemann, 1944

Bleackley, Horace, *The Hangmen of England,* Chapman and Hall, 1929

Birkenhead, Earl of (F E Smith), *Famous Trials Series,* Hutchinson, 1928

   More Famous Trials, Hutchinson, 1928

Bowker, A E, *A Lifetime with the Law,* W H Allen, 1961

Brice, A H M, *Look upon the Prisoner,* Hutchinson, 1928

Brown, Douglas G and Brock, Alan, *Fingerprints,* Harrap, 1953

Brown, Douglas G and Tullet, E V, *Bernard Spilsbury, his Life and Cases,* Harrap, 1951

Camps, Dr Francis E, *Medical and Scientific Investigations in the Christie Case,* Medical Publications Limited, 1953

Casey, Lee, *Denver Murders,* Duell, Sloan and Pearce, 1946

Cohen, Louis H, *Murder, Madness and the Law,* World Publishing Co, New York, 1952

Cullen, Tom, *When London Walked in Terror* (Jack the Ripper), Houghton Mifflin, 1965

Derleth, August, *Wisconsin Murders,* Mycroft and Moran, Sauk City, USA, 1968

Douthwaite, L C, *Mass Murder,* John Long, 1928

Famous Trials Series, ed. George Dilnot, Geoffrey Bles, 1927

Frank, Gerald, *The Boston Strangler,* New American Library, 1966

Furneaux, Rupert, *The Medical Murderer,* Elek, 1957

   Famous Criminal Cases, 6 vols

   Crime Documentary, 2 vols

Glaister, J, *Medical Jurisprudence and Toxicology*, Livingstone, 1956

Godwin, George, *Crime and Social Action*, Watts and Co, 1956

Gribble, Leonard, *Famous Manhunts, a Century of Crime*, Long, 1953

Griffiths, Major Arthur, *Chronicles of Newgate*, 1884
    Mysteries of police and crime, 3 vols, Cassell, 1898

Hayward, Arthur L, *Lives of the most remarkable criminals who have been condemned and executed. . . .* From papers published in 1735. Routledge, 1927

Hibbert, Christopher, *The Roots of Evil*, Weidenfeld and Nicolson, 1963

Hirschfeld, Magnus, *Sexual Anomalies and Perversions*, Encyclopaedic Press, London 1938

Holroyd, James Edward, *The Gaslight Murders*, Allen and Unwin, 1960

Humphreys, Christmas, *Seven Murderers*, Heinemann, 1931

Huson, Richard, *Sixty Famous Trials*, Daily Express publication, 1938

Jackson, J H, ed. *San Francisco Murders*, Duell, Sloan and Pearce, 1947

Jenkins, Elizabeth, *Six Criminal Women*, Pan Books 1958

Kingstone, Charles, *Remarkable Rogues. . . . Some notable criminals of Europe and America*, John Lane, 1921

Lilar, Suzanne, *Aspects of Love in Western Society*, Thames and Hudson, 1965

Lincoln, Victoria, *A Private Disgrace* (Lizzie Borden), Putnam, 1967

McCormick, Donald, *The Identity of Jack the Ripper*, Jarrolds, 1959

Makins, John R, ed. *Boston Murders*, Duell, Sloan and Pearce, 1947

Matters, Leonard, *Jack the Ripper*, W H Allen, 1950 (Pinnacle Book)

Mayhew, Henry, *London's Underworld*: extracts from Mayhew's *London labour and London poor*, ed. Peter Quennell, Spring Books, 1951

Newgate Calendar, T Werner Laurie Limited, 1932

Notable British Trials Series, ed. Harry Hodge, William Hodge and Co, London, 1905

Pelham, Camden, *Chronicles of Crime or the New Newgate Calendar,* 2 vols, Reeves and Turner, 1886

Penguin Famous Trials Series, ed. Harry Hodge, Penguin Books, 1941

Playfair, Giles and Sington, Derrick, *The Offenders: Society and the Atrocious Crime,* Secker and Warburg, 1957

Scott, Sir Harold, *Scotland Yard,* Andre Deutsch, 1954

Simpson, Dr Keith, *Forensic medicine,* Arnold, 1947

Smith-Hughes, Jack, *Nine verdicts on Violence,* Cassell, 1956

  Six Ventures in Villainy, Cassell, 1955

  Unfair comment upon some Victorian murder trials, Cassell, 1951

Sondern, Frederic, *Brotherhood of Evil: the Mafia,* Gollancz, 1959

Steiger, Brad, *The Mass Murderer,* Award Books, New York, 1967

Stekel, Dr Wilhelm, *Sexual Aberrations,* 2 vols, Vision Press, 1953

Svensson, Arne and Wendel, Otto, *Crime Detection,* Cleaver-Hume Press, London, 1955

Thorwald, Jurgen, *Crime and Science, the new frontier in criminology,* Harcourt Brace, 1967

  The Century of the Detective, Harcourt Brace, 1964

Traini, Robert, *Murder for Sex and Cases of Manslaughter under the new Act,* William Kimber, 1960

Index